Geopolitics

Geopolitics

Jeremy Black

THE SOCIAL AFFAIRS UNIT

British Library Cataloguing in Publication Data
A catalogue record of this book is available from the British Library

Printed and bound in the United Kingdom

ISBN-13: 978-1-904863-42-7

Social Affairs Unit
314–322 Regent Street
London W1B 5SA
www.socialaffairsunit.org.uk

To
Damian Green

CONTENTS

ABOUT THE AUTHOR

Jeremy Black is Professor of History at the University of Exeter. Graduating from Cambridge with a Starred First, he did postgraduate work at Oxford and then taught at Durham, eventually as Professor, before moving to Exeter in 1996. He has lectured extensively in Australia, Canada, Denmark, France, Germany, Ireland, Italy, Japan, the Netherlands, New Zealand, Norway, Singapore, Slovenia, Spain and the USA, where he has held visiting chairs at West Point, Texas Christian University and Stillman College. A past council member of the Royal Historical Society, Black is a Senior Fellow of the Foreign Policy Research Institute and a trustee of Agora. He was appointed to the Order of Membership of the British Empire for services to stamp design. In 2008, he received the Samuel Eliot Morison Prize of the Society for Military History.

He is, or has been, on a number of editorial boards, including the *Journal of Military History,* the journal of the Royal United Services Institute, *Media History* and *History Today,* and was Editor of *Archives*.

His books include *War and the World, 1450–2000* (Yale), *The British Seaborne Empire* (Yale), *Maps and History* (Yale) and *European Warfare in a Global Context, 1600–1815* (Routledge).

PREFACE

This book reflects two linked interests of mine. First, as a historian, I have always been fascinated by geography; indeed I nearly took the subject as an undergraduate. Subsequently, I have pursued the interest with a number of books on maps and also in my teaching. This concern with geography is relatively unusual among British or American historians, which unfortunately helps impoverish the subject. Second, in a number of works, including *The Curse of History* (2008) and *What If? Counterfactualism and the Problem of History* (2008), I have sought to rethink some of the key conceptual issues in history, indeed the intellectual architecture of the subject. In part, this aspiration reflects a concern with prevailing methods of interpretation.

In the case of this book, I am troubled not only by the lack of engagement with geopolitics on the part of most historians but also by the modish and somewhat politicised account of the subject provided from within the discipline of geography. Thus, this book can, in part, be understood as a sequence to my *Maps and Politics* (1997). I take the opportunity to introduce various understandings of geopolitics and to probe them over a longer chronological range than is conventional.

While working on this book, I have benefited from teaching my Maps and History course at Exeter. Opportunities to give outside lectures also helped me clarify aspects of my argument. These included the Carls-Schwerdfeger lecture at Union University in 2008, as well as lectures in 2009 to the Foreign Policy Research Institute (FPRI), Temple University, the University of Pennsylvania, to a Development, Concepts and Doctrine Centre/Mackinder Forum Workshop held at the Joint Services Command and Staff College at Shrivenham and to a conference, The Limits of Empire in the Early Modern World, in honour of Geoffrey Parker, held in Columbus, Ohio.

I would like to record the great intellectual value I have derived over many years from membership of the FPRI, for long as a Senior Fellow, as well as my pleasure at the good fellowship it has brought. The FPRI was founded by Robert Strausz-Hupé, a noted geopolitician, and the current President, Harvey Sicherman, is another, as well as a good friend. I have benefited greatly from discussing this book with Harvey.

I am also most grateful to John Andrews, Brian Blouet, Klaus Dodds, Colin Flint, Will Hay, Leonard Hochberg, Alex Johnson, Geoffrey Martin and Rupert Smith for their comments on all or part of an earlier draft, and to advice from Ahron Bregman, Peter Cain, Sean Carter, David Cohen, Art Eckstein, Jan Glete, Michael Grow, Stewart Lone, Peter Lorge, Edward Luttwak, Timothy May, Rana Mitter, Keith Neilson, Weichong Ong and Geoffrey Sloan. None is responsible for any errors that remain. I am most grateful to Liz O'Donnell for again proving an exemplary copy-editor.

It is a great pleasure to dedicate this book to Damian Green, a friend from university days as well as a distinguished parliamentarian.

CHAPTER 1

INTRODUCTION

Employed from 1899, geopolitics is an amorphous concept and a plastic or malleable, as well as controversial, term. Different working definitions have been advanced, but all focus on the relationship between politics, principally the composition and use of power, and geographical factors, especially space, location and distance. As a field on which policy-makers rest (or even unthinkingly base) their decisions, geopolitics calls attention to the context in which national security decisions are made and issues of war and peace are decided, and, more particularly, the relationship between strategy and geography. Thus, classical geopolitics discusses the key importance of geography for statecraft[1] and defines the relationships between, and among, the exercise of power, the changing geographic constraints and opportunities for success and failure – as perceived by actors engaged in conflict, the capabilities of adversaries, such as population and critical resources, their perception of their interests, the available technology for war (and now also terrorism), and economic competition.

At the same time, what these relationships meant to contemporaries, and also can be said to mean to subsequent commentators, itself varied, and this variation needs to be borne in mind. This point indeed provides a vital role for the historian. It is not that social scientists are unable to note changing values but rather that their subject specialism and methodology do not always lend themselves sufficiently to an empirical, source-based assessment of this dimension, an observation that is particularly the case for many specialists in International Relations. In part, this point reflects the tension between a desire, on the part of many social scientists, to look for universal entities which can then be analysed and, on the other, historical reservations about such an approach.[2] These reservations tend to focus on the nature of changing meanings, not least as a consequence of the specific discursive contexts within which entities and concepts exist and are to be understood. In the latter approach, geopolitics is thus historicised.

However, the argument that historical knowledge is a cure-all for ahistoricism, let alone for ideological-driven explanations, has to confront the degree to which historical scholarship has also been affected by self-conscious 'critical' studies which seek to subvert so-called dominant narratives.[3] Geopolitics as an academic sub-discipline reveals the problems created by the turn towards 'critical' social sciences and history, and the nature of much contemporary social theory. Indeed, geopolitics offers a valuable case study precisely because it is a field where long-term history ought to be deployed, but rarely is, because determinism is often favoured over freedom in explanations, because changing values and understandings of terrain are too rarely considered, and because the ambiguous and uncertain nexus of power, violence and strategy is (or ought to be) revealed, but today is often obscured in a rush by some leading writers to judge national security as unimportant, if not illegitimate.

Ironically, a historical placing of geopolitics as a subject throws a critical light on much of the geopolitical analysis produced by geographers. In particular, there is a general tendency among much social-science literature to adopt a politically partisan approach to the present, rather than attempting to engage with the complexities of a long-term historical dimension in which their own approach can indeed be contextualised. This partisan approach is as part of a self-conscious strand of critical studies, which challenges our understanding of our current ambiguous circumstances. This challenge is a problem because it relates not solely to academics but, rather, to students, the public and, indeed, policy-makers.

'Critical geopolitics', which is itself a diverse project but one better described as radical geopolitics, deliberately sets out to subvert the understanding of the categories and relationships mentioned in the first paragraph by calling into question fundamental distinctions as well as realist terminology, for example the state and society, military personnel versus civilians, and national security. 'Critical geopolitics' challenges our common understandings of definitions, categories and relationships, by replacing them with, in some cases, utopian wishful thinking, by political commitment instead of an objective appreciation of the causes of conflict, by foreshortened historical understandings and by a loss of clarity in communicating ideas. 'Critical geopolitics' self-consciously and aggressively stands today as a form of post-colonial study; and, although not all post-colonial work adopts a geopolitical stance, there is often an attack on American power, portrayed as hegemony, which is seen as the latest version of Western colonialism, an attack that involves calls for a different world order which has a distinctive spatial character.[4] Indeed, the aggressive nature of the condemnation may be justified by 'critical geopoliticians' on the grounds that this is criticism of hegemonic power.

'Critical geopolitics' is thus itself open to criticism. There is the risk in the subject of replacement of common sense by a particular jargon or discourse as well as of self-referential and self-reverential patterns of verification and endorsement within their own field, and such a replacement can be seen to undermine common action based on fear, interest and glory, the triad of motives taken from Thucydides. Objective reality, however, cannot be wished away. For example, alongside the political and cultural context, both, as this book seeks to demonstrate, crucial, objective factors counted and count: for example the nearby presence of coal really mattered for industrialisation, and the shift to oil and gas has had key consequences for power politics.

In contrast, a key theme in 'critical' studies, the subversion of realistic and common understanding, by denying any appreciation of an objective reality, challenges a capacity for action on the world stage in defence of a common fate in world history. More positively, the extent to which geopolitics can be seen as a way to help clarify assumptions, for example the imperial creed of many policy-makers in the late nineteenth century, offers an argument for employing it today to discuss international relations. Yet, in doing so, it is necessary to employ the caution appropriate if such decoding is to be successful in throwing light on the spatial aspects of power.

Moving from a geographical perspective, it is instructive to consider the writing of history from a geopolitical angle. The geopolitics of historical study includes the extent to which there is writing for national audiences, and indeed particular languages. This approach is inherently problematic, if not political, when addressing the history or present situation of once-contested or contested lands such as Silesia and Lithuania.[5] There is not space to develop this theme in this book, but *The Curse of History* (2008) considers some of its aspects.

A prominent book in the field of 'critical geopolitical' thought, Neil Smith's *American Empire: Roosevelt's Geographer and the Prelude to Globalization* (2003), provides a good example of some of the problems in the literature. British-born Smith was Professor of Anthropology and Geography at the City University of New York when the book was published. Although his book is large and complex, it is notable that Smith displayed scant reluctance in showing a commitment that apparently allowed him to overcome the ambiguities of debate or what a critic might call the constraints of empirical scholarship. Thus, Smith wrote that the Cold War 'was provoked amid a 1940s battle by U.S. capital and the U.S. government for global economic access to labour and commodity markets'.[6] Such simplistic, not to say misleading, arguments are an aspect of a wider problem with much 'cutting edge' i.e. modish, work in geography, for example on mapping,[7] and Smith's book appeared in the series California Studies in Critical Human Geography.[8]

Much of this fashionable work takes a politicised stance that is tendentious. Thus, Smith referred to 'deep sighs of epochal relief from the Western ruling classes after 1989'[9] and to the United Nations as 'the jewel in the crown of the postwar American Lebensraum',[10] a term presumably chosen to shock but one that failed to capture fundamental differences in intentionality and methods, akin to those of critics of Israeli policy in 2009 who mistakenly compared Gaza to the Warsaw ghetto.[11] The first was a forcible suppression of opposition involving civilian casualties but where these casualties was not the intention of the action, while the German action against the Warsaw ghetto in 1943 was part of a comprehensive genocide.

Smith was highly critical of the USA, and this criticism can be seen in the language he employed. Writing of Isaiah Bowman, a prominent academic geographer who was an adviser to President Roosevelt and the State Department during the Second World War, Smith noted of 1944: 'Pushed to the political wall by the strength of the Soviet come-back against Germany and by British colonialist obstinacy, which he quietly admired, his Wilsonian moralism became an ideological runt to an increasingly over-nourished nationalism. Americanness increasingly dominated his postwar vision of global Lebensraum.'[12]

Such a tone and approach was unfortunate because Smith's subject is important, and indeed he captured a central point, even if it could have been phrased better:

> By one account, then, the American Century took us beyond geography; by another, it *was* the *geographic century.* This contradiction between a spaceless and a spatially constituted American globalism is latent in the global history of the twentieth century . . . points to the powerful necessity of understanding the preludes to globalisation in a geographical register.[13]

Smith responded to the attacks on 11 September 2001 by arguing that they were a local and global event misrepresented as a national tragedy, indeed that the 'need to nationalize September 11th arose from the need to justify war'.[14] While

Smith's point that 9/11 had local, national and global scales worthy of consideration, especially how they interlinked with one another, is valid, his approach was in part set by his hostility to the American government. Moreover, his point offered a further example of how Smith wanted to assert the overriding importance of a global scale, one that overrode the local and the national. Therefore, to Smith, 9/11 was nationalised, despite the attacks being local and having a global meaning. This approach risked privileging the ideology of globalisation over the nation. Moreover, the attack on the Pentagon was clearly an attack on the USA, while the other plane brought down by the passengers before it could reach Washington was apparently also intended for a national target.

American power more generally appeared and appears to pose problems for academics who discuss geopolitics. In 'Oil and Blood: The Way to Take Over the World', a piece from *World Watch Magazine* (2003) reprinted in the second edition of *The Geopolitics Reader,* Michael Renner concluded:

> By rejecting U.S. participation in the Kyoto Protocol early in his tenure, George W. Bush sought to throw a wrench into the international machinery set up to address the threat of climate change. By securing the massive flow of cheap oil, he may hope to kill Kyoto. In a perverse sense, a war on Iraq reinforces the assault against the Earth's climate.[15]

It will probably not surprise readers to note that the volume included readings from Edward Said, Frantz Fanon, Osama bin Laden and Arundhati Roy, all worthy of serious analysis but equally evidence of the ideological bent of 'critical geopolitics'. Their views will probably be familiar, but what about Jennifer Hyndman, offering a feminist analysis of 9/11 in *ACME: An International E-Journal for Critical Geographies* (2003)?

> The events and aftermath of September 11th ineluctably ended the already precarious distinction

> between domestic space, that within a sovereign state, and more global space where transnational networks, international relations, multilateral institutions, and global corporations operate . . . Feminists have long argued that private-public distinctions serve to depoliticise the private domestic spaces of 'home' compared to more public domains . . . Terror in the US on September 11th has been met with more terror in Afghanistan . . . A feminist geopolitics aims to trace the connections between geographical and political locations, exposing investments in the dominant geopolitical rhetoric, in the pursuit of a more accountable and embodied geopolitics that contests the wisdom of violence targeted at innocent civilians, wherever they may be.[16]

Hyndman also argued the need to emphasise links between the CIA and bin Laden, via Pakistan's ISI (Inter-Services Intelligence). Hyndman's analysis can be unpacked by noting the consequences of her treatment of the 2001 attacks as supporting the feminist position on the private/public distinction. Hyndman proposed no clear definition of terror, leading the reader to suppose that terror equals violence; and, moreover, as the distinction is denied by feminist critical thinkers, equals violence in the home or by the state. In so far as the state was built on patriarchy and violence, it is illegitimate anyway for radical feminists.

More generally, there is a weary predictability about the ready resort to strident conclusions based on limited and problematic evidence. For example, Derek Gregory, in his *The Colonial Present* (2004), claimed that the use of the War on Terror created geopolitical spaces where the USA could use its massive firepower with impunity.[17] And so on.

Thus, in his *Geopolitics: A Very Short Introduction* (2007), Klaus Dodds, who had produced an account of Anglo-Argentinean geopolitical competition in Antarctica and the Falklands that is well grounded,[18] devoted much attention to American policy under President George W. Bush, and the language was clearly slanted. For example: 'In November 2004, much to the disappointment of many American voters, presidential candidate John Kerry was not able to deny the George W. Bush administration a second term',[19] a sentence that, while accurate, scarcely admitted that Bush's re-election reflected a democratic mandate reached by a significant majority of voters, approximately 5 million. Alarm was expressed by Dodds about the policies of the Bush administration,[20] and Dodds announced that 'the Bush Doctrine based on pre-emption and highly selective multilateralism is the single most important danger confronting the current geopolitical architecture.'[21] These were, of course, frequently repeated assertions, but such repetition did, and does, not amount to demonstration. Moreover, leaving aside its tendentious character, there is a terribly 'presentist' feel to the argument, and it may seem very dated in five years' time, let alone fifty; rather, indeed, as some of the approaches of 1960s academics appeared somewhat dated a decade later.

The partisan character of such work is possibly a comment not only on a lack of editorial rigour by publishers but also on a more general approach in much (but by no means all) geographical work, namely a tendency to offer a left-wing discourse approach that relies for evidence on guilt by association, rather than a critical evaluation of the various points of view, let alone empirical positivism. The call to action is scarcely downplayed. John Agnew, Professor of Geography at UCLA (the University of California at Los Angeles), and, as I write, the President of the Association of American Geographers, closed the second edition of his *Geopolitics: Re-Visioning World Politics* (2003), a popular work (i.e. possibly set often as a text), reprinted three times in 2006 and again in 2007, by writing:

> What is clear is that the state-territorial conception of power is not a transcendental feature of modern human history but, rather, a historically contingent feature of the relationship between geographical scales in the definition and concentration of political

> practices . . . Political geographers and others must finally choose whether to be agents of an imagination that has imposed manifold disasters on humanity or to try to understand geographical communalities and differences in their own right. In other words, it is past time to choose sides. But first we need to understand and overcome our own bad habits of thinking and doing: *vincit qui se vincit*.[22]

Agnew's argument captures the assumption, common to 'critical geopolitical' thinkers, that the world, as it is, is illegitimate and must be changed. As such, these thinkers differ in emphasis from realist or classical geopolitical thinkers, such as Mackinder, Mahan and Spykman, who sought to appreciate the world as it is, and then to describe, prescribe and predict. The perspective of the latter group was/is that power, conflict and violence all exist and cannot be banished. Temporary fixes are possible, and indeed desirable, and can be obtained through a balance of power or collective security or pre-emptive war or some action taken within an appreciation that all ends have costs and consequences and that means can overwhelm even the best of intentioned ends. Thus, realist geopolitics tends to base itself on the argument that principles and practices of strategic thought and action cannot be ignored or wished away.

It would be foolish to neglect the role of commitment in classical geopolitics, commitment in particular to the state. What is notable about the self-styled 'critical geopolitics' is that the commitment is different in type, especially with an attempt to reorient to 'a geography for peace'.[23] For example, commitment was also a theme in Colin Flint's *Introduction to Geopolitics:* 'Participation in geopolitics is also a matter of questioning and challenging the "common sense" assumptions generated by the geopolitical structures in general (difference, conflict etc) as well as by the representations and actions of key geopolitical agents, the US and British governments for example.'[24] Such examples could be easily multiplied.

My critique of the application of a binary conception of power politics by 'critical geopoliticians' also draws on my concern about their discussion of imperialism and of the role of geographers in the process. This hostile discussion tends to underplay the extent to which imperialism was also practised by non-Western powers,[25] as well as sometimes neglecting historical work that emphasises the complexities of imperialism and the extent to which it entailed compromises and negotiation, which are themes pursued in Chapters 2 and 3. These complex 'geographies of power'[26] cut across the crude strictures too often expressed by those propounding a binary approach.

Leaving aside the political slant, and a tendency to offer argument by assertion, tendentious statements and a lack of qualification, some of the modish work on political geography is written in a somewhat opaque fashion, a characteristic that is relevant not just to geographers but to self-consciously 'critical' work in a number of fields. Thus, Martin Brückner writes of early America:

> for the nation to become the perfectly regular alphabetic environment, the word maps had to reconcile a strain that lies at the heart of all cartographic representation: their formal arrangement had to negotiate the reader's imaginary freedom of movement offered by the hybrid textuality of the map. By reading the map as a quasi-blank and verbally elastic text, the apprentice map reader was able to create a space of his or her own . . . It is telling that at the historical moment of 1784, when language threatened to upend the new nation, the alphabet and alphabetic maps seemed to be insufficient tools for stabilizing the new American nation.[27]

Geopolitics itself can be variously defined and discussed, the latter a separate issue but one that also affects the question of definition. Geopolitics is commonly understood as the spatial dynamics of power, although there is a lack of clarity about whether this should be pursued in a descriptive or a normative sense. Moreover, what Harvey Sicherman termed 'the facts of geopolitics – the resources and locations of various peoples and states',[28] involve subjective as well as objective considerations,[29] although that does not mean that there is no objective reality. A human environment may be defined in terms of human needs, desires and capabilities for satisfying them from the materials at hand. This definition in part depends on the conscious awareness of the situation, but no amount of desire will enable the production of steel from coal and iron deposits if it is impossible to transport the raw materials, and at a reasonable cost. Nevertheless, the subjective appreciation of what is objectively available lends itself to historicising.[30] Coal deposits exist, and the French live in France, but the location of French and German coal and iron deposits played a role in their territorial aspirations and strategic planning in 1870–1945, while responses to the possibility of nuclear power or to France's interests involve ideological, cultural and political assumptions.

To take another example, the American government has found the notion of 'ungoverned spaces' useful as a way to classify the world, and the Pentagon's National Defense Strategy, issued in 2008, referred to 'ungoverned, under-governed, mis-governed and contested areas'. Yet, in practice, definitions are difficult because failure as a state occurs in different ways and with varied consequences, and there are differences between domestic and international perception, and different mechanisms at play, that might help us understanding something called state failure. Similarly, a murder rate that would be seen in Denmark as a sign of societal collapse is not perceived the same way in Brazil. Not all the supposedly weak states are centres for terrorism, although this issue underlines the problem of thinking in terms of states, as the key spaces are often parts of states, for example dissident regions and communities. This point underlines a concomitant need to think of geopolitics at least in part in terms of the spatial imprint and geographical shaping of ideologies.

Geoffrey Sloan, a student of classical geopolitics, has drawn attention to these different approaches by considering geopolitics as a policy science and as an appendage of political propaganda.[31] Such a use of geography for propaganda is long standing. For example, Augustin Fitzhugh's map of Newfoundland in about 1700 makes a political point, with the small area of 'English fishing boats' appearing to be entirely shut in by the huge part of the sea controlled by their French counterparts.[32] The Nazi map that shows Germany threatened by Czech airpower in the 1930s is a piece of propaganda, but a map depicting the utility of the Suez Canal for British shipping in the same period might be propaganda or mere description, depending on the use to which the map is put, how it is drawn and the accuracy of the data on which it is based.[33]

In the longer timescale, therefore, alongside the objective criteria discussed above, geopolitics, like other forms of geographical analysis and expression, can, in part, be seen as a belief system, not least due to the symbolic weight attached to methods of depiction, whether symbols on maps or geopolitical phrases, such as natural interests. Furthermore, the perception of power is centrally involved in issues of power; and even place, its constraints and relationships, is a matter of perception, as much as an element that can be objectively measured and displayed in terms of coordinates. As geography is a means by which political entities, including their populations, make sense of their situation, specifically, but not only, their territorial setting, so these perceptions are of key importance, and it is troubling to see the extent to which there is limited or no formal discussion of geopolitics in much of the literature produced by experts in Politics and International Relations.[34]

Perceptions of space are particularly significant for new states as they seek to define their interests. Alongside, for example, 'realist' issues of the strength of the Brazilian state, the role of such perceptions can be seen, in the contrast between Brazil's ability to retain cohesion after the Portuguese link was broken in the 1820s and the fissiparous character of former Spanish America in the same period. In the newly independent USA, geographical literacy played an important cognitive, symbolic and pedagogic role.[35]

Yet, to indicate the variety of directions in which geopolitics can be taken, the question of making sense of the spatial setting of states is made more complex when it is expanded from a simple notion of debating military strategy (now often termed geostrategy) to consider, in addition, domestic policy and its multiple locations, as a key aspect of geopolitics and strategy. Indeed, part of the value of 'critical geopolitics' is that discussion of practical and popular geopolitical culture plays a prominent role in some of the literature.

It is the very drive of the political system that is at question when domestic policies and the pressures for obedience and order are considered, and these factors have a spatial dimension. Moreover, to take the political aspect further, geopolitics and strategy can be understood in terms of a process of policy formulation, execution and evaluation, to which military purposes are frequently instrumental and secondary. In part, the definition and discussion in recent decades of an operational dimension to war and policy provide a key opportunity for emphasising a political approach to geopolitics and strategy. Conversely, the notion that military purposes are instrumental and secondary can be seen as a modern concept that underplays the extent to which such purposes can be of overwhelming significance. As noted earlier (p. 11), such values change with time.

This emphasis on domestic political issues also offers a possibility of dispensing with analytical models of international state and military development that assume some mechanistic search for efficiency and for a maximisation of effectiveness. One traditional strand of geopolitical argument can be located in this context by seeing it as designed to help secure such effectiveness and efficiency. Such ideas, however, can do violence to the inherently controversial nature of efficiency and effectiveness and to the complex processes by which interest in new ideas and methods interact with powerful elements of continuity. Much geopolitical discussion is in practice part of these debates.

Thus, replicating the situation in which geography, geographical relationships and maps can all be variously defined and presented, geopolitics has a range of meanings, from the geography of politics to the politics of geography; meanings, moreover, that relate to how it is discussed as much as to what is being considered. In part, this range reflects the porosity of geography as a subject, especially once public discussion of geographical factors are considered. Analysis of the range of meanings in terms of a typology of meanings would not be terribly helpful, as there is a sliding and elision between them, while, what to a practitioner may be an objective geopolitical analysis may be a subjective, rhetorical, politicised use of geopolitical ideas to commentators or other practitioners.

Similarly, of course, history, historical relationships and the periodisation of events can be variously defined and presented, also ensuring a range of meanings. Indeed, it is important not to criticise geographers in general when critiquing 'critical geopolitics'. Scepticism about the latter has been expressed by geographers.[36] Smith is seen by some as a Marxist, and many regard writings on 'critical geopolitics' as trying to reinterpret recent history from a contemporary left-wing viewpoint.

The historicism of geopolitics can turn in two different directions. It is conventional to focus on the period, of little over a century, in which geopolitics was discussed as a distinctive subject, an approach taken in Chapters 5 to 7. However, geopolitics can also be considered both as an issue throughout the history of organised human society and also as a means of analysis that is highly pertinent across time, themes pursued in Chapters 2 to 4. To do so poses risks but does not necessarily entail a failure to note the specificities of particular contexts, in other words both very different relationships between power and space and the need to vary the means of analysis in order to take note of the cultural dimensions of these relationships.

A good example of geopolitical thought is provided by one of the great successes of eighteenth-century political thought,

L'Esprit des lois (*The Spirit of the Laws*) by Charles-Louis de Secondat, Baron de Montesquieu. Published in 1748, this book, which was to have a considerable impact on contemporaries, was a comprehensive account of government systems. Montesquieu had a strong sense of the constant changes brought about by time in the fortunes of states and also believed that human society, far from being constant, was affected by environmental circumstances, such as climate, as well as by social forces, for example education and religion. Montesquieu therefore proposed an interaction of geography and peoples.

The sense that climate affected if not determined society, with heat inducing torpor and lasciviousness, was a key aspect of Western triumphalism, as well as of the Protestant rejection of Mediterranean culture. In the former case, this analysis was closely linked to the slave trade. Montesquieu, Buffon and others explained colour as a function of exposure to the tropical sun, but the ability of Africans to cope better than Europeans with disease in the tropics was believed to exemplify an inherent difference that was linked to a closeness to the animals that bred there. Thus, crude geographical determinism was linked to a form of anthropology, and both served to justify slavery.

Without going to this extent, there were also firm beliefs that particular environments, such as mountainous regions, had consequences in terms of social organisation and political control. These ideas were long-standing, and, indeed, Mackinder was to contrast the 'rooted provincialism' of island or peninsular provinces with the attitudes found in the great plains.[37] The notion of provincialism is one that is inherently bound up with the cultural and political consequences of spatial relationships. Modern counterparts include discussion of Afghanistan and the mountainous north-west of Pakistan in terms of the physical context of their societies and the problems these pose for attempts to control them. Political geography has also a key role in defining the parameters of society, as with borderlands (on which there is a big literature in geography) and their very different characters.[38]

Moreover, the external policies of states have often been traced to geographical concerns and interests, and these have been emphasised alongside, or instead of, ideological factors. For example, much Cold War geopolitics rested on the attempt to make sense of Soviet policy. Arguing a continuity with pre-Soviet Russian expansionism was a frequent theme and one that has been continued in subsequent scholarship.[39] Similarly, while allowing for frequent 'tectonic, apparently nonlinear, shifts in the geopolitical context', a distinctive geopolitical pattern to American national security has been discerned, with a focus since the 1940s on an anti-hegemonic policy towards Eurasia.[40]

The value of geopolitical concepts can also be seen in the discussion of Chinese policy, notably the relationship between East China, which can be presented as part of the Rimland (a term used by Spykman[41]) and Chinese Central Asia, which can be discussed as part of the Heartland. Thus, Hsiao-Ting Lin argued that China's reassertion of its sovereignty over Central Asia in 1937–45 was in part a response to Japan's success in overrunning much of the coastal Rimlands, a challenge that also led to the reshaping of relations between the Nationalist central government and regional power-brokers in west and south-west China. In turn, this process was seen by Lin as altering the geopolitical context by transforming modern China from a maritime economy rooted in East Asian trade to a continental one based on overland trade routes through Asia.[42]

More generally, the Heartland as well as China was changed. In the 1990s, the Chinese geopolitical drive into Central Asia was renewed as Russia ceased to dominate the region.[43] Moreover, the ideas of Mackinder and Spykman have been reconsidered in the context of present-day Central Asian affairs.[44] Alongside parallels, however, the geopolitical characterisation for one period is likely to be challenged, if not negated, by a characterisation for or in the period following. China, for example, shifted in the second half of the twentieth century from a continental strategy to an autarchic one, and then to a global one. These strategies also had internal regional implications.

At the same time, some of the literature, for example the Lin article, while arresting and instructive, suffers from a disinclination to hedge the use of geopolitical arguments with caution. Aside from the repeated difficulties of demonstrating the influence of geopolitical perceptions on policy-makers, there is the problem that more than one conclusion can be drawn from particular examples. Thus, for example, a Rimland approach to modern China, focusing on trans-oceanic trade and resource links, as well as on the greater Chinese world in the South-East Asian diaspora, and on strategic concerns with Taiwan, Japan and the USA, can be seen alongside Heartland interests within the interior of Eurasia.

It is appropriate to employ the term 'geopolitics' to discuss such subjects, despite this often being a case of using a term when discussing a period in which this term was not employed. Such usage is controversial, as can also be seen in the application of concepts such as strategy or descriptions such as class and enlightenment. For example, distinguished historians, such as Hew Strachan and Nicholas Rodger, have reservations about the use of strategy to analyse warfare in periods prior to the nineteenth century, as they are worried about 'backfitting' a modern conception of strategy upon eras that did not use the term. However, even if the word, or a synonym, is absent, the function of strategy – the relationships between ends, ways and means in power politics – was present.[45]

So also with geopolitics: a practice exists before a concept, and a concept exists before a term. For example, it is reasonable to ask what Christendom meant as a geographical space to Protestants and Catholics after the Reformation, during the Wars of Religion and thereafter. The value of a spatial dimension, in the shape of English confessional geography, understood by the study of travel books, was indicated in Tony Claydon's study of the late seventeenth and early eighteenth centuries.[46] Such studies help to establish the range and limits of concern, and this was a key aspect of geopolitics, both before the term and thereafter. Similarly, statesmen read Thucydides in order to hone a geopolitical sensibility, even if the word was not in use.[47]

It is also pertinent to consider why geopolitics developed as a self-conscious subject at the close of the nineteenth century, a subject valuably assessed by historical geographers, notably Felix Driver and Mike Heffernan.[48] There were clearly particular geopolitical circumstances that encouraged speculation in terms of an explicit geopolitical language, and these circumstances can be clarified by modern scholarship. In turn, studies on the period would benefit from an understanding of this work. For example, without mentioning the geopoliticians of the 1890s on, a recent account of 'the geopolitics of war in the mid-nineteenth century' repeated Mackinder's central theme of a binary difference between land- and sea-based powers. Michael Geyer and Charles Bright argued that 'a new breed of imperialist wars' drew on advances in technology in communications and transportation, especially telegraphy and steam shipping, and the resulting enhanced capabilities. They inscribed this general shift in terms of the pattern of power politics, with Britain allegedly having invented 'a politics of global power which no longer depended exclusively on the occupation of territory and the surpluses that could be squeezed from the land but aimed at controlling global lines of communication and exchange and living off the surpluses of this circulation.'[49]

As with many broad-brush approaches to imperial geopolitics, this account can be queried historically, especially with reference to the earlier and highly successful Portuguese and Dutch empires in the Indian Ocean, but Geyer and Bright captured the extent to which power in the late nineteenth century gained what they termed a new liquidity, so that 'what mattered was no longer the force at hand but the force that could be generated and put into place'.[50] Geyer and Bright suggested that 'the imperial premium on the control of space was replaced by a premium on the control of time',[51] a vital reminder that geopolitical considerations should not solely simply be understood in terms of varied accounts of the distribution of resources, opportunities and threats across space. These considerations were seen by Geyer and Bright as pertinent for both land and sea powers, but with important differences:

> Properly understood, the ability to sustain a global presence was the maritime equivalent of the newly acquired capabilities of military mobilisation on land by the new national states . . . the new nationalising land mobilisations moved along the inner lines of geopolitics, outward (and thus faced problems of dispersal), while the globalising maritime mobilisations moved along the perimeters, inward (and thus faced problems of concentration).[52]

Germany was presented as able to command the interior lines of global geopolitics but unable to transcend the landed nature of its power, whereas, in the twentieth century, the USA was able 'to fuse the capacities of the national state for mobilisation with the logistical capabilities of maritime power', and combined land-based and sea-borne power to become a 'global superpower'.[53]

As modern theoretical approaches need to be historically based in order to be accurate, so it is mistaken to restrict them to periods when a given term is used. This view guides what follows. It begins with three chapters on the understanding and role of geopolitics prior to the use of the term. These are lengthy because the contention here is that this period – most of human history – should play a key role in the discussion. Chapters 2 and 3 focus in particular on frontiers, a key concept in geopolitics, and on maps, a crucial tool in the understanding and presentation of geographical information, the analysis of geopolitical issues and the propagation of geopolitical arguments. Chapter 4 uses the case study of British power to assess the role and understanding of geographical factors in strategy, with particular reference to the Seven Years' War (1756–63; known in the USA as the French and Indian War), which was the key struggle in which Britain became the major world power. The chapter closes with a brief discussion of methodological points and of the geography of nineteenth-century imperialism.

In Chapter 5, we consider the classic age of geopolitical thought, and, in particular, the work of Ratzel, Kjellén, Mackinder and Haushofer. Their arguments are related to the power politics and geographical thought of the period 1890–1945. Chapter 6 takes us forward to assess the situation during the Cold War, Chapter 7 considers developments since 1990, including the work of Fukuyama and Huntington, and the War on Terror. Chapter 8 looks from present to future, and Chapter 9 offers some conclusions.

Readers will not agree with everything that follows, but, in disagreeing, I hope they will define why they think I am wrong. That is one of the great benefits of contributing to debate. There is valuable, but insufficient, debate between historians and geographers, in part because historians, chary of geographical determinism and ill informed on the literature, tend to ignore the first-rate literature by historical geographers. In addition, there is only limited criticism of 'critical geography'. I hope that this book contributes to a debate that will be conceptually fruitful as well as of value in public discussion.

CHAPTER 2

GEOPOLITICS BEFORE THE TERM: SPATIALITY AND FRONTIERS

One set of tramlines is that of past understandings of the geographical context and spatial nature of power, while another is that of the application of modern understandings to the many centuries under discussion. These approaches, historic and historical, are not completely separate because an aspect of the second rests on the ability to appreciate the cultural perceptions of the past. Indeed, there are profound differences between modern understandings of spatiality and past perceptions. The most fundamental difference relates to the issue of sacred space and the religious dimensions of power; and the pertinence of this issue is enhanced by the degree to which religious considerations cannot be treated as an anachronistic legacy of past superstition dispersed in a Whiggish fashion by the rise of knowledge. That approach underplays the continuing role of religious senses of space, and perceptions of religious space, in international and domestic politics, and also underrates the earlier extent to which the shaping of space and the understanding of power both owed much to a powerful belief in the existence of extraterrestrial forces operating in the here and now.

For example, medieval Christian thinkers, like many other religious commentators, saw inherent connections between the world and their salvation, saw God in their world, and their constant connection with, and dependence on, Him through the world.[1] St Augustine's book *The City of God* (412–27), with its presentation of good and evil as distinct and yet competing spheres, encompassing both the extraterrestrial worlds and human society, very much captured the geopolitics of spiritual power, as well as set a pattern for the understanding of human society as a competition between larger forces.

At the individual level, the sense of direct providential intervention, of a daily interaction of the human world and wider spheres of good and evil, of Heaven and Hell, of sacred places and saintly lives, is one that is today heavily constricted by secularism and science, but, for most of history, life and public morality were explicitly framed in terms of a struggle between good and evil, each of which was understood in religious terms. Moreover, good and evil were physically placed in terms of particular locations, and they were treated as able, indeed keen, to intervene in the human world, and with consequences that were both individual and collective.

Thus, the key spatial sense was of these relationships between good, evil and humanity, and of such aspects as the routes to salvation or damnation; and this was a spatial sense that was collective as much as individual. Moreover, these relationships were not only depicted visually, for example in wall paintings, but also aurally, in religious services and in the tales and conversation of oral culture, as well as being acted out. The Coopers' pageant in the 1415 York Corpus Christi play depicted 'Adam and Eve and a tree between them, a serpent deceiving them with applies, God speaking to them and cursing the serpent, and an angel with a sword casting them out of Paradise'.

The impact of printing, combined with the Protestant Reformation of the sixteenth century, ensured that in some areas the understanding of good and evil became more literary, and less oral or visual, but that change did not diminish the need for people to understand their world in terms of the struggle between the two, and the resulting spaces of and for good and evil.

One such spatial alignment was that between night and dark. The latter was a world of uncertainty, danger and menace, especially for the traveller literally unable to see his route:

The west yet glimmers with some streaks of day;
Now spurs the lated traveller apace,
To gain the timely inn.

(*Macbeth*, Act III, Scene 3)

More generally, the dark was a world outside human understanding and control. Macbeth's evil, in Shakespeare's play of that name, is measured by his willingness to call on the dark to cover the murder of Banquo: 'Come, seeling Night, / scarf up the tender eye of pitiful Day' (Act III, Scene 2).

If the natural contrasts, of night and day, and of the seasons, provided a time–space matrix within which past, present and future could be understood as a continuing process, the parameters were set by more fundamental sacral indicators of time and space, notably those of foundation myths and indicators that were often of cataclysmic impact, for example the Christian belief in the Apocalypse. In some cultures, such as New Caledonia, there were also subterranean countries of the dead, and therefore entrances to the underworld, which were spatially specific, as well as being understood as spiritual and psychological.

Religious accounts and animosities were also important in international relations. Thus, the Mongol concept of geopolitics eventually came down to the argument that Heaven had decreed that Chinggis Khan (d. 1227) and his descendants were to rule the world. This argument reflected the extent to which, as the empire expanded, so did the geopolitical perspective and strategy. The first step was that Chinggis Khan was destined to rule the Mongols, then all of the tribes of Mongolia, and then all of the tribes. For long, there was no interest in ruling sedentary populations. It was not until the 1230s that these ideas changed, probably as a product of the reality that the Mongols had conquered an empire and the assumption that they could not do it without the will of Heaven. Thus, it was argued that Heaven wanted them to rule the world.[2] More generally, sacred endorsement and support tended to be seen as requiring proselytism at the point of the sword as well as support for religious activity within the state.

Religious commitments and concerns, however, did not exclude other drives, nor did they provide the sole way to understand space. Jerusalem might be at the centre of medieval European 'T' maps, with the depiction of the world in terms of Europe, Asia and Africa, while medieval Indian cartography focused on astral bodies,[3] but that did not mean that the Crusaders had no understanding of the spatial geography of the Near and Middle East, nor the Lodi Sultanate of Delhi that of the geography of North India. Indeed, the location of Crusader castles suggests a very good appreciation both of the geopolitics of localities and of their broader relationships, although, alongside issues of control, especially over communication routes, there are also questions about the role of political symbolism in castle-building.[4]

Castle location, like that of walls, was a sharp edge of geopolitics but also one that underlines the difficulties of readily applying modern concepts of space, because, in this case, the notion of the frontier has varied across time, which means that the notion of the castle as a form of frontier consolidation and defence has to be seen in a changing context. These variations throw considerable light on the importance of geopolitics but also on its changing application. The salience of frontier consolidation and defence also serves as a reminder of the difficulties of distinguishing geopolitics from geostrategy.

Frontiers are a key site of concern in the study of geopolitics, but, like most of the vocabulary employed and applied by geopoliticians, that of frontiers is neither unique to them nor shaped by them. Indeed, frontiers, originally and primarily a legal concept (as a place locating sovereignty and authority) and also a geographical idea, now provide a basic language for linguistic and social studies, not least because of the interest, in these studies, in concepts of control and contention. The interchangeability of frontiers and borders contributes to this situation.

In a point that is of wider relevance for the study of geopolitics, linguistic and social-studies approaches, however, have relatively little to offer, except in so far as they demonstrate a central point about frontiers, namely that they are places of compliance as well as control, opportunities for eliciting cooperation as well as for asserting power and for achieving peaceful success as well as waging war. Indeed, for geopoliticians, there is an essential typology at stake, one, moreover, that covers both external conquest and internal rule. This typology encompasses two key understandings of the idea of force as an enabler of power, each of which is crucial to geopolitics: one of force as an assertor of control, the more usual emphasis, and the other of force as an expression of cooperation.

In practice, of course, there is a continuum of circumstance and also an overlap of definition between these understandings. This overlap, furthermore, adds a powerful element of complexity to geopolitical thought and the use of geopolitical language. Indeed, the resulting ambiguity should operate as a restraint on some of the more didactic use of geopolitical arguments by commentators not keen to probe the complex reality and understanding of terms such as control, dominance and expansion, let alone imperialism. Cooperation, for example, often rested on an asymmetrical relationship based on the stronger force of one power, while, in turn, control required compliance.

Nevertheless, the typology above offers a model that can be widely applied. The model is particularly valuable as it also addresses the internal dimension of control and contention, a dimension which is generally ignored in conventional accounts of geopolitics and frontiers, because internal lack of control rarely had (or has) a jurisdictional expression. Similarly, although not to the same extent, such lack of control rarely excited the attention of geopoliticians (at least prior to the work of 'critical geopoliticians') unless it extended to a large-scale insurrection, or, even better for most of their purposes, a civil war between regular or mostly regular forces, in the manner, in particular, of the English and American Civil Wars.

In practice, the denial of obedience short of such action was (and is) far more common, and this denial also lessened the authority and power of the state, but without being so clearly understandable in terms of the binary divisions that geopolitical writing tends to favour. Variations in authority and power within states led to internal frontiers[5] that were important, particularly, but not only, to large states. Indeed, a crucial aspect of empires was that they had to be able to adjust to the role of such internal frontiers.

Internal frontiers had varied consequences for geopolitics. Irrespective of whether they were characterised by rebellion, they were a challenge to the authority and, even more, power of states, and these frontiers could be the site of large-scale military activity, as with sustained and unsuccessful Mughal conflict with the rebellious Marathas in India in the seventeenth and eighteenth centuries. Ironically, internal frontiers could also be the site of military strength as the frontier relationship was frequently mediated, even defined, by the recruitment of auxiliaries for service with regular imperial forces, for example by imperial Rome.

This service was a key aspect of the rule of European and other imperial powers, although the recruitment of auxiliaries was not restricted to this method nor to these regions. To illustrate the complexity already referred to, this recruitment was an aspect of both strength and weakness, an expression of the need of the imperial power to negotiate for support, and yet also a product of its ability to do so. Taking this further, the military service could be on terms, explicit or implicit. This conditionality was another aspect of the internal frontier and a further reminder of its complexity, and, therefore, of the mistake of thinking or presenting power in terms of undifferentiated blocs.

Such presentation is an unfortunate tendency in much conventional geopolitical writing, especially by political commentators, and is, in part, a product of its role in the literature of political persuasion and, indeed, propaganda. The relationship between the Nazi empire and Vichy France in 1940–2 provides a recent instance of such conditionality, most obviously in the case of control over the French fleet and the French colonies in North Africa. Another example is that of the Soviet Union and Romania in the 1960s–1980s, or the exclusion, until 1918, of Ireland from conscription when it was introduced in Britain in 1916 during the First World War.

Both conditionality and complexity can also be seen at the level of international frontiers, and they serve as a reminder that interpretative geopolitical models that seek to simplify conflict and make it unidimensional, whether those of the European state system of the nineteenth century or, more recently, of the clash of civilisations,[6] are flawed. Much revisionism indeed has come from work on frontiers between civilisations and those they deemed barbarian, notably between China and its neighbours, and this work is pertinent for classical geopolitics with its emphasis on binary divides, as well as because of the interest, from Mackinder on, in the idea of a Eurasian Heartland pressing outwards on other societies in what would later be termed the Rimland.

Analysis of raids on China by steppe people (a subject where research bridges military and non-military history, indicating the tenuous character of the distinction) have emphasised the quest for politically useful luxury goods, rather than for subsistence, a quest also seen with Native Americans negotiating with Europeans in North America in the seventeenth to nineteenth centuries. More generally, the steppe people raided China to build alliances and to force the acceptance of commercial links. The relationship between the Russian princelings and the Tatars from the thirteenth to the late fifteenth century has also been presented in symbiotic terms.[7]

Work on the Eurasian steppe, for over a century a key area of geopolitical discussion, suggests that, rather than separating hostile blocs that were internally undifferentiated, frontiers were generally zones of interaction, and, moreover, that conflict was only one part of the interaction. Trade and other aspects of symbiotic behaviour were, also, very important. Furthermore, nomadic attacks frequently arose because the commercial and other relationships had been disturbed or the terms were no longer acceptable to one party; in short, these attacks were not the 'natural' characteristic of the relationship but a product of its failure. Most of the nomad rulers who controlled the northern borderlands wanted to extract resources from China, rather than to conquer it, this extraction was most efficient if relations were peaceful, and intervention was usually a response to political fragmentation within China.

Instances of failure occurred in the Ming–Mongol conflict of the 1440s and also in the refusal of the Ming to trade with the Mongols in the mid-sixteenth century, a refusal that has been traced to xenophobia and a determination to appear strong, both of which play a key role in international relations and need to be incorporated in geopolitical analysis. Partly as a result of poor relations with the Mongols, Ming China abandoned the voyages to the Indian Ocean from 1438 and focused on conflict to the north and not with other potential targets, for example Japan or the states on the southern borderlands. This geopolitical 'tasking' was highly significant not only to military goals but also to the pattern of Chinese military development.

From another perspective, geopolitics relates to the extent and range of polities with which a state interacts, and these change. Thus, earlier, the Northern Song empire (960–1126) dealt with the Tanguts in the north-west and the Kitan in the north-east, which ensured a much more extended sense of politics than that of some previous dynasties, but, in turn, one that was much less extended than that of the conquering Mongols.

When resort was had to war by the steppe people or China, there was a relationship between means and ends that affected the nature of the frontier and the character of geopolitics. Thus, the building of defensive walls by China altered the expression of the frontier. To turn to the most prominent attacker, the Mongols, in the thirteenth century, tended to invade and devastate a large region before withdrawing, thus creating a buffer zone that made it impossible to attack them and that also weakened the enemy's resource. This policy allowed the Mongols to fight on multiple fronts without overextending themselves.

Similar points to those raised in a discussion of China can be made about Imperial Rome, an empire that has attracted geopolitical discussion that is more widely relevant. Not all parts of the empire had frontier structures, such as Hadrian's Wall or the wall between the Rhine and the Danube, the role of which is anyway debated, and, more generally, it is argued that the Roman frontiers should be understood as permeable and shifting frontier zones. Thus, although the expansion of Roman power is generally shown in historical atlases in terms of a series of provincial 'annexations', this approach is misleading since it has little connection with contemporary perceptions of the *imperium populi Romani.* The notion of a political boundary for the Roman empire has itself been questioned.[8] It is also unclear how far the *provinciae* were thought of as territorial entities or had clearly defined boundaries.[9]

In addition, there is uncertainty about the Roman usage of maps, not that maps define spatial awareness. The Peutinger map, a medieval copy of Roman origin dating to about 300 CE, indicates that the Romans felt the need for cartographic sources, rather than merely written lists, with the map also placing accurately the main junction settlements on the roads. Yet, in practice, this map would have served travellers, administrators and generals poorly, and, instead, it should be considered as an idealistic, not to say propagandistic, item for display.

Moreover, Byzantine frontiers (those of the Eastern Roman Empire) have been presented as best understood as the shifting consequence of a number of dynamic elements that include the role of tribal transhumance.[10] These points about frontiers need to be borne in mind when assessing geopolitics and strategy, especially as there is a risk of ahistorically ascribing modern notions. Geopolitics and strategy indeed are centrally linked to frontier concepts as frontiers classically provided definitions of threat and opportunity, as well as sites for concern or advance.

Debate over the 'grand strategy' of the Roman empire is in part a discussion of geopolitics but one that is problematised by two historical issues, each of which is relevant across the range of historical examples and into the present; first, the limited nature of the sources, especially (but not only) as far as intentions are concerned, and, second, the difficulty of determining how far modern analytical approaches are appropriate. The latter has been a vexed issue in the debate over Edward Luttwak's influential, but also controversial, *The Grand Strategy of the Roman Empire from the First Century* AD *to the Third*, a work that has just been followed by *The Grand Strategy of the Byzantine Empire.*[11] In an interesting guide to the way in which geopolitical arguments can be regarded in a contrasting fashion by different specialists, military historians have found Luttwak more helpful[12] than other ancient historians have done. The latter have assumed that a systematic plan should be in evidence, and, in its absence, that there was no grand strategy.

In contrast, drawing on Luttwak, there have been attempts to classify Roman policy and to link apparent changes in policy to broader geopolitical issues. In particular, there was a shift towards a strong frontier defence based on permanent border garrisons, which was the norm from the late first century CE. This defence became more important when the Emperor Hadrian (r. 117–38) abandoned the Mesopotamian conquests of his predecessor, Trajan, whose war with Parthia to the east in 114–17 had exposed Rome's overreach. Moreover, alongside the requirement of a movement of forces from other frontiers to fight specific eastern wars, there was a permanent shift in the distribution of legions between the mid-70s CE and the mid-second century, particularly from the Rhine to the Danube and the East.

Manpower, a term that Mackinder was to develop,[13] and an indication of means relative to securing ends, was therefore a key element in geopolitics. The limits on Roman manpower exposed Rome's weakness to war on two fronts, which events were to force on them in the third century CE. The problem offers an instructive prefiguring of current American problems about relating force structure and strategy to the number of geopolitical commitments, and, indeed,

Luttwak was to go on to write and advise on American geostrategy. In turn, this prefiguring of current American problems can be inscribed onto current debates about priorities, as with the argument that Rome fell due to 'Barbarian' attack and not war with empires, such as Parthia, to the east; and, therefore, that the USA should focus on the War on Terror and not on symmetrical great-power conflict with China and Russia. Such a rereading of history into present and future, however, takes the practice too far, although rereading has proved, and will continue to prove, very attractive to publishers and to commentators who find ahistoricism a positive release.[14] Moreover, there is a tradition in American political discussion, as earlier in that of Britain when it was a great power, of looking at Roman examples.[15]

In about 235 CE, the frontier system of Imperial Rome was abandoned in favour of a defence in depth, relying on mobile field armies as the key element providing a strategic reserve in a system that included fixed fortifications. Cavalry played a greater role in these armies than hitherto in Roman warfare. A scholarly focus on patterns of troop movement indicates that imperial decision-making about grand strategic issues did occur. Prioritisation among objectives, and the resulting allocation of resources, were key factors,[16] and this allocation was inherently spatial as both challenges and opportunities were seen in terms of particular frontiers. The same was true of other empires, such as Philip II's Spain,[17] imperial Russia,[18] and imperial Britain.

Yet, as a reminder of the need to understand both geopolitics and strategy in their political context, although the ostensible purpose of these Roman field armies was to move out to meet invaders, their primary function often became the protection of the emperor from internal rivals. This emphasis ensured that provinces were left susceptible to invasion, a process that sapped both resources and political support, and that indeed can be seen as a form of negative geopolitics, a concept that would repay development. Moreover, the political role of the army was such that many of the emperors in the third century CE, for example Diocletian (r. 284–305), were

Illyrian soldiers from the western Balkans, a region that was a major recruiting base for the army. Thus, the geopolitics and strategy of the Roman empire became in large part a matter of the geopolitics of power within the empire, a point more generally true of states and one also relevant to the question of strategic overreach.

The relationship between the understanding of frontiers, geopolitics and warfare clearly varied, and this variation draws attention to controversies over the causes of war, not least the respective role of, and relationship between, structure and agency, as well as between the determination to fight and the specific factors that can cause war.[19] For example, the nature of geopolitics and boundaries in early modern African states, a contentious subject, help explain a key context of conflict there. In the approach of John Thornton, African law did not recognise landed private property and states did not assess land taxes.[20] State jurisdiction became critically important in defining who was taxable and who not, and the key goal of control was over labour, rather than land. This goal involved concepts of frontiers and boundaries and purposes of conflict that were different to the conventional European ones. Nevertheless, in early modern Africa, jurisdiction was ultimately territorially bounded, so that subjects of states could, and often did, cross the borders to escape taxation, though usually this only put them within the taxable boundaries of another similar state.

This situation was an aspect of the equation of force and labour control that was so important to the slave trade within and from Africa, a trade that very much reflected a type of geopolitics, namely the spatial dynamics of control over labour.[21] The emphasis on labour control was related in Africa to another aspect of the use of force, that by larger political units which typically agglomerated mini-states, either by charging them tribute or by interfering in their institutional, judicial or leadership functions. As a reminder of the value of a broad working definition of frontiers, the point at which such a state lost sovereignty and became a part of a larger unit is problematic: it is unclear whether it was when one state recognised the supremacy of another with nominal presents, or when significant tribute was assessed, or when judicial functions or leadership positions were taken over and appointed from outside, or when boundaries were completely redrawn.[22]

Moreover, the notion of a transforming interference by a more potent force is one that can, in part, be understood in terms of informal empire. Again underlying the potential value of historical scholarship for geopolitical work, this concept is one that was insufficiently deployed in the early twentieth-century age of classical geopolitics. In contrast, the idea of American imperialism has been employed more frequently since, notably (yet not only) in critiques of American power; but this description has not been employed with sufficient care, nor with adequate knowledge of the literature about informal empire.

It is all too easy to see European (and, after that, Western) international history as in some way different to that of the rest of the world, often with some Whiggish reference to the Westphalian system that supposedly began in the mid-seventeenth century. Yet, leaving aside the value of this system both as an analytical construct and as a set of norms, the European 'mind-set' was centred for long on an approach to territory in legal/feudal, rather than more modern, spatial terms; or, rather, space, and thus frontiers and the goals of conflict, were considered in these legal/feudal terms.[23] This situation pertained both before and after the Peace of Westphalia of 1648.

This emphasis on legal and feudal claims and issues was linked to a system in which there were areas of transition from one authority to another, often via several stages, as with the medieval Welsh March, which was militarily important. The March was the result of late-eleventh-century Norman invasion and conquest, but it remained part of Wales and not a kind of no-man's land between Wales and England. As territories and their relationships were the building blocks of spatial consideration and geopolitics, so the difficulty of assessing them is worthy of note, as it underlines the point already made about the need to handle terms with care. For example, Marcher lordship has been seen as essentially Welsh political authority exercised by Anglo-Norman lords by right of conquest, in short Welsh royal rights in baronial hands. More recently, however, Marcher lordship has been presented as compact feudal lordships, with much in common with lordships in northern France (whose lords made war and peace, and exercised 'high justice'), and with the 'castleries' of early Norman England, and with conflict organised accordingly.

A chronological dimension in judging spatial identities and related values is also of value. Marcher lordships came to look increasingly odd as the March stayed outside the orbit of the developing common law and centralised government in England, but that was not yet the case in the eleventh century. However, although the March had its own law and Marcher lordships were part of Wales rather than England, they came to be regarded as held of the English Crown, which exercised rights of wardship, marriage and escheat over feudal vassals. Indeed, in the twelfth and thirteenth centuries, many lordships spent lengthy periods in the king's hands, or were pushed towards his supporters through marriage to heiresses.[24]

More generally, the widespread medieval practice of overlapping jurisdiction and divided sovereignty challenged an approach to territory in modern terms. As a result, territorial divisions are difficult to represent clearly on modern maps, a point that is worth bearing in mind when trying, without qualification, to employ modern methods of exposition in order to explain, let alone analyse, geopolitics in the past. As a prominent medievalist pointed out:

> it is well known that even when the course of a frontier can be accurately plotted – and that is rare for the Middle Ages – it meant less than it does now, being more often than not simply the boundary between the lands of the villages which owed returns to lords who were the subjects of different powers. In

> some regions, indeed, frontiers were characterized by broad belts of *condominia*, in which lords of different nationalities, and in Palestine and Syria of different religions, shared the ownership of great swathes of villages. Customs posts were sometimes to be found . . . but they were often not on the border itself.[25]

The same was true of many other cultures.[26] Even in the Italian states of the early Renaissance, then the epicentre of European scientific and geographical discourse, 'mapping was not a common conceptual tool', and this point was important to the understanding of what frontiers meant. At the same time that mapping was developing in Europe even before the impact of the Age of European Exploration,[27] subjects such as the division of ownership of open-field farmland or directions for a journey 'continued to be expressed through verbal details of boundaries and topological lists of travel days'.[28]

Nevertheless, medieval and Renaissance states clearly had a concept of the spatial dimension of power. For example, the rulers of the House of Aragon displayed such a concept both in in-house-type statements among the royal family and officials and in public, political statements meant to persuade. Among the in-house statements, a remark of Pere III (r. 1336–87) to his heir in 1380 is typical: 'If Sardinia is lost, Majorca, without its food supply from Sicily and Sardinia, will be depopulated and will be lost, and Barcelona will also be depopulated, for Barcelona could not live without Sicily and Sardinia, nor could its merchants trade if the isles were lost.'[29]

Pere was in this trying to convince his heir to keep up the dynasty's long and intractable effort to conquer Sardinia, as well as trying to persuade him to seek a bride among their own cousins in Sicily. Part of this geographical awareness certainly came from the dynasty's long Mediterranean involvement in the islands and its ties to merchants and sailors. The famous cartographic school in Majorca, which came under royal patronage, after Pere conquered the island in 1342–3, was an aspect of this involvement. This school focused on the production of portolan maps, some of them luxury presentation-type items on royal commission.

The dynasty also showed as much geographic awareness about its landward side. Thus, in 1363, Pere told an assembly that the Castilians were about to conquer the whole Crown of Aragon:

> Now we give ourselves to great disaster and great misadventure, and what we have striven to conquer for five centuries, we lose in fifteen days. And we consciously tell you fifteen days, and not more, because according to the news we have had today before the meal, the king of Castile comes to these parts with great power, and we understand that he will come to Zaragoza. . . . If it [Zaragoza] is lost in consequence, we do not reckon that he will stop until [he reaches] the sea, even to Barcelona, and Barcelona is not a city that can withstand a long siege, because it is not in a place that has or can have much food, but instead it would be lost in a long siege through lack of food.[30]

This kind of domino-effect statement was very frequent: Pere frequently told captains that they had to defend a castle at a ford because of what the enemy could reach if they gained the ford; or he lamented the fall of one castle because that made specific others extremely vulnerable; and so on. Likewise he would argue that it was better to attack in one place or another because of terrain or logistics.

Pere's chronicle was also meticulous about tracing the stages of his itinerary around his kingdoms; this was in accordance with the King's instructions to the secretaries who wrote the chronicle for him. He appears to have thought of the chronicle in part as a book of advice for future rulers.

The court also displayed a sort of chess-like sense of power and power-rankings, which offer an aspect of spatiality. Thus, in one letter, Pere tried to persuade the King of

Portugal to abandon his alliance with the King of Castile, by arguing that the latter was reaching for domination of the whole peninsula. Similarly, he tried to persuade the Foix to stop attacking him, reminding them that their nearby enemies, the Armagnacs, were always watching for an opening. This geopolitical awareness, however, existed alongside more stereotypically 'medieval' features, as when Pere, looking for funds to fight in Sardinia, treated an assembly to a long scholastic discourse on all the meanings of 'ingratitude'.[31]

The nature of frontiers was linked to the conceptualisation of territory, a key element in geopolitical thought, and this conceptualisation was related not only to issues of sovereignty but also to the goals of conflict. In Western Europe, in the medieval and early modern periods, the essential unit of diplomatic exchange and strife was jurisdictional-territorial, and not geographical-territorial. This focus was reflected in the dominance of succession disputes in the international relations of the period. For example, most of the major wars in Western Europe in the pre-Revolutionary eighteenth century were succession conflicts – the Wars of the Spanish (1701–14), Polish (1733–5), Austrian (1740–8) and Bavarian (1778–9) Successions, while the Seven Years' War (1756–63) can be seen, at least in Europe, as an attempt to reverse the principal territorial consequence of the War of the Austrian Succession, the Austrian loss of Silesia to Prussia, and thus as an extension of that war. Succession conflicts focused on who ruled territory rather than on how that territory was defined.

For the pre-Westphalian period, there was a major emphasis on ideology, in the shape of the Wars of Religion of the 1540s to 1648, although the territorial building blocks at dispute were jurisdictional-territorial. In addition, succession disputes were important in this period, for example with the War of the Mantuan Succession (1628–31), which involved France and the Habsburgs, or indeed with the French royal succession in the latter stages of the French Wars of Religion in the 1590s. A focus on succession issues serves as a reminder of the salience of dynasties. They, rather than the abstract concept of states, were the key determinants, and it is unclear how far subsequent theories of international relations are really appropriate when considering the geopolitics of dynastic interests and of *gloire* in past societies. Moreover, the modern resonances of the geopolitics of *gloire* repay consideration.

For pre-modern societies, an understanding of the spatial understanding and bounding of notions of honour is problematic, other than in dynastic terms, which tended to equate with legal and feudal considerations. The dynastic dimension, however, was very varied, not least because of the tensions between opportunistic and legitimist dynasticism.[32] The former lends itself to discussion in terms of the geopolitical goals of particular rulers. Honour was also bound up in other issues such as confessional conflicts.

Yet such religious wars offered a different context for geopolitical issues in that the issues at stake were less subject to compromise than disputes over dynastic concerns. Thus, the European Wars of Religion of the 1540s to 1648 created and reflected a geopolitics that did not propose jurisdictional boundaries, but, instead, an ideological world view and urgency that transposed into Europe rivalries hitherto seen when confronting the infidel outside, notably Islam in the long series of conflicts that began with its expansion from the seventh century. The phrase 'created and reflected' presents the analytical problem of determining the agency involved in geopolitics, a problem that is latent in the literature but not always explicitly discussed. How far do issues create a geopolitics, or how far does whatever is understood to comprise the latter lead to particular issues becoming important? A non-linear approach to the past, one that notes discontinuities in policy and circumstances, would suggest the former, but much geopolitical literature emphasises the formative power of geopolitical factors.

There might appear to be a parallel between the Wars of Religion and late-twentieth-century Cold War confrontations, not least in terms of the frequently complex relationship between ideological clarity and the particular strategies of rulers and ruling groups. Thus, there could be cooperation with the outside group against co-religionists, as in medieval Spain (for both Christians and Moors) or with the Crusader kingdoms (again for both sides), or in the sixteenth and seventeenth centuries with rulers of France allying with German Protestant Princes and also the Ottoman Turks against the Habsburgs: thus Francis I cooperated with Suleiman the Magnificent while Henry II's successful siege of Metz in 1552 was designed to benefit from confessional conflict in Germany. Richelieu was to pursue a similar policy, notably in subsidising Gustavus Adolphus of Sweden to attack Austria in 1630. Such cooperation offers a qualification to attempts to argue for the centrality of ideological division.

At the same time, at the general or systemic level, there was scant attempt to work out limits or compromises, containment or détente, until the Wars of Religion ended with only local and regional victories. In the meanwhile, debates over policy could (and should) not be seen solely as part of the ordinary waft and warp of adversarial politics, whether ministerial, court or public. Instead, given the problems posed by, or believed to be posed by, religious division, both international and minorities within states, these debates focused on more serious questions of ideology and loyalty.

While the Wars of Religion dramatised the role of ideological factors in international and domestic power politics in early modern Europe, this issue did not exhaust the place of religious considerations in geopolitics. In addition, sacred space involved fundamental questions of legitimacy, such as that enjoyed by the Ottoman Sultans as a consequence of their custody of the Muslim holy places of Mecca, Medina and Jerusalem. They had gained this custody as a result of the conquest of the Mameluke empire in 1516–17, a conquest that transformed the geopolitics of the Islamic world and also of the Mediterranean. Similarly, the Dukes of Savoy-Piedmont, in moving their court and capital from Chambéry in Savoy to Turin in Piedmont in the 1560s, also moved the Holy Shroud, a relic that gave the dynasty particular prestige. Moreover, the dukes sought to patronise shrines whose saints could be seen as working for the state as a whole and not for only part of it. The cult of relics was another aspect of the pursuit of status, as well as of the ranking of places and institutions within the state.[33]

The absence of ideological triumph in the Wars of Religion led to a different tone in the geopolitics of international relations in the second half of the seventeenth century, as well as looking towards a new definition of Europe, one that moved away from a Christian understanding of goals, external limits and internal organisation, and, instead, towards a secular geopolitics. Moreover, as a result of the decline of the religious rift as a key element in international relations, there was a stronger concern with the specific and regional that had been the case over the previous century, although, even then, this element had been very important.

The historical legacy was a difficult one. Aside from the emphasis on territory as a jurisdictional entity, frontiers, such as that of France in Alsace, were frequently highly complex and remained characterised by divided sovereignty. This point can be appreciated if it is stressed that abstractions such as France described the patrimonies of ruling dynasties, whose possessions and pretensions extended as a result of, and in the context of, feudal overlordships,[34] rather than a situation of 'natural' linear frontiers, such as rivers. Thus, medieval experience remained very relevant.

This point serves as a reminder that the continuity of spatial elements that is a key point in geopolitical literature is not a continuity restricted to the physical environment nor to resources. Looked at differently, claims to territory are an important aspect of spatial resource, one moreover that was not necessarily swept aside by, nor subordinated to, ideological considerations.

Geopolitics in part entailed the understanding of spatial issues, and thus perception and information were important to this process. An important endeavour to understand and rationalise jurisdictional-territorial prerogatives was instigated in Louis XIV's France. In 1663, Jean-Baptiste Colbert issued an instruction to all provincial officials ordering them to send all available maps and geographical information to

Paris. This knowledge was then used by Nicolas Sanson, the *géographe du cabinet,* to devise an unprecedented series of maps which would clearly 'illustrate the divisions between military, judicial, fiscal and ecclesiastical administrative units' of the realm.[35]

In Eastern Europe, in contrast, geographical-territorial issues played a larger role than their jurisdictional counterparts. The major states in the region lacked good historic claims to the areas in dispute, the texture of sovereign polities was less dense (and increasingly less dense) than in Western Europe, not least because hitherto autonomous regions, such as Ukraine, were brought under control,[36] and dynastic succession was not the major diplomatic idiom, nor generally a means by which large areas of territory changed hands and through which relative power could be assessed. For example, succession disputes were not the issue at stake between Russia and its rivals. The idiom of disputes in Eastern Europe, instead, was geographical-territorial, and this emphasis put a premium on spatial considerations, and on the framing of senses of opportunity in spatial terms.[37] International relations and war became in part a measure of the pursuit and impact of such considerations.

The implication of this contrast between Western and Eastern Europe, for geopolitics, military tasking and the planning and conduct of operations, has not been teased out but requires research and discussion. A focus on jurisdictional-territorial goals probably led not only to an emphasis on the gain of particular territories (rather than territory as a whole, let alone the destruction of the opponent's army), but may well also have encouraged sieges of the cities that were the centre of jurisdictions, for example Besançon (over Franche-Comté), Lille (over what became French Flanders), or Perpignan (over Roussillon), irrespective of their abstract military value. The way of grasping control, symbolically as well as practically, needs to be assessed, not least in terms of the international response that would register and legitimate a transfer of territory. Concepts of decisive victory in battle are not terribly helpful here, and, instead, as so often, represent an unwarranted extrapolation of a particular type of conflict, and, specifically, the reading back of the views of a distinct period. Modern counterparts suggest themselves, particularly the importance of symbolic factors in wielding control and exerting influence, and also the difference between military output and outcome.

Alongside the issue of goals came that of means, and spatial considerations were particularly important in terms of communications and logistics, notably routes used for movement and supply. Thus, the 'Spanish Road', the route along which 10,000 Spanish troops marched north in 1567 from Italy to the Low Countries, was a key factor in strategy and strategic capability,[38] as, subsequently, was the Valtelline Pass through which Spanish troops could march from Milan to Austria.

A more spatially territorial approach to frontiers developed in Europe in the eighteenth century, although this process remained incomplete at the time of the outbreak of the French Revolution in 1789. The process was related to the consolidation of territorial sovereignty, the increasing state monopolisation of organised violence, and the mapping of frontiers, all of which can be seen as crucial preparations to the stage of international relations that was to give birth to modern concepts of 'realist' international behaviour, including geopolitics as classically understood. This process extended to the Turks, with Ahmed Resmi, in the 1760s, mapping the frontier province of Wallachia, a province the control of which had been contested earlier in the century.[39]

There was an important military component in Europe, as the implementation of firm frontiers was bound up with the existence of more assertive states and growing state bureaucracies, which sought to know where exactly they could impose their demands for resources, including recruits, and where they needed to create their first line of defence. At the same time, the control of frontier zones by states enhanced their military capability, not least by strengthening the provision of supplies that was so crucial for operating in and beyond these zones. Geopolitical capacity thus involved governmental as well as military strength. There was a widespread symbiotic relationship similar to that identified by Brian L. Davies in his remark that

> the single most important contribution to Muscovy's imperial project in the southern steppe in the seventeenth century was less directly linked to the field army than to the spread of the *voevoda* system of local government, which greatly enhanced the central chancelleries' control over resource mobilisation at the local level and thereby allowed Moscow to pursue an ambitious program of planned military colonisation.[40]

Moreover, international competition helped drive both state formation and also, as a consequence of the interaction of geopolitics, war and state formation, led to pronounced differences between states. These differences related to internal structure as much as apparently objective measures of strength in terms of territory or population. Indeed, the capability for effective governance suggested by these factors of internal structure and political culture helped determine the benefit, in terms of revenue and troops, that could be obtained from these measures of strength.[41] These differences between states, in turn, created opportunities for expansion, notably by Prussia, Russia and Austria in the three Partitions of Poland in 1772–95.[42] Much of the discussion of international relations became a matter of considering how best to respond to these differences and also how to secure their continuance to the benefit of particular states. Both ideological and practical issues played a role in this discussion.

CHAPTER 3

GEOPOLITICS BEFORE THE TERM: MAPS

In the interaction between geopolitics, war and state formation in the European world, geographical information became increasingly prominent in the early modern period and was regarded as important by contemporaries. In the case of Sweden, for example, there was a marked change between the sixteenth century and the first half of the seventeenth in which military map-making and naval cartography began, both by collecting maps and by the training of professional mapmakers. The Swedish war archives contains a collection of maps from the Thirty Years' War (which Sweden entered in 1630) and later, reflecting the army's need of maps for planning and information during operations in foreign countries. Moreover, the National Land Survey of Sweden, which began in 1628 under the guidance of Anders Bureus, mapped not only Sweden in large-scale but also lands occupied by the Swedes.

The varied potential of maps as information systems repays consideration, as this issue throws considerable light on the extent to which geographical knowledge could be involved in the formulation and execution of policy. A map presented such knowledge at a distance. War was the prime focus for such knowledge, and General Henry Lloyd argued in 1766 that the 'most important object of any, to those who aspire to the command of armies, is geography'. For Lloyd, this was a matter not only of topography and natural resources, but also of 'form of government' and its consequences for the society in question.[1]

To be effective tactically – in short, to have power over a locality – it was necessary to understand the terrain. Maps could help in this,[2] and terrain was already being mapped in manuscript in the mid-1540s, as in John Rogers's technically advanced plans of the environs of Boulogne in the Cotton Collection in the British Library. Such mapping did not need to be precise in order to meet the needs of the planners, and, by the late sixteenth century, the mapping of terrain was commonplace in manuscript mapping. The mapping of topography was to be more common and more precise by the late nineteenth century, by when the surveying and mapping of height had improved, not least with the use of contours. Nevertheless, there were useful devices prior to that, for example using numbers to indicate the relative height of the ground, a technique known as relative command and taught by François Jarry, a French émigré who became Topographical Instructor at the British Royal Military College in 1799. He influenced the teaching of reconnaissance to the Royal Engineers, as can be seen in the reconnoitring sketches that were used by the Duke of Wellington to plan his successful dispositions at the battle of Waterloo in 1815.

Maps were particularly important for the use of artillery, not so much at the tactical level (because of the problems of mapping height), but, instead, at the operational one, as maps provided indications of where artillery could be transported. Maps could be unhelpful in their depiction of roads,[3] but this need was being well catered for in manuscript mapping by 1710, and there was an awareness of it in the 1530s, as in Thomas Elyot's *The Boke Named the Governour* (1531), a work that praised the utility of maps. More generally, the need for information on where cannon could be transported was a product of the operational issues posed by the greater scale of war, and by the need, despite this scale, to retain mobility. Thus, an understanding of routes was crucial to war, and maps provided a key aspect of this.

The eighteenth century featured conflicts in which the operational theatre spanned hundreds of miles. Notably in North America, European forces had to traverse vast distances often through wild, inhospitable terrain, making large armies vulnerable to enemy tactics of *petite guerre*, by which small, highly mobile, detachments carried out fleeting attacks and ambuscades on the flanks of their larger adversary. Commanders therefore required maps which conveyed very practical knowledge that would allow their forces to move quickly without being overexposed to enemy action. This gave rise to what Brian Harley subsequently termed 'the cartography of military movement', which included two distinct practices of cartography: reconnaissance maps and route maps. With reference to the former, commanders would dispatch troops, sometimes disguised as civilians, to record observations which were 'closely related to the requirements of troops moving through and subsisting in unfamiliar terrain. By means of sketches and written notes, only relevant information was to be collected.'[4]

While such maps and instructions would include details such as major roads, bridges and obvious sources of supplies, in addition to serious obstacles, these maps, although drawn to a rough scale, were invariably crude, being executed with some degree of haste. Nevertheless, such reconnaissance mapping was often not done in anticipation of any specific military movement but rather in anticipation of activity in that general theatre. For example, in February 1775, just months before the battle of Bunker Hill, General Thomas Gage dispatched two amateur surveyors to reconnoitre the countryside around Boston, their maps and notes today being preserved in the Library of Congress.[5] The need for maps was recognised and British officers were to be issued with the *American Military Atlas* (1776).[6]

The second type of cartography in North American warfare, route maps, were usually executed by professional military surveyors, laying out the intended course of a specific armed force under set conditions: 'As a generator of cartographical by-products, such troop movement was a formal activity that had more in common with fortification planning than with reconnaissance.'[7] While they may have incorporated intelligence gleaned from reconnaissance maps, these maps laid out specific routes for the army to take, often also drawing on information from (sometimes already existing) topographical surveys conducted under scientific conditions. This mapping was often undertaken with specific reference to an intended itinerary which considered daily progress and the most appropriate sites for encampments and resupply of the force. As a result, an accurate and formal detailing of distances and features of the landscape was critical. Perhaps the finest set of route maps produced during the period are the refined manuscript copies of the maps by the Comte de Rochambeau's engineers which painstakingly charted the route of the French forces from Newport, Rhode Island to Yorktown, Virginia in 1781. This carefully chosen route afforded the force the speed and stealth which allowed them to arrive at their objective at an ideally opportune moment, while avoiding British detection.[8]

Indeed, in so far as warfare provided a central aspect of the expanded use of maps for planning purposes, it was route-planning that was fundamental. The Gough Map of England of c. 1360 and, even more convincingly, because route planning for invasion purposes was the stated purpose of the maps, the Hardynge maps of Scotland of c. 1420–50 showed military invasion routes. Signot's map of Italy, which appeared in manuscript in 1498 and in print in 1515, was explicitly an invasion plan for Louis XII and then Francis I of France during the lengthy Italian wars. Maps of Franche-Comté were produced in order to help plan the route for Spanish units moving through the province en route between Italy and the Low Countries in the late sixteenth century. The maps showed relief features, which crucially affected routes and timing along part of the so-called 'Spanish Road'.[9]

This process was not restricted to Western Europe, although the use of military mapping by non-Western societies appears to have been limited.[10] The first Polish campaign to rely on theatre maps drawn up expressly for the campaign was King Stefan Báthory's successful 1579 campaign to retake Polotsk from Ivan the Terrible (Ivan IV) of Russia. In this case, maps of the Lithuanian–Muscovite border were prepared by Maciej Strubicz, Stanislaw Pacholowiecki and the Wallachian Petr Frankus. The Russians made increased use of mapping in the seventeenth century, especially towards the close. For his march on the Crimean khanate in the successful campaign of 1689, Prince Golitsyn made use of a primitive wagon-mounted odometer and compiled a *versta* or distance-book that was intended to be used to prepare a map. This book is preserved in the archive of the Military Chancellery and is useful in retracing the route Golitsyn's army took.[11]

Maps that could aid campaigning were more common, however, further west. Under Henry IV of France (r. 1589–1610), the *ingénieurs du roi* produced detailed manuscript maps of the major frontier provinces, maps that were designed to aid campaigning against Spain and Savoy and that were soon printed. One of the engineers, Jean de Beins, who was also a fortification expert in Dauphiné, drew maps based on his surveys of the different valleys which he then linked into a master map. A map of Ireland survives in the French archives, showing the major military moves made in the campaign there in 1690. By then, the French had established a permanent collection of maps for military purposes, the Dépôt de la Guerre being founded in 1688. The records of fortifications there included the *Recueil des plans des places du roi,* also known as the *Louvois Atlas* of 1683–8.[12]

War led up to an increased demand for geographical information. Thus, the silk maps printed for military use in northern Italy at the Milanese press of Marc' Antonio Del Re in the 1730s and 1740s, during the Wars of the Polish (1733–5) and Austrian (1740–8) Successions, for example *Italiae Septentrionalis* (1735) and *Nuova Carta Corografica, o sia centro del gran teatro di guerra in Piemonte Savoia l'anno 1744* (1744), were very useful for route-planning as well as for indicating the geographical relationship of the numerous principalities. As war involved the pursuit of military advantage in terms of the politics of this complex territorial world, so it was necessary to understand the geopolitics of the latter. The war in northern Italy could also be followed in Johannes Covens and Cornelis Mortier's *Le Cours du Po* (1735), which may have helped the negotiators at The Hague seeking (unsuccessfully) to settle the War of the Polish Succession in negotiations during the winter of 1734–5.

Similarly, it is no accident that Georges-Louis Le Rouge published in Paris in 1768 a *Carte Militaire de l'Isle de Corse,* for that was the year France purchased the island from the republic of Genoa, only to face a rebellion that led to large-scale, and ultimately successful, military intervention. Le Rouge was a military engineer and cartographer, and his wall map of Corsica marked the military posts. He was also to publish *Cartes des Troubles de l'Est* (1770), at the time of the Russo-Turkish war of 1768–74, a conflict followed with attention further west where it appeared to usher in the beginning of the Eastern Question. The activities of Le Rouge were an instance of the growing importance in eighteenth-century Europe of large-scale military surveys. These were part of a larger economy of knowledge, which expanded considerably, helped by the diffusion of information through print.[13]

This cartography and literature became more prominent from the 1750s and seems to be related, at least in part, to the expansion of the zones of war away from an emphasis on positional conflict (and zones), classically sieges of fortified positions, to larger, theatre-wide operations, as well as transoceanic campaigning, which became more important for Britain from 1755. This significance of maps for route-planning was particularly true of operations beyond the area of existing European territorial control, not only Russian advances against the Turks southwards into the Balkans but also European transoceanic expansionism. An absence of maps hindered the Dutch in their unsuccessful operations into the interior of Sri Lanka in 1764, and, as a result, Lubert Jan Baron Van Eyck, the Dutch Governor, had new maps drawn while his forces operated.

An emphasis on the significance of maps for route-planning helped ensure a degree of 'non-specificity' that is one of the characteristics of military cartography and, indeed, an aspect of its more general importance to the development and practice of mapping. This non-specificity relates to the extent to which maps were not solely of value for military purposes, nor only part of a wider geopolitical agenda. Indeed, a key problem with the issue of warfare and cartography for Enlightenment Europe and, more generally, is that there is a tendency to understand it in terms of military cartography – maps produced specifically for the military or for related state purposes – whereas this cartography was only a fraction of the usage of maps, and, as will be discussed later (see pp. 55–62), wartime cartography involved more than military operations.

A wider geopolitical agenda can be readily grasped in the case of British military mapping, as during the period between the Seven Years' War (1756–63) and the American Revolution (1775–83), 'military mapmaking tended to undergo a process of "civilianization," characterized by subtle adaptation, conscious or unconscious, of military objectives, surveyors, and technical skills to serve the wider needs of colonial government.'[14] This point can also be seen with the mapping of coasts and waters, which served commercial as well as military ends. In turn, an instance of the ownership of such maps by a key figure is shown in the copy of the *Atlas Maritimus and Commercialis; or, a General View of the World* (1728) by Nathaniel Cutler and Edmond Halley that belonged to John Clevland, a commissioner of the Navy from 1743–6 who became Joint Secretary to the Admiralty from 1746, and sole Secretary from 1751 until his death in 1763. This work included a coasting pilot for mariners with fine charts of most trading areas of the world. Geographical knowledge was clearly linked to naval and economic power.

The Royal Navy came to play a major role in encouraging the production of charts. After the Seven Years' War, the Swiss-born Joseph Frederick Wallet DesBarres, who had been trained at the Royal Military College, Woolwich, and served as a military engineer in North America, was instructed to survey the coastlines of Nova Scotia, Newfoundland and the Gulf of St Lawrence, which became a basis for his *The Atlantic Neptune*, a survey of the east coast of North America.[15]

Earlier, in the late sixteenth century, there was much awareness of the utility of charts for warfare and defence. Anthony Ashley, the Secretary to the English Privy Council, sponsored the translation into English of Waghenaer's rutter and charts in the months before the Spanish Armada in 1588. Established commercial chart publishers were called on in the seventeenth and eighteenth centuries to meet official needs for charts, as with the activities of the Blaeu dynasty in connection with the Dutch East and West India Companies in the seventeenth century,[16] and the publication of the *Neptune François* and the Dutch pirated version in the early 1690s.

In a direct and ultimately successful challenge to Dutch hegemony over the sea-chart market, a challenge that can be linked to the movement of maritime hegemony to England, the initial issue of *The English Pilot, Book Four,* covering American coastlines, was published in London in 1689. Eventually running to four books encompassing the known globe, numerous editions were published throughout the eighteenth century. Although many of the maps dealing with European waters were derivatives of earlier Dutch charts, the work proved enormously popular, not least due to the charts' accompaniment with sailing directions written in the English language. The project had been conceived in the 1670s by John Seller but was only realised by the cartographer John Thornton in collaboration with the publisher William Fisher. Most of the subsequent editions of *The English Pilot* were published by the firm of Mount & Page.[17] Official hydrographic offices followed in Britain, France and Spain in the eighteenth century. The pace of development varied by state, but there was a clear direction of change.[18]

Naval operations were heavily dependent on maps. The Swedish navy used Dutch maps of the Baltic Sea until 1645 when the first Swedish map was published by the navy's Senior Master Pilot Johan Månsson. This map was greatly reliant on the Dutch maps. A much better map was published by Petter Gedda in 1695 after extensive surveying operations, and, from then on, the navy continually surveyed and updated maps of the Baltic and the Swedish coast.

As a testimony to the importance attached to geographical material, there were attempts to restrict the availability of maps, and indeed of information, especially about distant areas. In particular, the Spanish government tried to keep other Europeans out of the Pacific, which it regarded as a monopoly, and to restrict likely information about the ocean. However, in 1680, a band of English buccaneers under Bartholomew Sharp crossed the Isthmus of Darien from the Atlantic to the Pacific. Using a Spanish vessel they had seized off Panama, they then attacked Spanish shipping, before navigating the waters south of Cape Horn from west to east (Pacific to Atlantic) and returning to England in 1682. The band included Basil Ringrose, who both wrote a journal of the expedition that was published in 1685 and compiled a substantial 'waggoner' – a description in the form of sailing directions – to much of the coast he sailed along as well as to some parts he never visited. This description stemmed from the *derrotero* or set of official manuscript sailing directions, illustrated by a large number of coastal charts, that Sharp seized from a captured Spanish ship in 1681 and that he presented to Charles II of England in order to win royal favour. Such atlases had been regarded by the Spaniards as too confidential to go into print.[19]

Earlier, Jan Huyghen van Linschoten, who had worked as a clerk and scribe for the Portuguese Archbishop of Goa, being involved in mapmaking, returned to the Low Countries, in the 1590s, and passed on the cartographic information that the Portuguese had consistently striven to keep a secret. His commercial espionage helped enable the Dutch East India Company to deploy its naval force in the Indian Ocean. Van Linschoten published his findings in *Itinerario: Voyage ofte schipvaert van Jan Huygen van Linschoten naar Oost ofte Portugaels Indien, inhoudende een corte beschrijvinghe der selver landen ende zeecusten* (1595–6). In turn, the maps of the Dutch East India Company were secret and therefore not printed. Secrecy was also the case for maps of forts, and indeed for detailed maps of important ports, which, for example, the Swedes kept secret. Controlling geopolitical knowledge was a strategic concern.

The emphasis on only fractional usage of maps for military purposes, or, looked at differently, on the wide parameters of geopolitical information, can be expanded by considering two other dimensions of warfare and cartography, the strategic and the public. The degree to which strategy existed in this period is a matter of debate, and there have been arguments that strategic planning is not a helpful concept. Certainly, in terms of the institutionalisation of planning seen by 1900, with the development of General Staffs on the Prussian model, and indeed with strategy as a formal military process, there was scant strategic planning in the early modern period. However, that is possibly not the most helpful basis of comparison, not least because the issue of allocating military resources between competing commitments was a serious one, and it is difficult to see how this issue can be understood other than in terms of strategy. More generally, information about resources played a role in planning.[20]

Furthermore, there are instances of strategic planning, as by the British in 1726–7 when considering how best for the Anglo-French Alliance of Hanover to resist likely Austrian and Prussian advances in Germany.[21] In such cases, a sense of place was crucial as British ministers wished to prevent such advances from threatening Hanover, the ancestral territory of the Hanoverian dynasty then on the British throne. To that end, the value to the Alliance of Hanover of seizing and using the Rhine crossing point at Rheinfels was emphasised.[22] If archives, printed primaries and secondary literature were systematically searched for such material, then it is likely that far more would be uncovered. Maps played a role. In the early 1760s, the French navy used a map for a planned invasion of England. This showed how particular French squadrons were designed to blockade Plymouth and Portsmouth, while another covered an invasion near Hastings. The location of the invading troops was also depicted.[23]

This is a rare survivor, but Philip II of Spain must have had something like an invasion plan of England, while Henry VIII appears to have sought maps of the Boulogne area from John

Rogers with a view to deciding on the most advantageous boundary line between his and Francis I's forces during their peace negotiations in 1546. In the next reign, Thomas Seymour is recorded as trying to use a manuscript map of England in the late 1540s to demonstrate the extent and strategic nature of his support as a means of persuading his friends to join him in revolt against his brother, the Protector Somerset. Royal and princely collections of maps were a major feature of early modern courts, notably with the painted maps that decorated audience halls. The use of maps for overlapping utilitarian and symbolic purposes was matched by that of globes, for example those displayed in the Escorial, Philip II's major palace. Rulers were particularly interested in maps of their own estates but also amassed collections of battle plans and maps. Maps were to record triumphs, for example those of the French Crown in the seventeenth century, which were depicted by Jacques Callot, Stefano della Bella, Nicolas Cochir, Sébastien de Pontault and Romeyn de Hooghe. The Landgraves of Hesse-Cassel amassed an excellent collection of maps[24] which are very revealing about the visual depiction of military operations. Clearly, the Landgraves actively collected information about earlier battles.

There are also examples of the use of maps by ministers in order to understand the military dimension of international crises. In response to the crisis of war with Spain (1585–1604), Lord Burghley's map of Lancashire depicted the seats of both Catholic and Protestant gentry, a clear indication of the security problems believed to be posed by the loyalties of the former.[25] Two centuries later, the use of maps can be seen, during the Dutch crisis of 1787, in the advice offered the British Cabinet in person by Charles, 3rd Duke of Richmond, the Master-General of the Ordnance, and Sir James Harris, the British envoy in The Hague, and later 1st Earl of Malmesbury. Richmond demonstrated the contrast between the distance allied Prussian troops would have to traverse from their base in Cleve, in order to mount an invasion of the Netherlands, with the greater distance which French forces need take from Givet in order to intervene on behalf of their Dutch protégés.[26]

In 1800, George Canning wrote to his successor as Under-Secretary in the British Foreign Office about French campaigning in Italy, 'What do you think of the Italian news? And what consolation does Pitt point out after looking over the map in the corner of his room by the door?'[27]

The public dimension of the use of maps fits most easily with the theme of the development of a public sphere[28] in which map consumption was driven by the interaction of public demand and entrepreneurial activity. Such a public sphere is a commonplace in discussion of Enlightenment culture and, although it may be overplayed,[29] the thesis has considerable value. War provided a key issue for the public, which, in part, reflected a different political agenda to that of the modern world, with far less government attention devoted to economic management, social welfare or health and education as public issues. Second, despite claims about pre-Revolutionary warfare as limited and indecisive, there were key issues at stake, not least fears about hegemony in Europe, as well as the fate of transoceanic power. Indeed, the crucial nature of these issues is an important qualification of the argument of limited warfare, which, anyway, is of questionable value given casualty rates and also the impact of hostilities on civilians.[30]

Public interest encouraged the production of two types of maps, first the plans of prominent battles. In 1590, an account of the defeat of the Spanish Armada two years earlier was illustrated by a set of plans by Robert Adams showing the successive stages of the campaign on a background of scale maps of the English Channel. Illustrative plans and maps were being published with official connivance in England by at least 1689, when Thomas Phillips published plans of Londonderry, which was then being blockaded by forces loyal to James II. That plans were produced was an instructive variant on the earlier focus on pictures, although the latter remained prominent.

Furthermore, there was the important fusion type: of the illustration of the conflict that included a map of the battle. In this format, the illustration provided the dynamic quality and sense of vigour and could also throw light on the topography of the battle. The map, however, was clearly part of the authority of the scene. Such a fusion was also seen in depictions of naval battles such as that between the British and Franco-Spanish fleet off Toulon in 1744.[31] The limited number of ships involved in naval battles facilitated this process.

Second, public interest encouraged the production of maps showing the region of contention and hostilities, in short the placing of the contestation of power, a key theme in geopolitics. In 1635, a map depicting recent Dutch operations in Brazil and Curaçao was published in The Hague. It provided both details of particular sites, such as Recife (captured by the Dutch from the Portuguese in 1630), and a large-scale map of Brazil on which the general campaign could be followed. Wars in Europe were understood with the help of maps such as *A True and Exact Map of the Seat of War in Brabant and Flanders with the Enemies Lines in Their Just Dimensions* (1705), a detailed map on which the moves of Anglo-Dutch-German forces commanded by John, 1st Duke of Marlborough and of his French opponents could be charted. This map was followed by the issue, by John Harris, of *A New Map of Europe Done from the Most Accurate Observations Communicated by the Royal Societies at London and Paris Illustrated with Plans and Views of the Battles, Sieges and Other Advantages Obtained by Her Majesties Forces and Those of Her Allies over the French*. Insets included plans of the battles of Blenheim (1704) and Ramillies (1706), both key victories for Marlborough.[32]

Similar maps appeared for particular battles, enabling readers to understand the general context, as well as the course of the battle. Thus, the battle of Falkirk in 1746, a major clash in the Jacobite rising that had started in 1745, was rapidly commemorated in a map showing the general area. It included a plan of the battle of Falkirk and of the subsequent battle at Culloden; the latter was also the subject of a separately published plan.

Sieges were frequently shown in printed maps and had been since the sixteenth century, although not by non-

European societies. Fortifications readily lent themselves to mapping, and this provided a ready source of material for entrepreneurial publishers such as the Huguenot exile Abel Boyer who published, in London in 1701, *The Draughts of the Most Remarkable Fortified Towns of Europe . . . with a Geographical Description of the Said Places; and the History of Sieges They Have Sustained*. This was a propitious moment in international tension as the wide-ranging and lengthy War of the Spanish Succession was beginning. Four years later appeared in Paris a collected edition of Nicolas de Fer's fortification plans, *Les Forces d'Europe*, which had first appeared between 1690 and 1695, during the Nine Years' War. Similarly, in 1727, the second edition of Jacques Ozanam's *A Treatise of Fortification* was published in London with the addition of *A New and Exact Plan of Gibraltar with all its Fortifications* by Hermann Moll, the latter plan made topical by the Spanish siege of that year, the highpoint of the unofficial war between the two powers. Encampments could also be depicted in maps. The relationship between mapping, public interest and the military was taken further with dedications, as of Moll's *A New Map of Germany, Hungary, Transylvania and the Suisse* (1712) to Marlborough.

Naval battles were also commemorated with maps, although, as a static presentation of a more complex and fluid set of events, they generally had only limited value, as for example with the maps of the Anglo-Bourbon battles of Malaga (1704) and Toulon (1744). Difficulties in establishing location at sea accentuated the problems of planning, conducting and recording naval operations. Thus, in 1708, when a French squadron carrying the so-called James VIII and III, the Jacobite Pretender to the Crowns of Scotland and England, succeeded in avoiding the British blockading squadron off Dunkirk in the mist, reaching Scottish waters before its pursuers, the initial landfall was made not, as intended, at the mouth of the Firth of Forth, but, as a result of error, 100 miles further north. Seeking, in 1741, to enter the Pacific in order to attack Spanish positions, George Anson of the British navy nearly ran aground on the island of Tierra del

Fuego: dead reckoning had put his position more than 300 miles out to sea.

As a result of the difficulties of mounting blockades, the British navy made major efforts to produce accurate charts of the waters off France and Spain. More problems were encountered in planning or mounting operations far from home waters. When, in 1791, the British planned war with Russia in the Ochakov Crisis, they discovered that they had no charts for the Black Sea and had to turn to the Dutch for advice. Indeed, the lack of knowledge, which reflected not the lack of detailed contemporary maps of the area, but the deficiencies of the British information system, left the British unclear whether the fortress of Ochakov, the crucial issue in the negotiations, really controlled the entrance to the river Dnieper, as was claimed. Ochakov is, in fact, on the northern shore of the Dneprovskiy Liman, a nearly landlocked section of the Black Sea into which the estuaries of both the Bug and the Dnieper open. Ochakov is situated at the narrow strait that forms the seaward entrance of this section of bay, but the British lacked adequate maps and coastal charts to illustrate this location, and this deficiency affected diplomatic discussion and military planning.[33] The government sought to argue, to both domestic and international audiences, that the return of Ochakov to the Turks, from whom the Russians had captured it in 1788, was a key goal, but the limited information at its disposal made this a difficult argument to substantiate. This episode demonstrated the relationship between knowledge and geopolitics.

The creation of popular printed maps of areas of conflict goes back to the early sixteenth century, with Vavassore's map of Lombardy of about 1515, the year in which Francis I of France invaded. Adverts from the *London Gazette* indicate that war-induced special cartography was thriving by the 1680s, although the limited nature of the technology available for the printing of illustrations in newspapers, as well as the extent to which illustrations were not expected, were such that few maps were published in a newspaper format then or in the next century.

The interrelationship of war and cartography was demonstrated by conflict in North America in the second half of the eighteenth century which greatly increased interest in maps of the region. Already, the capture of Louisbourg on Cape Breton Island in 1745 had led to the publication of broadsheet maps in Britain. New maps of North America were announced in the issues of the *Daily Advertiser* of 3 August, 5 September, and 10 September 1755. John Clevland also had a copy of a series of tracts of 1755–6 that dealt with the geography of North America, bound in one volume, being supported by maps. These works moreover reflected the contention that maps could lead to. One of the tracts, Lewis Evans's *Geographical, Historical, Political, Philosophical and Mechanical Essays: The First Containing an Analysis of a General Map of the Middle British Colonies in America and of the Country of the Confederate Indians* (1755), was criticised in New York, especially by the *New York Mercury,* for acknowledging too many French claims, but was used by General Edward Braddock in 1755.

Maps and the politics of space were closely linked. Criticism of Evans's map led in 1756 to the publication of a second essay by Evans. Clevland's volume also included Ellis Huske's *The Present State of North America* (1755), which backed the cartographer John Mitchell in his pro-British *Map of the British and French Dominions in North America* (1755),[34] and Thomas Jefferys' *Explanation for the New Map of Nova Scotia . . . with the Adjacent Parts of New England and Canada* (1755), which took issue with the accuracy of Mitchell's map. Public interest can be gauged from the fact that two editions of Huske appeared in Boston in 1755 and two in London.[35]

The capture of Québec in 1759 led to the production and sale in Britain of more maps on North America. A *Universal Geographical Dictionary; or, Grand Gazetteer* (1759) was, the title page proclaimed, 'Illustrated by a general map of the world, particular ones of the different quarters, and of the seat of war in Germany.' At the end of the Seven Years' War with France, a conflict discussed in the following chapter, the *Universal Magazine* of March 1763 provided a map of the extent of territory Britain now controlled in North America. This map was both a triumphant display of British achievement and a response to reader interest.

Meanwhile, readers of the *London Magazine* who wished to follow the course of the war of 1760–1 between the Cherokees and British and colonial forces could turn to *A New Map of the Cherokee Nation . . . Engraved from an Indian Draught by Thomas Kitchin* in early 1760.

Interest, of course, was not restricted to the public, but, instead, overlapped with military concerns. In 1760, Colonel James Montresor wrote to General Jeffrey Amherst, the British commander-in-chief in North America:

> I think it my duty to acquaint your Excellency that I have got in great forwardness a general map of that part of North America which has been the seat of war wherein is distinguished the roads that have been made by the troops, the navigation of its rivers, its carrying places, the new forts and posts constructed, the several hospitals, barracks and buildings for the soldiers, the marches of the army, the places where have been engagements, attacks, sieges and camps, interspersed with useful remarks. The most part laid down by actual surveys with geographical and military observations made in that country from the year 1754 to 1760. As this map will show at one view what has been done in that country, I hope that it will be very acceptable, as well to the ministry as to the military, as your Excellency's march from Albany to Montreal, and Brigadier-General Murray's from Quebec is only wanting to complete it.[36]

Montresor sought information on the details of these successful advances in 1760.[37]

Post-war interest in North America continued to encourage the publication of maps and strengthened with the War of Independence, which broke out in 1775. Jefferys published a number of atlases, including *A General Topography of North America and the West Indies* (1768), and, using his maps, Robert Sayers and John Bennett published *The American Atlas, or a Geographical Description of the Whole Continent of America* (dated 1775), with subsequent editions dated 1776 and 1778.[38] The first major altercation of the American Revolution, the battle of Bunker Hill in June 1775, was rapidly followed in London by the publication of maps of the battle, the earliest appearing four days after the report of the engagement reached London. The struggle for Boston was also followed on the Continent, with Samuel Holland and George Callender's *Chart of the Harbour of Boston*, published by J. F. W. DesBarres, being used by Jean, Chevalier de Beaurain. The latter's map was soon re-engraved and printed in Leipzig, making it the sole German map of Boston made during the period.[39]

In 1776, detailed maps of New England enabled British readers, anxious about the civil war in the empire, to follow the course of the conflict in its initial theatre,[40] while, in 1777, William Faden published a large-scale map of New Jersey, and, in the following year, a plan displaying the recent campaign on the Delaware river, which had been waged by the British in order to ensure Philadelphia's access to the sea. Faden did the same for other campaigns and engagements, such as the unsuccessful British attack on Fort Sullivan, South Carolina in 1776 and George Washington's operations at Trenton and Princeton in New Jersey in the winter of 1776–7.

Several plans depicting the decisive altercation of the war, the successful American and French siege of the British position at Yorktown in 1781, appeared shortly after the event, notably including Sebastian Bauman's masterly work, printed at Philadelphia in 1782. An interesting contrast in perspective is evident when comparing two important French maps of the siege, *Carte de la partie de la Virginie ou l'armée combinée de France et des États-Unis de l'Amerique a fait prisonnière l'Armée Anglaise* (c. 1782), which put much emphasis on the battle between the British and French fleets near the mouth of Chesapeake Bay, whereas Georges-Louis

Le Rouge's map closely focused on the action immediately surrounding the besieged town.[41]

Reviewing Lewis Evans's *Analysis of a General Map of the Middle British Colonies in America*, in 1756, Samuel (Dr) Johnson wrote that 'the last war between the Russians and the Turks [1736–9] made geographers acquainted with the situation and extent of many countries little known before',[42] a reference to the lands on the northern shore of the Black Sea. This relationship between war and knowledge continued to be the case. Conflict encouraged both supply and demand: military mapping and the commercial production of maps. Thus Louis Félix Keralio published *Histoire de la guerre entre la Russie et la Turquie, particulièrement de la campagne de 1769* (1773) and *Histoire de la guerre des Russes et des Imperiaux contre les Turcs en 1736, 1737, 1738, 1739* (1780), works that included maps. The *Journal Politique de Bruxelles* of 2 February 1788 advertised a map of the northern and north-western littoral of the Black Sea that would help those interested in the Russo-Turkish war (begun the previous year) to follow its course. In 1792, George III of Britain used a map to follow the Prussian invasion of France.[43] Returning to Russian expansion, critics depicted Russia as an octopus spreading its tentacles in cartoon maps such as Fred Rose's *Serio-Comic War Map for the Year 1877*, as well as Japanese maps produced at the time of the Russo-Japanese War.

In many respects, the use of maps to follow wars was an aspect of a general map culture, with rising map consumption being focused on particular interests. At the same time, this focus involved not only conflicts in which one's own country was a participant but also others, a reminder of the different audiences for geopolitics. Cartography served as an aspect of the news, and that in a Europe in which the provision of news was becoming more central, and its presentation more clearly scientific and rational, rather than providential and impressionistic. At the same time, there is need for care in distinguishing between the popularity of 'science' and the real situation. While there were an increasing number of map publishers, like Faden or d'Anville, who took accuracy seriously, there were plenty whose considerations remained purely commercial and who disguised this lack of accuracy behind grand claims made in map titles and/or the new austere form of map decoration.[44] The relevance of a distinction between the popularity and the reality of 'science' and scientific cartography is open to consideration for the discussion of geopolitical journalism during the twentieth century.

There was a general shift in cartography during the Enlightenment from pictorial to book forms and conventions, although this shift should not be exaggerated: small-scale maps had used conventional signs for centuries, while pictorial maps of small areas were still being employed for military-planning purposes in the mid-nineteenth century. Indeed, the British Library has recently acquired manuscript experiments along these lines made by the Newton family for King Louis-Philippe of France in the 1840s.

Encouraging the map culture in eighteenth-century Europe, there was also a general downgrading of theory in favour of facts, not least as the notion of applied knowledge acquired definition and prestige, especially thanks to the development of political arithmetic and political economy. This intellectual shift was linked to a situation in which information, rather than received wisdom, had greater currency, both as a source of authority and as a practical guide to policy-making. This shift is generally treated as an aspect of the history of science but was far wider in its sources and application.[45] Indeed, the deployment of information to support geopolitical analyses and arguments can be related to this process.

The relationship between war, geopolitics and cartography can be traced to a developing consciousness about planning, with warfare providing instances of using information both for policy prescription, in the shape of planning and for policy discussion. Scientific methods entailed not only the concern of generals with artillery and sieges but also the use of scientific knowledge at the operational level, with the need to plan foraging and marches requiring an understanding of agronomy, surveying, celestial navigation, botany and forestry. Military technology and practice were thus influenced by the larger economy of knowledge, which expanded considerably, helped by the diffusion of information through the culture of print. Locational skills were important to the staff-planning that was at an increased premium, for example with the Austrian army during the Turkish War in 1737–9.[46] The Austrians took this planning forward after 1748, establishing, during the Seven Years' War, under the direction of Field Marshal Lacy, Inspector General of the Austrian army, what became an effective proto-General Staff.

At the same time, the use of the military as the major source for mapping, and indeed as a key basis for map publication, provided another important dimension of military cartography. The long-standing surveying and charting facilities and interests of armies and navies varied, but they were certainly important in the eighteenth century. The French *ingénieurs-géographes* had been busy with this sort of mapping, and in an organised way, since the 1600s, but, in terms of scale and, more arguably, of accuracy, the eighteenth-century surveys were in a different class. Drawing on the cartographic traditions of their varied possessions, especially Italy and the Austrian Netherlands (modern Belgium), the Austrians were particularly prominent in this mapping, notably in Sicily, Lombardy, Austria, Bohemia, Hungary and the Austrian Netherlands. Ruling Sicily between 1720 and 1734, the Austrians used army engineers to prepare the first detailed map of the island. As an aspect of defence preparations against Prussia, a major military survey of Bohemia was begun in the 1760s and completed under Joseph II. Lower Austria was surveyed from 1773, and an enormous survey of Hungary completed in 1786. The use of the military in this fashion was important in societies where, ordinarily, attempts to gain information were dangerously dependent on the cooperation of others.

The resulting detail was often considerable. The maps of the Austrian Netherlands, drawn up in 1771–4, supervised by Joseph-Johann-Franz, Count of Ferraris, the Director-

General of the Artillery, were based on military surveys and comprised 275 leaves. As an instructive instance of the relationship between military activity and commercialisation, a relationship focused on entrepreneurs, Ferraris was then permitted to produce his own commercial version, which was published in 1778.

Military engineers from other countries were also important. The French military engineers of the period, such as Pierre Bourçet, tackled the problems of mapping mountains, creating a clearer idea of what the Alpine frontier looked like. He also mapped Corsica, this mapping an expression of the assertion of French control on the troublesome island, a process that also included road-building. Bourçet's work on the Alps was continued by Le Michaud d'Arcon, and this mapping helped the French Revolutionary forces in their successful campaigns there in the 1790s.[47]

Following the suppression of the 1745 Jacobite rebellion, William Roy of the British Royal Engineers carried out a military survey of Scotland that served as the basis for more accurate maps. Survey and maps were designed to help in the British military response to any future rebellion and also to assist in the process of governmental reorganisation of the Highlands. As such, they complemented both fortification and legislative action.[48]

The Russians were less to the fore than the Austrians, but Russia was far larger and there was a widespread lack of reliable information. Nevertheless, the army was employed to produce relatively good maps of the western provinces. The government regularly dispatched groups of officers to conduct surveys and prepare maps. This was particularly done in 1810–12 when the western provinces were thoroughly surveyed as part of a process of defence that included an improvement to the existing fortifications. In contrast, there was a lack of maps of the eastern provinces, especially beyond the Ural Mountains: this indicated the needs-based nature of cartography, and, more generally, of geopolitical information, which is a problem if conflict or interest suddenly shifts, as to Afghanistan in the 2000s.

A separate issue for Russia in the 1800s was posed by the shortage of maps for offensive operations, because this shortage reflected a dependence on army sources and the difficulty of securing information about foreign countries through these means. Thus, in the 1800s, the Russian army lacked maps of Central Europe. When an army under Kutuzov marched to support Austria in 1805, he was desperately short of maps of the Habsburg dominions and asked the Ambassador in Vienna, Prince Razumovsky, to send any maps of the theatre of war. The Prince sent him general maps of the area which he had purchased in a shop, but he could not find the detailed maps that would have been useful at the operational and tactical levels.[49]

The role of the military was often more directly entrepreneurial, as with Johann Jaegar, Captain of the Artillery and an Inspector of Arsenals in Frankfurt, who opened a map shop there in 1762 and, from 1766, published eighty-one sheets providing a map of Germany and its surrounds. There are many earlier examples of soldiers with time on their hands teaching cartography and publishing commercial maps. Alongside an emphasis on entrepreneurial interests, it is pertinent to note continued peacetime military concerns. Longstanding Prussian intervention in Mecklenburg was given a cartographic dimension when Friedrich, Count von Schmettau, a Prussian colonel, produced a *Carte Chorographique et Militaire du Duche de Mecklenburg-Strehlitz* (1780) followed by an engraved survey, *Topographisch, Oeconomisch und Militarische Charte des Herzogthums Mecklenburg Schwerin* (1787).

Similarly, but on the other side of the Atlantic, Lieutenant John Ross was sent, in 1765, on an expedition up the Mississippi that led to his *Course of the Mississippi* (1775). So also with the party sent down the Ohio Valley in 1766 which led to Thomas Hutchins' map of it.[50] Alongside cartographic interest in North America, military activity elsewhere led to an expansion of the mapping of other areas about which the Europeans lacked reliable cartographic knowledge. For example, Napoleon's successful invasion of Egypt in 1798 led to the first accurate map of the country. The French army carried out the trigonometric survey of the Nile Valley and the Mediterranean coasts of Sinai and Palestine, all of which were areas in which it operated. The resulting map, on forty-seven sheets, was designed to help military planning, as well as being part of a geographical enquiry that was intended to ennoble Napoleon in enlightened opinion. In addition, the French occupation led to the production of a map of Cairo in which the French had a garrison. That French rule of the city included a heavy bombardment in response to a rebellion there indicated the range of activity that information was designed to further.

More generally, Napoleon regarded maps as a key operational tool. In his numerous criticisms of his subordinates, Napoleon often commented that, if they simply looked at a map, they would see the error of their ways. Describing his headquarters in 1813, Baron Odeleben wrote:

> In the middle . . . was placed a large table, on which was spread the best map that could be obtained of the seat of the war. . . . This was placed conformably with the points of the compass . . . pins with various coloured heads were thrust into it to point out the situation of the different *corps d'armée* of the French or those of the enemy. This was the business of the director of *bureau topographique*, . . . who possessed a perfect knowledge of the different positions . . . Napoleon . . . attached more importance to this [map] than any want of his life. During the night . . . was surrounded by thirty candles . . . When the Emperor mounted his horse, . . . the grande equerry carried [a copy] . . . attached to his breast button . . . to have it in readiness whenever [Napoleon] . . . exclaimed 'la carte!'.[51]

The extensive use of mapping and maps seen during the French Revolutionary and Napoleonic Wars[52] was not a new development, as already-existing patterns of behaviour continued in a European society and military culture that were carto-literate.

Geopolitics was a matter not only of international conflict but also of the attempt to make uniform both governance and the internal politics of states and, as such, was an instance of the application of knowledge for the service of government, a key theme in the self-image of the latter in the seventeenth and eighteenth centuries.[53] Despite the continuation of internal differences, many geographically linked, the increasing demands of sovereign states also helped to reconfigure power relationships within their boundaries, notably in border areas, and thus to take them closer to being blocs of territory. For example, in the Val d'Aosta in 1767–8, Charles Emmanuel III of Savoy-Piedmont transferred duties and powers from the Conseil des Commis, the executive body of the Estates, to royal delegates. The scope of Piedmontese law was extended in the valley; obligatory taxes were decreed, which effectively neutralised the Estates; and the state-appointed office of *intendant* was introduced.

This process made the areas comprehended by state frontiers on maps more real as units, and the crystallisation of European frontiers was both real and mappable. By the end of the seventeenth century, it was common to distinguish between traditional provincial borders and contemporary international frontiers by marking the latter on maps when they occurred within historically united provinces. The redrawing of boundaries was an aspect and means of power. Thus, in Galicia, the area Austria gained from Poland in 1772, Joseph II followed a policy of centralisation in which administrative boundaries were redrawn. Moreover, Joseph reorganised the system of Hungarian provincial administration, in part to increase his power as well as to create units dictated by geographical and demographic convenience.[54]

At the same time, the suggestion of consolidated blocs of territory helped lead, from the late seventeenth century, to a mechanistic concept of international relations, one understood and described in terms of a balance of power. This understanding had a clear geographical dimension, not least as it could be readily transposed into spatial terms. The balance seemed an appropriately modern conception in a Europe of Cartesian mathematics and Newtonian physics. The concept seemed to offer an apparently rational way to arrive at a scientific analysis of international relations. Once quantified, power could be understood in mechanistic terms that corresponded to those being popularised for Newtonian physics.[55] The notion of the balance assumed that hegemonic power would meet with a matching reaction, rather as, in his laws of motion, Sir Isaac Newton (1642–1727) had revealed that the action of a force created an equal and opposite response.

In some respects, the balance of power was also a radical geopolitical understanding as, taking forward the opposition to the 'universal monarchy' supposedly threatened by the Habsburgs in the sixteenth and early seventeenth century, it suggested that the theme of an empire, made normative by the legacy of Classical Rome, as well as the subsequent search for hegemonic power, was unnatural. To treat this shift simply in terms of geopolitical thought would be naive, as key elements in the politics of the day were involved, notably opposition to Louis XIV of France (r. 1643–1715), especially from the mid-1670s, as well as what might be understood as the changing European political thought of the age about international relations. Yet, to separate these elements out is not overly helpful with regard to the thought of the age. There was far less specialisation in terms of sub-disciplines[56] than there was to be in the late nineteenth century, when geopolitics is generally seen as beginning. As a consequence, the balance of power can be seen as a part of the geopolitical thought of the period without implying that the latter was a distinct strand.

Yet, as a concept, the balance of power indicated some of the issues and problems that were to attach to later geopolitical discussion. There was the important question of whether the balance was descriptive, explaining what happened naturally, or prescriptive, outlining what ought to happen but, nevertheless, required human volition to take effect. The prescriptive approach was, in part, an aspect of the more general move, also seen in cartography and science, to regarding the natural world as an analysable, knowable and controllable structure.[57] Yet, the role of balance-of-power language in calling for policies supposedly in pursuit of such a balance underlined its place as polemic as much as analysis and prefigured the use of the language of containment during the Cold War. There was also the problem that power could not be readily defined or measured, and thus balanced, a fundamental issue for rationalist use of geopolitical arguments.

The balance also carried with it the concept of natural interests, goals that stemmed from inherent characteristics. This argument, however, underplayed differences in opinion over interests, while also raising the prospect that rulers could be criticised for failing to understand interests, and thus potentially challenging the idea that governments were best placed to choose policies and to change them. This approach could be seen as providing an intellectual pedigree for modern 'critical geopolitics', but a key difference was the belief in the late seventeenth and eighteenth centuries, that there were inherent national interests and, therefore, a correct policy, which could be objectively assessed and which governments could be criticised for failing to understand. Modern 'critical geopolitics' is wary of this commitment to objective reality.

As a key aspect of the territorialisation of European states in the eighteenth century, and of the particular geopolitics of Enlightenment and Revolutionary Europe, the concept of natural frontiers – readily grasped geographical entities, principally mountains and rivers – became an established aspect of geographical description and political discussion. This change encouraged a determination to enforce control in frontier zones, as such zones no longer seemed conceptually as valid as linear frontiers. In the 1790s, it was under this ethic that Revolutionary France justified its invasions of its neighbours, including annexing most of Savoy and the left bank of the Rhine, as France's 'natural boundaries' were said to follow the heights of the Alps and Pyrenees, and the mid-channel of the Rhine. The eighteenth-century anticipations of such ideas of natural frontiers serve as a reminder of the need to see French Revolutionary warfare (1792–9) in terms of continuity as much as change. Indeed, the Revolution has been presented as 'old wine in the old bottles of French geopolitical pride',[58] as well as a product of geopolitics in the shape of international competition.[59]

Most of the geopolitics with which we are familiar relates to the concept and practice of clear frontiers that arose in Europe in the eighteenth century, but the extent to which it is helpful to apply this concept and practice more widely is questionable, as is the notion of this situation as a terminus of historical development and/or a best practice for all time. In short, we face the position, familiar with much geopolitical thought and also military history, of a desire to apply a chronologically specific descriptive and analytical criteria more widely, and to derive notions of state interest and relative military capability as a result. This issue relates to the situation across space as well as time, with an asymmetry of understanding based on Western Whiggish concepts.[60]

Turning to non-Western concepts and practices of frontiers, geopolitics and war, there is much excellent work on asymmetrical conflict, and it covers much of the world, although it is fair to say that the emphasis is anglophone and that, at least in relative terms, there is far less on the frontier conflicts and understandings of non-Western societies with and towards their counterparts, particularly if neither was, or is, in the first league of power. Thus, the nature and role of warfare and the related geopolitics in South-East Asia in the eighteenth century, such as the fierce conflicts between Burma and Siam, has not received the attention devoted to such conflict involving China, while the latter is modestly covered compared to the extensive and excellent work on the situation in North America in the eighteenth century.

The discussion of advancing Western frontiers of settlement, and the resulting conflict of land claim, appropriation and clearance, are themes pursued in the self-styled 'critical geopolitics', with its tendency to treat geography, both as subject and as practice, as an adjunct of imperialism. Yet this discussion can underplay the extent to which, alongside conflict, colonies, such as those of British and French North America, also involved cooperation with non-Westerners, in this case the Native Americans. Underplaying this cooperation can lead to a simplification of frontier society and 'the frontier', with consequences for an exaggeration of the role of warfare. Frontier society, anyway, is an aspect of European imperialism that receives insufficient attention because better records survive for those of the colonial population who lived in port cities, and their linkage with frontier conflict was often indirect. Moreover, the port cities, and their trade with imperial metropoles, engaged most fully the attention of the home governments.

Thus, the Anglo-French crisis of the mid-1750s, which arose from the rivalry over the remote Ohio Valley, a rivalry that led in 1754 to the conflict discussed in the next chapter, was an aberration for the British government. Looked at differently, the extent to which the British government in this crisis was largely responding to developments, in part, reflected its earlier lack of attention to the frontier issues. Yet, what became a new determination on the part of the government to take these issues into its hands, and to enforce its views in the borderlands of empire, clashed with colonists' assumptions, not least a zeal for land speculation.[61] Indeed, the destruction of the geopolitical bloc of Anglo-America in the War of American Independence (1775–83) in part rested on tensions within that bloc already visible in mid-century.[62] Such qualifications about coherence and unity in policy and practice are more generally pertinent in the discussion of geopolitics, as some of the literature is prone to underrate political tensions within geographical units or blocs, and also take specific episodes, for example particular surveys or publications, and see them as more generally significant, without devoting sufficient attention to the need to evaluate evidence in context.

The geopolitics of frontier zones were complex because their economy and society were inherently unstable and prone to be absorbed by the controls, practices and ethos of more colonised areas, especially as immigration gathered pace. Nevertheless, however unstable, frontier societies were not some mere fag end of empire. Instead, in North America, the phrase 'frontier society' encapsulates complex relationships, both between colonists and Native Americans, and between colonists and their governments.

Furthermore, these frontier societies have been presented as providing what has been termed a 'middle ground' of shared cultural space between colonists (especially if traders rather than settlers) and Native Americans. In this space, individuals and groups have been seen as playing an active role in organising relations, instead of being in conflict, or indeed simply victims of a distant imperial power. This approach is part of an understanding of empire, and geopolitics more generally, in terms of processes rather than structures. These were processes in which not only those immediately engaged in colonisation played a crucial role but also those affected by imperialism. In other words, Native Americans as well as colonists had agency.[63] As a separate point, there was also a Native American pursuit of advantage and geopolitics that can be seen as a variant on imperialism, and this point repays examination before focusing exclusively on the supposed ills of Western imperialism.

There was also an ethnic dimension to geopolitics on the imperial frontier, a dimension in both practice and classification. Many individuals prominent in the 'middle ground' were the product of European-Native American marriages, which helped them to act as translators and to play a major role in trade and raising auxiliary forces. In addition, as more mixed-race children were born, so the prospects of marrying mixed-race women increased. The process of participation in the 'middle ground' and, more generally, in the imperial system, however, was both unstable and unequal. European mores were strongly asserted, which played a role in considering the role of allies, and Native American views were slighted. As a consequence, mixed-race relationships faced opposition to what was seen as concubinage.

The 'middle ground' with the Native Americans was key to the reality, if not concept, of the frontier, but the situation was to change radically with American independence in 1776. No longer constrained by British power, the newly independent Americans were able to define and pursue a distinctive geopolitics within North America, a geopolitics that was as much a matter of the specific tone of the relations with the Native Americans as of particular geographical considerations. Nevertheless, the spatial consequences of American political culture were also significant, not least a strong desire for territory and influence that manifested itself as land hunger.

As so often with the geopolitics of expansion, there was a gap between the self-perception of the expansionist period and the perceptions held by others. As Robert Kagan pointed out, Americans have cherished an image of themselves as, by nature, inward-looking and aloof, only sporadically and spasmodically venturing forth into the world, usually in response to external attack or perceived threats. This lack of self-awareness was presented by Kagan as a problem in another way: not only had Americans frequently failed to see how their actions could provoke reactions from others, but they had not even accurately predicted their own responses. In the quintessential American way, Kagan expressed an optimism about the value of self-understanding: 'On balance, Americans would be better off if they understood themselves, their nation, and their nation's history better. This applies especially to the early history of American foreign policy.' Kagan argued that the War of 1898 with Spain, in which America conquered Cuba and the Philippines, and became a transoceanic power, was consistent with his central themes: 'the war was the product of deeply ingrained American attitudes toward the nation's place in the world . . . It reflected Americans' view of themselves, stretching back to before the nation's founding, as the advance guard of civilization, leading the way against backward and barbaric nations and empires.'[64]

In practice, as with so many works, including those that discuss geopolitics, there was a tendency on Kagan's part to simplify American attitudes and politics in order to offer a misleading consistency, one, moreover, that depoliticised the national space, which is an instance of a well-established practice of doing so, including, but not only, by geopoliticians. The reality, instead, in the USA, was of very different views, as in the 1812 Seminole, Mexican and Spanish–American wars. Indeed, there was often opposition to expansion. Thus, Kagan's *zeitschrift* approach was (and is) questionable.

Much modern geopolitical theory is concerned with the asymmetries of power, especially (but not only) their spatial dimensions. Frontiers can be understood as the zone of asymmetrical interaction. This point leads directly to two issues of geopolitical interaction that locate and are located on frontiers and are yet also of wider applicability: the recruitment of native auxiliaries and the diffusion of Western arms, organisation and technique. In the nineteenth century, the two overlapped to help produce potent armies, as for the British in South Asia and the French in West Africa. European success in this respect (like that of the different case of the Manchu in China from the seventeenth century) extended greatly what can be seen as another definition of the frontier, that of strategic reach: the frontier of the militarily viable, which is a key issue in modern strategy and geopolitics, as seen with the debate over the value and practicality of Western power-projection in Afghanistan.

The opposite to strategic reach, strategic overreach, is a concept much employed by key scholars of empire, most prominently Paul Kennedy and Geoffrey Parker.[65] This concept provides them with a frontier of practicality which, when exceeded, helps to provoke crisis, although the idea is not always employed so mechanistically. The idea is an apparently plausible one, and one that can be readily translated to geopolitical discussion, but the idea faces the serious conceptual difficulty of assuming a clear-cut measure of strategic reach and geopolitical concern, whether in military or in other terms. The extent to which, however objective resources and distances may be, overreach is, on the contrary, a matter of perception, both for contemporaries and subsequently, should lead to a questioning of any ready application of the concept, not least by returning it to the sphere of contention in which policy was formulated and discussed.

Financial problems or a lack of adequate military resources are not helpful as measures of overreach, as both are true of most combatants. Systems do not have to work well, but just well enough to achieve their objective or avoid collapse.

Moreover, it is unclear that restraint (the presumed opposite of overreach, and a description generally applied as praise) can be readily abstracted from the political culture of the age. To take early modern Europe, there was a stress on honour and dynastic responsibility, and a concern with *gloire* and the normative values of combat. Furthermore, in prudential terms, war and expansion appeared possible, successful and necessary. The modern emphasis, in contrast, on restraint not only clashes with the cultural assumptions of the period but also presupposes that compromise could have been reached and sustained short of large-scale conflict. That is implausible, not only for early modern Europe but also, for example, for Britain when faced by a victorious Germany in 1940. Thus, frontiers of power were inherently unclear and, therefore, unstable, both in practical and in cultural terms, and this situation helped lead to confrontation, if not conflict.

Geopolitical discussion needs to take note of the cultural assumptions of particular periods, rather than assuming the same set of values, or evaluative criteria, across time. Looked at differently, the classic geopolitics of the early twentieth century, its Cold War revival, and 'critical geopolitics', can all be seen, at least in part, as critiques reflecting the cultural assumptions of particular period; although it is important not to reify the situation at any particular moment, nor to assume a measure of determinism. Instead, concepts at any given time varied, and there was a degree of autonomy in the relationship between ideas and circumstances.

The problematic nature of the scholarly assessment of appropriate frontiers of aspiration is indicated by the case of the Ottoman Turks in the Indian Ocean. There is the obvious contradiction between the charge of strategic overreach that would have arisen had the Turks projected power more consistently in the sixteenth century, and the fact that, because they did not do so, this policy is taken to indicate limited goals and, in particular, a failure to appreciate the oceanic destiny of empires, or indeed to recalibrate their geostrategy in the face of a new geopolitical situation.[66]

Like other cases, this contradiction exemplifies the need, in advancing geopolitical judgements, to reconcile the military historians' perspective on operational practicality and strategic norms, with the knowledge offered by scholarship on 'foreign policy', in so far as the latter can be separated from strategic norms. Whichever perspective is adopted, it is crucial not to argue the existence of coherent policies in the past by tracing them to the choices and actions that were taken, without employing due care in assessing the relationship between policies and actions, and the problems more generally of ascribing cause from effect. This point is pertinent in understanding what frontiers and other geopolitical elements meant to contemporaries, in terms of purpose and practicality, norms, problems and possibilities.

The naval dimension of frontier geopolitics has attracted relatively little attention as the emphasis, instead, has been on shifts in naval dominance and on symmetrical conflict between similarly armed fleets, an emphasis that owes much to the prominence of Western concepts of naval power, as well as to the impact of the writing of A. T. Mahan in the nineteenth century (see pp. 116–17). Similar points can be made about maritime frontiers as for their land counterparts, although the extent to which ships are not a permanent presence like forts and frontier walls also introduces an important contrast. So also does the ability of warships to refuse battle by not sailing forth: it is harder to force battle on naval opponents than on their land counterparts.

The standard narrative of naval power and geopolitics focuses on ships of the line and proposes the superiority of Western navies and naval systems from the early sixteenth century, a superiority that was only compromised in 1904–42 when the Japanese used their borrowing of Western systems with considerable success. This account has considerable force but underrates the extent to which Western warships, with their deep draughts, were unable to bring their force to bear readily upon much of the maritime environment of the world, notably shallow coastal, deltaic and estuarine waters, let alone rivers and lakes. Along the coasts of Africa, South-East Asia, the East Indies, New Zealand and Pacific North America, there were polities that controlled shallow-draught boats which enjoyed a local range denied Western warships. These boats were quick, manoeuvrable, beachable and inexpensive. Their crews usually fought with missile weapons, which, in the eighteenth century, increasingly meant muskets, and some canoes also carried cannon. The ability of such forces to achieve operational goals was seen in conflict between the New Zealand Maori in the early nineteenth century and, even more clearly, in the earlier unification of the Hawaiian archipelago. Operational goals drew on a capacity for troop transport and amphibious operations.

This situation did not change until the mid-nineteenth century, when steam-driven, iron-bottomed shallow-draught gunboats gave the West a greater capacity, at the same time, crucially, as there was a strong determination to use this power, the latter a reminder of the need to locate the spatial considerations of geopolitics in terms of the political culture of the age. Shifting frontiers of maritime power then came to be rapidly apparent. Looked at differently, the maritime sphere as a restraint on, and thus frontier to, Western power ceased to operate. Instead, Western power could now be projected into the heart of continents, as evinced by the French and Belgian navigation up the Congo River in the late nineteenth century, and the British up the Nile with gunboats playing a role in the battle of Omdurman in 1898.[67]

Western power could also be projected along new sea routes made possible by the digging of canals. British concern about French ambitions led to the mapping of the Suez isthmus in 1836, and a canal across it was opened in 1869. Now, as a similar instance of power altering geopolitical structures, there is talk of China sponsoring a canal across the Kra isthmus in Thailand, in order to improve security on the maritime route from the Indian Ocean, to shorten the route and to further the deployment of Chinese naval power.

Power projection into the heart of continents was an important aspect of the reordering of frontiers across the world in the nineteenth century, as the Western matrix of knowledge, as well as Western equations of force, were employed in ordering the world on Western terms and in Western interests. Force and legitimacy were brought together, for example, in the drawing of straight frontier and administration lines on maps, without regard to ethnic, linguistic, religious, economic and political alignments and practices, let alone drainage patterns, landforms and biological provinces. The reconceptualisation of the frontier and the redrawing of frontiers were thus crucial aspects of the expression of Western power as Western norms and conventions were applied globally. Non-Western states followed if they wished to survive.[68] The development of geopolitics as a formal discourse, system of analysis and call for action, can all be located in this process.

CHAPTER 4

THE GEOPOLITICS OF BRITISH POWER, 1500–1900: A CASE STUDY

In 1791, King George III was told by the French envoy that it was appropriate for the French Revolutionary government, pursuing a new radical course, to abolish feudal rights in Alsace, as, 'for the sake of public utility, governments should seek administrative uniformity'. This claim led the temperamentally and intellectually conservative George to reply 'that such uniformity could exist only in small states, and that in kingdoms as big as France any attempt to introduce it would create problems'.[1] The exchange serves as a reminder that geopolitics, as a form of both analysis and policy, like strategy as an aspect of policy, has a strong domestic dimension as well as the more common international one.

In the case of the French Revolution, which had broken out in 1789, the exchange also demonstrated the degree to which the systematisation of knowledge posed the danger (as it still does) of encouraging a politically misplaced utilitarianism. Indeed, the abolition of these feudal rights, mostly enjoyed by German rulers, while appropriate from the perspective of French revolutionaries, with their commitment to uniform modern systems and their opposition to feudalism,[2] was to help alienate German support and to encourage a breakdown in relations with German princely rulers, contributing to the outbreak of a lengthy war in 1792.

In the case of British geopolitics, the standard emphasis for the period covered by this chapter was (and is) on a narrative and analysis focused on the expansion of the British empire. While understandable, this approach underplays the role of geopolitics as a means of understanding domestic power politics. As far as the latter are concerned, the frames of reference were both England and the British Isles, but the two were joined by a common narrative of the rise of London and the south-east to dominance and control, first over England and then, from the mid-seventeenth century to the mid-eighteenth (Oliver Cromwell's conquests to the battle of Culloden) over the British Isles.[3]

This domestic geopolitics was deliberately subordinated by an emphasis on the English and, later, British state as the unit for discussion and, subsequently, analysis, but this approach is seriously misleading. Thus, it was no accident that the struggle to impose the Reformation in England had a powerful geographical component, with related hostile risings against the Tudors in the north and Cornwall from the 1530s to the 1560s, while, on the British scale, there was powerful opposition to the Reformation in Ireland.

Support for the Parliamentarians or Royalists in the Civil War of 1642–6 also reflected marked spatial variations, as did backing for Jacobitism within the British Isles between 1689 and 1746. Moreover, the consequences of these spatial variations helped explain the result of the conflicts, with control over London and the south-east proving a key element. Similar points about spatial variations could be made about key episodes in other countries, for example support for, or opposition to, the French Revolution, and for particular stages of the Revolution such as the Civil Constitution of the Clergy in 1790.[4] This conflict featured an especially severe regional variation in the form of the bloody and unsuccessful royalist counter-revolution in the Vendée. Most discussion of geopolitics, however, treats the state as the unit and focuses on international affairs, with, for example, a willingness to treat the American Civil War (1861–5) in terms of two competing states.

As far as England was concerned, there was also an agenda of international concern driven by competitive power politics as well as by the expansion of empire. Drawing, however, on a point made in Chapter 1, both processes need to be approached not only in modern terms but also in those employed by contemporaries. Indeed, part of the history of geopolitics is that of the changing understanding and usage of terms, both in the past and between past and present. In the early modern period, and in part as a consequence of both the Renaissance and the interest linked to European expansion, the ability to discuss and interpret spatial issues rose with the development of geography, both as an intellectual subject and as a sphere of publication. Moreover, carto-literacy rose greatly with the production of large numbers of maps and atlases.[5]

The relationship between these developments and shifts in the language used about territory was indirect, but the latter occurred in some key areas, notably the understanding of the term 'empire'. Originally employed in England when discussing essentially dominion over the British Isles and the surrounding sea, empire was reconceptualised to include transoceanic possessions.[6] Such a reconceptualisation was not required for the latter to be pursued, but it helped make such a policy appear normative.

Yet the use of the term 'normative' can reduce what was in practice the contentious political character of the pursuit of empire, not least in particular contexts. Such a reduction should be seen as parallel to the downplaying of the geopolitics of domestic dissension. These points can be pursued by looking at an example, British geopolitics during the Seven Years' War (1756–63), which is the central, but by no means the sole, topic in this chapter. The understanding of geopolitical goals and issues was a matter of strategic culture. The latter, however, should be understood not as a readily apparent objective reality, but rather as a key public mythos, in short an instance of geopolitics as political rhetoric. This treatment of strategy and strategic usage is at variance with its standard use in the literature as the context within which military tasks were 'shaped'.[7] Paralleling understandings of geopolitics in terms of particular national traditions, this usage of strategy reflects discussion of distinctive ways of war (a form of exceptionalism)[8] and draws on the authority of cultural interpretations of warfare.[9] However, it is argued here that, at the national level (as at the international) the concepts of geopolitics and strategic culture have to address the issue of coherence and consistency in face of the contested character of national (as of international) interests, the rage of debate, and the roles of politics and contingency. In short, there is a revenge of history on theory.

The very existence of geopolitics, strategy, strategic culture and strategic policy in the eighteenth century is highly problematic as far as some well-informed scholars are concerned.[10] The delay in the development of the idea of strategy is held to have reflected conceptual and institutional limitations. Yet, paralleling the treatment of geopolitics in the past two chapters, such an approach mistakes the absence of an articulated school of strategic thinking or doctrine of strategy for the lack of strategic awareness. For example, as far as the British navy was concerned, there was considerable experience of choosing, indeed balancing, between tasks, in a process of prioritisation that, as with the Roman army, involved spatial considerations. This process can be seen with the detachment of squadrons from home waters for the Baltic, and the Mediterranean and the Caribbean. Moreover, a strategy of commercial interdiction played a role in operations against the Dutch in the late seventeenth century and, including a powerful transoceanic dimension, in the Anglo-Spanish crisis of 1725–7. Furthermore, the planned use of naval power in international crises, as in 1718, 1730, 1731 and 1735, can be seen as wide-ranging and reasonably sophisticated, given limitations with communications and institutional support.

The same is true of planned operations on land, although here there was a degree of greater complexity because such operations involved coalition warfare. Thus, there was an intertwining of military planning and diplomatic exigencies. This intertwining can be seen with the War of the Spanish Succession, in which Britain was involved from 1702 to 1713, and again in the War of the Austrian Succession, in which Britain was involved from 1743 to 1748.

Therefore, an important background to the issue of geopolitics and strategic culture during the Seven Years' War is to appreciate that strategy existed as a concept, even if the word was not used in English until about 1800 when it was borrowed from the French. The earliest citation in the second edition of the *Oxford English Dictionary* is from 1810.

If the contemporary understanding of strategy as a concept is one context for the subject, a second is provided by a treatment of geopolitics and strategy in a wider sense, namely as being seen to relate to the health and strength of the country as a whole. Indeed, Churchill was to argue that 'at the summit true politics and strategy are one.' From this perspective, the British role in the Seven Years' War was a symptom, albeit a very significant one, of a wider anxiety about the country, while there was again a clear relationship at the time of the French Revolutionary War (1792–9; for Britain from 1793), for all the combatants, between strategy and concern with domestic circumstances. This approach may seem far removed from the habitual consideration of the Seven Years' War and other conflicts, but the approach repays attention because it helps explain the contours of contemporary public political concern. These, in turn, helped drive the politics of the conflict and, thus, the contemporary understanding and discussion of geopolitics.

The anxiety about the country referred to reflected the extent to which organic theories of the state were important. There is a tendency, in contrast, when considering the eighteenth century, to emphasise mechanistic themes, not least because of the intellectual thrall that century of Newtonian physics, and the extent to which notions of balancing power were regarded as of importance. This importance was the case both for international relations, not least the understanding of what would be subsequently termed geopolitics, and for domestic constitutional issues.

As far as the former were concerned, states were seen as sovereign but linked as if within a machine. This system was seen as self-contained, and as part of a static and well-ordered world. The concept was based on the model of the machine which, in turn, was regarded as well ordered and enabling its parts to conduct activities only in accordance with its own construction. The mechanistic concept of the system of states was well suited to the wider currents of thought of the period, specifically Cartesian rationalism as well as its successors.

These currents of thought provided not only an analytical framework but also a moral context for international relations. For example, balance-of-power politics, as generally presented, appear as selfishly pragmatic, bereft of any overarching rules and lacking any ethical theoretical foundations, in other words as a prelude to Cold War containment, at least in the eyes of critics of the latter. In practice, however, the situation was somewhat different, notably in terms of the felt need to oppose hegemonic expansionism, both as far as the balance of power was concerned and with regard to Cold War containment. There was a widely expressed theory of the balance of power, as well as rules for its politics, outlined in tracts, pamphlets, doctoral dissertations and explanations of the reasons for the resort to war. The relationship between such theoretisation and rules on the one hand, and decision-making processes on the other, is obscure, and clearly varied by ruler and minister, but such discussion set normative standards that helped shape policies and responses.[11]

Without denying a central role for such mechanistic notions, it is necessary to complement them with an awareness of the organic assumptions of the period. These were important not so much at the level of the international system (until the nineteenth century), but at that of individual states. Moreover, these assumptions helped provide a dynamic component that was (and is) generally lacking with the more structural nature of the mechanistic themes. This contrast is more generally important for geopolitics, with, in crude terms, organic concepts of international relations lending themselves to expansionism, while mechanistic concepts tended to be more defensive or, at least, reactive. On the other hand, mechanistic concepts of balancing could lead to the aggression and expansionism of equivalent gains, as in the Partitions of Poland (1772–95), or in European imperialism, for example the Anglo-Russian agreement of 1907 over zones of influence in Persia.[12]

The dynamic component of organic assumptions was vitalist in intention. In particular, there was a sense of a state as the expression of a nation, of the latter as linked in a national character, and of this character as capable of change and as prone to decay. The last looked in part to cyclical accounts of the rise and fall of empires, which drew much of their authority from the commanding role of Classical Rome in the historicised political thought of the period, but there was also a strong input from contemporary ideas of health. Thus, a traditional sense of the nation as akin to a person remained important.

This idea translated into the international sphere with a sense of nations as competitive and as under threat from challenges that were foreign as well as domestic in their causation and mechanism. As far as the Seven Years' War was concerned, anti-Catholicism was important in affecting British attitudes,[13] and this point is worth underlining because it encouraged a sense that the struggle should be persisted in even in the face of news that was very negative, which was the case in the first two years of the war.[14] Anti-Catholicism led to a sense of existentialist and meta-historical struggle, and, more generally, such emotional drives should not be divorced from the discussion of geopolitics. Instead, they are important when evaluating the reality behind such geopolitical concepts as environmental determinism and also when assessing the language and tone of geopolitical analysis. Thus, in looking for parallels, it is instructive to consider the relationship between ideological drives, such as anti-Catholicism and anti-Communism, and power political issues, such as opposition to France and the Soviet Union. However, no single classification of such relationships is valid, and there is extensive and long-standing historiographical debate over such questions as the role of ideology in the foreign and military policies of the governments of Revolutionary France and also in those of their opponents.

In Britain, the politics, and thus geopolitics, of the Seven Years' War drew on the character and dynamic of public political concern, to an extent that was not matched on the Continent where politics were generally more authoritarian and a sense of nation less apparent in public discourse. In Britain, governmental and public sensitivity to imperial issues rose in mid-century. Economic competition led to the foundation of the Anti-Gallican Association in 1745, a body that joined manufacturing and trade in its goals. Through design, this competition was linked to aesthetic rivalry which was given economic point through a conscious process of public support, particularly by the Society of Arts, Manufactures and Commerce established in 1754. Enthusiasm for imperial expansion reflected both political positioning and the strengthening of the public engagement with such expansion as a way to ensure commercial strength and maritime destiny.[15]

In part, however much linked by opposition to France, the running together of 'an empire of the seas', the traditional idea of British power, with the new goal of territorial empire in North America represented a geopolitical conflation that posed serious problems in policy as well as conception. Partly as a result, it is necessary to be cautious in presenting an undifferentiated account of British public attitudes, not least because it is unclear how extensive was pre-war interest in territorial expansion. Nevertheless, various government officials in both the colonies and London were very interested in British claims to land in the Ohio Valley prior to the outbreak of hostilities between Britain and France.[16]

Yet the war, like many other conflicts, helped foster ambitions which preceded the war, and powerfully so, not only at the governmental level but also in terms of public discussion. Thus, the geopolitics and strategic culture were changed, indeed transformed, during and by the war, as much as causing it, or setting its alignment. To argue this point, which is more commonly true of the relationship between geopolitics and conflict, does not deny the role of earlier interest in imperial expansion, but it does suggest a major change.

Moreover, the argument above is not intended to deny the value of linking expansionism and, more generally, other geopolitical themes to longer-term socio-cultural shifts, including, in this case, a growing assertiveness on the part of the expanding middling orders and the accompanying repositioning of trade as a political interest and sphere of discussion.[17] However, there is a need for specificity in offering such an account of the geopolitics of empire. This specificity should be not only chronological but also with respect to particular spheres for expansion and different mercantile interests. The relationship between the latter and imperial expansion was complex, not only due to these differences but also because merchants were wary of the burdens that might arise.

Rivalry with France provided a common issue, linking diplomatic, mercantile, imperial and cultural anxieties and themes. Rivalry, moreover, resonated, with a strong context of popular assumptions. This overarching rivalry also affected this context, as the rivalry made it possible to minimise tensions between these different anxieties and themes. In part, this dominance of France in British geopolitics reflected France's greater prominence as a dynamic power, although the rise of Austria, Russia and Prussia led to competing concerns, most particularly by those concerned about power politics in Germany and the Baltic. France's commercial and colonial revival after 1748, and the failure of the Dutch or Spain, the other leading maritime powers, to match this, whether objectively or as far as British commentators were concerned, were important. So also was the extent to which an easing (although not ending) of Anglo-Spanish political and commercial tensions after the War of the Austrian Succession[18] helped throw the focus on France. This focus on France encouraged an important shift in the public imagination of Britain as an imperial power, one towards a greater role for transoceanic interests and concerns.

Public opinion was, and is, open to multiple definitions. It is most helpful to think of a number of widely held opinions that lacked specific force, such as the wish to be seen to do well and the need to protect national territorial and commercial interests, the platitudes of policy, as well as of more particular notions that were not so widely held but which were presented as public opinion by their protagonists. In Britain, the goals of policy were crucial themes in public debate, and geopolitics and strategic culture were thus centrally linked to questions of public politics. The politics of strategy helped provide a considerable measure of continuity, with issues and problems interpreted and debated in terms of the experience of conflict. This experience was perceived through the perspective of collective (and contentious) public myths, such as the hopes invested in blue-water policy (the primacy of maritime and colonial goals and conflict), hopes that constituted a valid and vital geopolitics, based on the national interest, as far of its supporters were concerned. The role of geopolitics as an idiom of public debate and policy underlined its importance.

An expectation of a public debate influencing policy presupposes a linear process of influence, albeit one affected by important feedback mechanisms in terms of the attempt to produce material for, and in, this debate. Yet, the relationship between debate and policy was more complex and less automatic than this model assumes, and that situation provided more opportunity for those who sought to shape both debate and policy. Arguments, for example, about the salience of imperial issues might appear more prominent to contemporaries in particular conjunctures that, in practice, were at variance with any attempt to produce a developmental model of changing attitudes with all the teleological implications of the latter.

Debate, politics and policy thus were in a complex relationship,[19] and shaping this relationship in terms of geopolitics and strategic culture, or rather a particular understanding of them, may lead to an underplaying of this complexity. For example, in 1754, the specific political impact of the shift in public consciousness towards a greater concern over colonial disputes with the Bourbons, especially with France in North America, was limited, but, in late 1754, the prevalent opinion in political and governmental circles was of a need to stand up to France in these disputes. Again, as a reminder of the complexity of debate, politics and policy, this view was not really, or even closely, related to the more general issues of Britain's diplomatic standing towards France and other European powers. Indeed, these issues were less acute in 1754 than they had been earlier in the decade. Thus, in 1753, Anglo-French hostility still revolved around European issues, but without the political or public resonance within Britain that could lead ministers to expect support if they pressed for action.

North America had been a cause of diplomatic activity, ministerial concern and mapping[20] for a number of years, but its sudden rise to prominence in the summer of 1754, with the outbreak of fighting in the Ohio valley, was a surprise to many in London (though not to colonial officials such as Virginia's governor Robert Dinwiddie), rather than the product of geopolitical forces apparent to all. This change underlines the non-linear character of geopolitics: geographical factors may have a long-term role, but they are operative in particular political circumstances. The prominence of North American issues in 1754 was politically significant in Britain precisely because it matched with a powerful and politically loaded theme of public debate, one that joined, or could join, Whig critics of the (Whig) government with Tory opponents. Thus, there was frequent emphasis on a threat from France, and this emphasis preceded the mid-1750s. The pseudonymous 'Camber' referred to the 'encroaching ambition' of the French when warning of their moves in the West Indies in the *London Evening Post* of 27 May 1749. He warned of the possible loss of the sugar trade and also drew attention to the threat to the Newfoundland fishery posed by the French recovery of Cape Breton. Pressing for efforts to separate Spain from France, *Old England* claimed on 21 December 1751 that 'the exorbitant power of the House of Bourbon is a subject worn . . . threadbare by my indefatigable brethren of the quill.'

Such an emphasis could also serve domestic political purposes by creating the impression that the government was failing to respond and was thus part of the problem, and in fact a threat. Ministers did indeed respond, although this response was shaped by their own attitudes and experience, and here the notion of a geopolitics and strategic culture can appear unduly unitary, hegemonic and based on an unsubtle notion of influence. For example, Thomas, Duke of Newcastle, the First Lord of the Treasury and leading minister, was keener on focusing on Europe, while a rival, John, 4th Duke of Bedford, Secretary of State for the Southern Department and, in 1762, negotiator of the Peace of Paris, was a supporter of 'blue-water' policies, with their stress on maritime destiny and transoceanic interests. In 1749, Bedford responded to news of Spanish warships searching British merchantmen in the Caribbean by writing to Benjamin Keene, the envoy in Spain, 'You know how extremely jealous this nation is of the least encroachments of this nature – the least spark of this sort must, if not timely prevented, kindle a flame.'[21]

It is easy to leap from such remarks to William, Duke of Cumberland, complaining in 1757, 'I am very fully convinced that the Tory doctrine of a sea-war, which we are following, will be repeated by our children's children.'[22] Rather than being an unengaged commentator, Cumberland, the sole surviving son of George II, it must be remembered, was part of the politics of the situation. An opponent of William Pitt the Elder, he felt that he was starved of support in his German command because of the influence of Pitt's blue-water ideas. Cumberland sought to condemn these ideas by labelling them as Tory, although that proved a difficult case to sell to the public.

It is the argument here that Cumberland's explanation in terms of doctrine is both correct and insufficient. Ideas were important to geopolitics, which helped explain the controversy over differing maps of the North American interior (see p. 59), but, to move to policy, it is necessary to explain their interaction with the politics of the period. While this included a public sphere, there is also the extent to which politics was a matter of ministerial manoeuvres, what one might term five men and the Duke of Newcastle, and the complex relations between them. Here a crucial shift in recent scholarship has been the positive re-evaluation of the role of monarchy and the impact of monarchs in eighteenth-century Britain.[23]

Although elderly, George II (r. 1727–60) was still fit and committed both to his royal prerogatives and to his interests as Elector of Hanover, to which he paid long visits in 1753 and 1755, providing him with opportunities for negotiations. In Britain, the political role of the King was crucial because of the lack of collective ministerial responsibility and cabinet cohesion. Instead, ministers were appointed by, and answerable to, the King. His role was more significant when ministries were divided and weak, and the death of Henry Pelham, the First Lord of the Treasury, in 1754 began a period of serious instability that was only ended by the formation of the Pitt[24]–Newcastle ministry in 1757. Throughout that period, but particularly in 1756–7, George was crucial politically, and any discussion of geopolitics and strategic culture has to take note of him.

Personnel issues were related to complex questions of policy, and these constrained the parameters within which George could operate. The vulnerability of the Electorate of Hanover, a fundamental geopolitical issue and idea, the significance and consequences of which were (and are) contestable, ensured that he did not want war with France, but the deteriorating situation in North America limited his options. Hanover was indeed vulnerable to attack in what was a fast-deteriorating international situation. Although conflict between Britain and France had broken out over the Ohio country in 1754, full-scale war was not declared until 1756. However, alongside the concern that it could break out, there was a specific worry that France might attack Hanover in order to put pressure on Britain, including counteracting any British gains in North America. It was assumed that this would also involve an attack by France's ally Prussia, to which Hanover was particularly exposed.[25]

In response, the British government sought to strengthen relations with Austria and its ally Russia, each of which bordered Prussia and was in a position to threaten military pressure on it, as Russia had done in 1748, another key aspect of the geopolitical situation. George II was associated with this policy, which had indeed been a significant theme in his views since the early 1730s. To him, the empire that counted was the Holy Roman Empire (essentially modern Germany, Austria and the Czech Republic), and not the British empire, although, alongside his continued interest in Hanover, he became more concerned about the latter during the course of the Seven Years' War. Already, in June 1755, Robert, 4th Earl of Holdernesse, one of the two Secretaries of State, had written 'entre nous' to Newcastle, that 'the King seemed overjoyed at the probable success of his measures in America',[26] a reference to the decision to deploy more troops there and to attack French positions, in short to a militarisation of policy, which was frequently George's instinctual response.

Attempts were made by politicians (and subsequently have been by scholars) to lessen the tension between European and imperial goals in British foreign policy and to argue that they were fundamentally compatible and, indeed, mutually beneficial. This was indeed the argument Pitt made from 1758, when he claimed that the dispatch of British troops to Germany distracted France and thus eased British operations in North America, but it was not an argument that captured George's attitude in the mid-1750s. He saw a clash in commitments, and, despite his interest in North America, clearly favoured the European dimension. Such a clash was indeed particularly apparent in the mid-1750s. Nevertheless, when the war went well, George was to press for the conquest of Canada from the French.

George's role might appear marginal if the focus is on the crisis for the British empire in North America, but that is mistaken as George's determination to keep attention directed to Europe influenced both British policy and politics and raises questions about how strategic culture should be discussed. Thus, part of the analysis of the geopolitics of a situation depends on the geopolitics of the perspective. The Cabinet recommended that the Austrian envoy be informed 'that His Majesty has lately given the strongest orders for concluding, forthwith, the treaty with Russia, and greatly augmented the terms hitherto offered, both with regard to the preliminary subsidy, and to the sum to be allowed for the

Russian troops, when in motion',[27] the last a reference to the wish to deploy Russian troops in order to put pressure on neighbouring Prussia. George was regarded by Frederick the Great of Prussia as having a great predilection for Austria, as well as considerable concern for Hanoverian interests and views. Ironically, this concern, a concern that was also to influence Newcastle's views, was to help lead to an alliance with Prussia in 1756.[28]

On 10 January 1755, George told the newly arrived French envoy, Mirepoix, that he sought a continuation of peace, but he also spoke to him with warmth about the situation in North America. Characteristically, George presented this in terms of honour and obligations, with the monarch appearing in the traditional light of a defender of his subjects, themes that are difficult to analyse in geopolitical terms if the emphasis is placed on honour. George told Mirepoix that, in response to repeated complaints from the American colonists, he could not dispense from providing them with the protection he owed them. George claimed that he had no intention of expanding his possessions, but he stated that he could not accept that others should infringe the territorial rights of his subjects, an approach that Mirepoix declared was shared by Louis XV.[29] George, therefore, very much took the government's view.

Offering a reminder of the key role of personal views, and particularly priorities, Mirepoix claimed in correspondence that George did not care much about the colonies and did not want war, but that he had no intention of trying to improve the situation for Hanover by making concessions over North America, and indeed had no power to make such a suggestion,[30] which was an accurate account both of George's position and of his views. George was in line with the development of government policy in the growing crisis over North America, and British diplomatic instructions were not simply using the Crown as a fiction; although in 1757 George and ministry were briefly to follow different courses.

Turning to Frederick in 1755 reflected George's quest for security for Hanover and his perception of the state of these alliances and, in particular, his anger with Austrian policy.

Alongside loyalty to the constitution of the Holy Roman Empire, an ambivalence towards Austria ran through his reign from the outset, and it was certainly apparent in 1755. Ambivalence is not a category that readily lends itself to the often-misleading clarity of geopolitical exposition. Without specifically mentioning his own experience of battle at Oudenaarde in 1708, it is clear that the vulnerability of the Low Countries to French attack was an important consideration to George, not least because it would weaken the role that Austria, the ruler of the Austrian Netherlands (Belgium), might take in protecting Hanover against Prussia. In May 1755, there was a noticeable tone of complaint: 'every measure the King is taking with the different powers of Europe must be at a stand until Her Imperial Majesty shall come to the necessary resolution of sending, without loss of time, a strong reinforcement into the Low Countries.' With clear-cut reproach, the envoy in Vienna was accused of going native. He was informed that the King could not see why he referred to the Austrian government as having a good disposition, 'when you see a refusal, on the part of the Court of Vienna, of coming into the only measure in which His Majesty's interest is concerned'.[31]

Yet, in turn, the French occupation of Hanover in 1757 led George to consider negotiations with Austria for neutrality for the Electorate. This departure indicated the dependence of strategic culture on events. Hanoverian neutrality, however, was rejected by Pitt as likely to wreck Britain's alliance with Prussia and as posing the danger that Frederick would leave the war. This episode is a reminder of the need to consider geopolitics in terms of alliance dynamics and also that the geopolitics of participants interacted in a fashion that was shaped by events and politics.[32]

As a reminder also of the political dimension, Pitt, in the winter of 1757–8, played a major role in securing a political settlement that tied the defence of Hanover to British direction and identified it with the more popular Prussian alliance. He proposed that Britain pay the entire cost of the 'Army of Observation' intended to protect Hanover and in 1758 won support for the dispatch to Germany of British troops which were designed to assist this army. Landing in Emden that August, the British forces saw action the following year. The dispatch of this force was an important concession to George, although it also fixed Hanover as a principal in the war, ending the option of neutrality, and leaving the Electorate vulnerable to renewed French attacks.

Nevertheless, provision for protection of Hanover was part of the settlement of domestic political differences, and this provision reflected George's importance. Considering the geopolitics of the Seven Years' War in the light of the contested character of national interests emphasises the extent to which political contention and politics make geopolitics and strategic culture a means of debate, rather than categories that encompasses politics.

By the close of George's reign in 1760, British forces had smashed the French navy (at the battles of Lagos and Quiberon Bay, both in 1759) and also captured much of the French empire, most dramatically Québec in 1759, becoming the dominant European power in South Asia and North America. War patriotism helped to keep the nation moving forward. The Reverend Samuel Pullein took time from his publications on silk cultivation to write the poem 'On the Taking of Louisburgh', which was published in *Owen's Weekly Chronicle* on 9 September 1758, as well as in the *Gentleman's Magazine*. Pullein saw the capture of the fortress, which was believed to be the key base in the French outer defences of Canada, as a decisive moment in world history, and presented the war as part of a struggle against tyranny and superstition. This presentation entailed a location of geopolitics in terms of ideological conflict, which is one of the strands in the use of geopolitics, albeit not a consistent strand:

> Hail Western world! begin thy better fate,
> Hence let thy annals take a happier date . . .
> liberty, released by heroes hands . . .
> gives the new-known worlds a second birth.

Montréal and the French forces in Canada capitulated in 1760.

A key element of contingency was provided by the rapidly changing nature of the war, both in Europe and overseas. This strong sense of contingency was true for Britain and for the other powers, and their interaction created a system that was also an unpredictable element. War, its presence, changes and consequences, thus set the pace for the diplomacy of France and other states. Much of this diplomacy became a matter of keeping the rival coalitions together, which, in turn, added another element of unpredictability. Thus, defeats in late 1757 destroyed early French enthusiasm for the war, leading the French Foreign Minister, Bernis, at the start of 1758, to see the alliance with Austria as a failure. These problems obliged the allies to consider new options. The French government sought that spring to persuade Austria to make peace with Prussia, while Austria was determined to fight on, increasingly relied on Russia and displayed limited interest in the French war. Such diplomatic tensions are difficult to capture if the emphasis is on geopolitical blocs.

Similarly, relations between France and Spain affected those between each and Britain. At the same time, they also underlined the role of individuals. Ferdinand VI of Spain (r. 1746–59) resisted French pressure to act against Britain and warnings that the Spanish colonies would follow those of France in being conquered by her.[33] His attitude is a reminder of the dangers of adopting a schematic approach to international relations. Far from being driven to align with France, by fear of British expansion or by dynastic links, Ferdinand was reasonably close to Britain. In contrast, his half-brother and successor, Charles III (r. 1759–88), was concerned about a fundamental shift of oceanic power towards Britain. His accession represented a major shift in Spanish policy reflecting a different geopolitical assessment, a shift that greatly encouraged French firmness in abortive Anglo-French peace negotiations in 1761, because it gave point to this firmness. In turn, Spain joined France against Britain that winter.

British success therefore helped transform not only attitudes there but also those of Britain's opponents. This sense of geopolitics and strategic culture as dynamic is one that needs to be captured. It is particularly appropriate when considering the latter years of the war, for the parameters of debate in Britain were very different to those at the outset. In part, this difference reflected the consequences of campaigning, but there were also key external developments in the shape of the new political environment surrounding the accession of a new king (George III, r. 1760–1820) who was determined to see through changes. There was an important interaction between campaigning and politics, with choices in relations with Prussia and Spain seen in political terms.

George III, his key adviser, John, 3rd Earl of Bute, and the Duke of Newcastle, decided to seek to revive the 'Old System' of pre-war alliances, notably with Austria, a policy that entailed distancing Britain from Prussia. However, as a powerful reminder of the impact of ideas, George and Bute did not envisage the extensive and costly Continental commitments of Newcastle's pre-war diplomacy. The defence of Hanover was no longer to be a central feature of Britain's Continental policy, and thus its geopolitics was to change. Conversely, the argument that the Anglo-Prussian alliance was unlikely to have survived the war anyway throws light on the policies of Bute, who can be seen as an intelligent and effective minister forced to deal with the commitments of war, including the Prussian alliance, and obliged to adapt policy to the peacetime exigencies of domestic political and financial constraints.[34] Geopolitics drew in with the coming of peace, a phrasing, however, that suggests a natural process at work, when, instead, the domestic and international politics of the episode should be emphasised.

A sense of geopolitics and strategic culture as dynamic, or at least changing, makes sense not only of the politics of the period, for example the response to George III's wish to end the commitment to Hanoverian expansionism and to the deployment of British forces in Germany, but also of politics in a more widely defined sense of attitudes to state and country. The consequences of the Seven Years' War in this respect were more profound in France where public debate became more prominent than hitherto. In Britain, the key change was a greater salience for imperial issues which led to post-war attempts to make empire work. These, however, were attempts that helped cause the American Revolution.

In part, this revolution, which broke out in 1775, was an expression of tension between different 'kinds of spaces', notably the oceanically oriented British Atlantic and the settler empire of 'the American Frontier', with the intermediate eastern seaboard providing a crucial sphere of tension. Although English merchants and proprietors had begun the colonisation of New England, the Chesapeake and the Carolina low country in the seventeenth century, they had subsequently lost control over the process of settlement, defeated by the enormous availability of agricultural land and the difficulty of commanding immigrant labour. As a result, more autonomous economies had developed. Moreover, the spaces of the American interior provided colonial elites with a 'much greater geographic context in which to manoeuvre than existed on the islands of the British Atlantic'.[35] Much of the work on the American Revolution has been on ideology and politics, but it is also possible to see geography as playing a key role: 'the fracturing of empire was along structural faults embedded in the continent's evolving human geography.'[36] The interior came to the fore in British politics in 1772, when the Privy Council supported the creation of a new colonial province in the Ohio Valley.

That the discussion above of the Seven Years' War and of its consequences could be repeated for other episodes and indeed, allowing for changes in political system and culture, throughout the period, indicates the problem with broad-brush analytical formulations, such as those commonly employed in geopolitical literature. The intention here is not to undermine the latter but simply to point out that the detailed application of theory in particular contexts faces serious problems.

For all scholars, serious issues are created by limited space, not least the difficulty of explaining the context, process and contingencies of each choice of policy and then of analysing it in accordance with the chronological specificities of the debate at any particular juncture. Arguments take on meaning in that context, but this approach poses problems of analysis, exposition and space. As a result, factors of convenience encourage a frequently misleading tendency to emphasise the continuity of arguments, as indeed do academic fashions as well as the strategies or culture of particular disciplines, including that of political geography and, more specifically, geopolitics.

This problem of simplification is also an issue that involves historians. The common problems are not only the selection and analysis of texts in accordance with a predetermined thesis but also the very notion of a *zeitgeist* (Spirit of the Age). This, indeed, is a notion which, unless care is taken, can be the basis for a misleading use of the concept of geopolitics. Those considering the past (and indeed also present and future) may stress the power of particular sets of ideas, but, to go beyond this, and to suggest that one vision became a dominant discourse, runs considerable risks. Such an approach may become self-validating; it has severe limitations in describing what was generally in fact a diverse situation; it may neglect the complexity and compromises within discourses itself; and it may miss the extent to which supposedly hegemonic world views were actually divisive and polemical.

Indeed, to take the period of Whig hegemony under George I and George II, 1714–60, far from there being a zeitgeist, the contested nature, among the Whigs, of the concept of national interest makes it easier to understand Tory criticism of the methods and objectives of foreign policy. The role of contingency in affecting the formulation and execution of policy contributed to this criticism, as well as reshaping the debate. To again underline the problem with the idea of a dominant discourse, albeit in a very different context, contemporary claims that German geopolitics were a monolithic support for Nazi expansionism underrated serious differences between their emphases, as the discussion in the next chapter indicates.

A historian in the British empirical tradition would therefore argue that an awareness of particular interest and specific conjunctures should take precedence over the fascination with discourse. In doing so, it is also important that the reality was more complex and fractured than those who search for a *zeitgeist* might suggest. This sceptical view, however, is a fundamental challenge to the standard approach across so much of the academic world, with its tendency both to employ discourse as a hegemonic concept and (as a related, but different, issue) to argue by assertion. As an aspect of this problem, it is unhelpful to ascribe policy to a climate of opinion unless the subjective nature of the definition of the climate is accepted and the problematic concept of moving from climate to policy allowed for. Such methodological challenges need to be addressed explicitly.

An instance is provided by the treatment of geography as an adjunct, indeed enabler, of imperial power. This view was taken by radical figures in cartographic studies, notably Brian Harley,[37] and has subsequently been adopted more generally by geographers, including those re-examining geopolitics. Thus, Gearóid Ó Tuathail began *Critical Geopolitics,* which is, possibly more aptly than he intended, subtitled *The Politics of Writing Global Space* (1996), by stating 'Geography is about power. Although often assumed to be innocent, the geography of the world is not a product of nature but a product of histories of struggle between competing authorities over the power to organize, occupy, and administer space.' He subsequently added that geography was 'an active writing of the earth by an expanding, centralizing imperial state'.[38]

The intention here is not to focus on the general flaws of this argument, several of which are considered in Chapter 1, but, rather, to assess British imperialism specifically in this light. The charge sheet here, and the term is employed advisedly to discuss the critical, if not accusatory, nature of much of the literature, is a presentation of geography both as an adjunct for the process of imperial conquest and as a key aspect of colonial rule.[39] Geography, as practice, analysis and discourse, is seen by its critics as empowering the imperialist and as weakening native culture, not least by ensuring that space is conceived in the terms of the imperialist, with native geographical consciousness driven to the shadows, usually the shadows of an oral culture. Thus, there is much discussion of imperialist appropriation through naming, of geography's role in land seizure and distribution, of the drawing of colonial boundaries without concern for pre-existing alignments and affinities, and of geography as an aspect of control.

This process is a key instance of geopolitics to some commentators, and thus, in this view, the modern subject should address itself to the process. Furthermore, in an extension of the argument that the conflicts within Europe in 1914–45, specifically the eastward expansion of German power in both world wars, owed their origins to transoceanic European imperialism, a similar point was made about the usage of geography for imperialism first outside and then within Europe. The former argument was frequently offered by critics on the left pursuing Western guilt through ascription and association, and this process was taken up by those interested in a critical account of the usage of geography.

In the next chapter, the classic period of geopolitics, that of the first half of the twentieth century, will be considered. Here it will suffice to note that a key problem with the treatment of geography in this fashion is that it adopts a simplification and instrumentalism that permits the avoidance of the hard work of moving from the drawing of links to the weighing of influence. More particularly, it is also unclear how far what is castigated was no more than the commonplace rationalisation of what had already occurred; in short that the key element was conquest, and not subsequent intellectual strategies.

The variety of geography, geography in short as medium and not message, also needs to be underlined. For example, it is possible to link the development of the subject in the late sixteenth century to that of English imperialism. Attempts to understand the wider world led to the study of geography, which offered a new ideal of science as a tool for understanding and controlling nature, while the need to confront the information acquired by exploration and the issues raised posed problems for classification.[40] Service of the state fostered an interest in mathematical geography, while descriptive geography encouraged readers to regard the world as a source of wondrous tales and new goods; and there was a relationship between the study of geography and the development of ideas of English power and imperial growth.[41]

A sense of maritime destiny was pressed in a number of publications, including John Dee's *General and Rare Memorials Pertaining to the Perfect Act of Navigation* (1577) and Richard Hakluyt's *Principal Navigations, Voyages, Traffiques and Discoveries of the English Nation* (1598–1600). Hakluyt's work served in its field a function akin to John Foxe's *Book of Martyrs* (1563), which provided an account of England as a kingdom that had been in the forefront of the advance towards Christian truth. Such works offered those open to the culture of print an awareness of the oceans and the overseas world that provided a potent vision of present interest and future glory; but, crucially, the impact of such works on government policy is difficult to assess.

A similar point can be made about the high tide of imperialism in the nineteenth century. Policy and contention focused on issues such as whether Britain should adopt a forward policy, notably, but not only, in Afghanistan, Sudan, Uganda or southern Africa. The literature about British greatness and imperial destiny did not ensure specific governmental, political or public responses in these and other debates. Nor did specific initiatives. For example, the British-led Survey of India may have sent North Indian geographical spies and explorers into Tibet and Central Asia between 1863 and 1893, but that did not mean any agreement on a forward imperialist policy; indeed, in many respects, accurate information could be seen as a crucial prerequisite also for those who urged policies of caution.

Yet, allowing for the difficulty in drawing a consistent causal relationship between geography and imperial policy, as opposed to imperial activity, it would be naive to neglect the relationship between imperialism and knowledge. Territoriality required knowledge – locational specificity – and the construction and acquisition of that knowledge were parts of a more general process by which the Europeans sought to understand the world in their own terms.[42] As so often, terminology can convey different meanings with, for example, the word 'understand' in the last sentence replaced by 'grasp'.

Geographical advances, moreover, did not necessarily lead to imperial sway. For example, Ethiopia resisted conquest despite a marked increase in Western knowledge about it. Indeed, to survey part of the country between 1837 and 1849, Antoine d'Abbadie invented a rapid survey method and critically reviewed his instruments. His later development of a simplified theodolite, the ata, and his continued stress on simplicity and lightness in instrument design, derived from his Ethiopian surveying. Back in France, d'Abbadie wrote on Ethiopia, including a *Géographie d'Ethiopie* (1890), and also prepared ten maps. Ethiopia, like Japan, is an instance of the extent to which imperial expansion in this period was not restricted to Western powers.[43]

Even when there was a close link, it was geographers who were subservient to the expansionist impulses, rather than giving rise to it. Thus, the Berlin Conference of 1885 established the principle that the hinterland of a stretch of coast occupied by a European power was legitimately part of its sphere of influence, an approach adopted by statesmen that encouraged territorial expansion and found work for geographers. Moreover, the local spatial patterning of imperial rule and settlement, particularly the different racial, gender and social spaces of land use and settlement,[44] were scarcely dependent on surveyors, mapmakers and other geographically linked trades, however much they assisted in a commodification of land that helped lessen non-Western rights to it. In addition, although earlier spatial configurations were downplayed,[45] and the superiority of Western instruments was stressed,[46] Western surveyors, mapmakers and others were often dependent on local assistance,[47] and, indeed, were welcomed as well as opposed by local people.[48]

Geography, as the acquisition of spatially linked information and, even more, its organisation and analysis, was, in the nineteenth century, an aspect of the systematisation of knowledge also seen in subjects such as ethnography and geology. For example, the physical geography of the world was understood in terms of measurement, and measured accordingly. Seas were charted, heights gauged, depths plumbed and rainfall and temperature graphed; and all was integrated, so that the world was increasingly understood in terms of a European matrix of knowledge, contributing to an integrative science of the Earth, as in Alexander von Humboldt's *Essay on the Geography of Plants* (1807).[49] Areas were given an aggregate assessment – for example, wet, hot, mountainous, forested – that reflected and denoted value and values to Europe. Similarly, regions were grouped together, most prominently as continents, in response to European ideas. Thus, the South Atlantic world of the west coast of Africa, Brazil, the Guianas and the West Indies, was subordinated to a European model in which Africa and the New World were separate.[50] The voyage of Humboldt and Aimé Bonpland to South America in 1799–1804 was an especially important example of this approach, as described in Humboldt's *Vue des cordillères et monuments des peuples indigènes de l'Amérique* (1810) and *Atlas géographique et physique du royaume de la Nouvelle Espagne* (1811).

Geography, in the sense of the collection, understanding and analysis of spatially linked information, was part of the process by which, alongside, and indeed antecedent to, technological developments, notably the telegraph,[51] there was a crucial development in the perception of the plasticity of nature and of the world itself. Moreover, this development had a major impact on the political imagination, notably in dissolving distance and encouraging what has been seen as globalisation.[52]

Changing intellectual and cultural suppositions remoulded assumptions about place, and about national, ethnic and geographical hierarchies, with everything then entailed that stemmed from a notion of hierarchy. Such notions were particularly important in a period in which cultural superiority was explicitly taken to justify control and the use of control.

In the broadest sense, this process can be seen as political, but without assuming that a particular political narrative arose as a result.

CHAPTER 5

GEOPOLITICS AND THE AGE OF IMPERIALISM, 1890–1945

Geopolitics as a self-conscious subject began at the close of the nineteenth century. It would be misleading to ascribe this development to one specific cause, but international competition was clearly the key element. The ability of Western states to expand without conflict between them, other than the Crimean War of 1854–6, can lead to a failure to heed the extent to which European international relations were intensely competitive. Moreover, this competition increased towards the close of the century, not only because most of the world had already been divided up, either as colonies or as spheres of influence, but also as a result of the rise of new imperial powers – Germany, Italy, the USA and Japan – to add to the expanding imperial powers earlier in the century – Britain, France and Russia, powers that were still actively expanding. Indeed, Britain went to war with the Boer republics of Transvaal and the Orange Free State in 1899, a conflict that was to lead to their annexation.

Geopolitics provided both a means to understand this competition and also a way to urge particular policies, generally in the shape of national destinies. Geopolitics as a self-conscious intellectual tradition rested on the realist theory of international relations, and on the geography of states, as developed by Friedrich Ratzel (1844–1904), a professor of geography in Germany and the country's leading political scientist. The key element was an approach to state competition in which the territorialisation of space was presented as an expression of conflicting political drives and was held in tension by them. Ratzel, who was trained in the natural sciences (like Mackinder), and who had served in the Franco-Prussian War of 1870–1, presented international relations in the Darwinian terms of a struggle for survival, although arguing that Darwin had failed to devote due attention to the issue of space. War, to Ratzel, was natural. He also saw states as organic and thus ignored divisions within them, let alone the play of individual political and military leaders, who, in practice, provide the key level for understanding geopolitical pressures.

The struggle for space was central to Ratzel's *Die Erde und das Leben* (*The Earth and Life*, 1902). In this, Ratzel deployed the concept of *Lebensraum* (living space) that had been devised in 1860 by the biologist Oscar Peschel in a review of Darwin's *The Origin of Species*. Ratzel emphasised the role of environmental circumstances in affecting the process and progress of struggle between states. Ratzel was also much engaged in German maritime and colonial expansion, supporting a large fleet and overseas bases as means to secure Germany's 'Place in the Sun'.[1] Ratzel's *Politische Geographie* (1897), with its stress on the close relationship of people and environment, was a crucial text for the development of geopolitics, not least because of its influence on Rudolf Kjellén (1864–1922), who held the chair of political science at Sweden's leading university, Uppsala, and who coined the term *Geopolitik* in 1899. Ratzel's book was also to be recommended to Hitler.

Kjellén's early work focused on the conventional treatment of the state, in terms of historical identity and constitutional character, but he rethought his views in accordance with Ratzel's emphasis on the role of geographical factors. To Kjellén, full, like many, of *fin de siècle* pessimism about the future of both Western civilisation (and, in his case, concerned about the fate of Sweden) in the face of international competition and ascendant democratic populism, it was necessary to understand geopolitics in order to appreciate the true nature of national interests. The strong sense of *fin de siècle* also produced an assumption that the new century would lead to new beginnings and that the resulting discontinuity required new analytical concepts.[2] Emphasising the value and application of scientific methods, Kjellén presented the state as taking on particular significance in terms of its existence and effectiveness as a geographical entity. To him, both rested in part on the state's relationship with other states as geographical entities.

This approach took forward Ratzel's emphasis on territorial expansion as both product and cause of a state's success as an organic phenomenon. Indeed, to Ratzel, this union of expansion and strength, the two being crucial to the state's existence (rather than simply controlling space itself), was expressed in terms of its pursuit of *Lebensraum,* or living space. Success in this pursuit would guarantee, as well as define, power, and thus permit the pursuit of great-power status. Power, in short, was cumulative, with space a crucial means and measure.

Kjellén provided the vocabulary and theoretical term of *Geopolitik,* opening the way to formal geopolitical reasoning in terms of an explicit methodology and specific literature. Kjellén saw this new-coined term as one offering a new understanding for a new age, an advance through classification on the existing subject of political geography. The emphasis, as in other intellectual fields, was on a universal law that would provide both explanation and a key to reordering circumstances. A belief in the possibility of the latter, moreover, was to help make geopolitics fashionable.

To Kjellén, such an advance in understanding was necessary because of the pronounced flux in world affairs, one of transformative international political and economic changes, notably the rise of the USA. In explaining them, Kjellén argued that geopolitics took precedence over the other forms of politics. Such an argument represented a departure from historicist accounts of states in terms of particular constitutional, legal, diplomatic and political legacies, rationalisations and legitimations; and Kjellén indeed argued that these accounts were overly narrow and drew on a particular political and intellectual strand, that of French bourgeois republicanism and Enlightenment ideas. Instead, Kjellén pressed for a wider concept of states as communities, communities that were geographically grounded. To Kjellén, the legitimation offered in geopolitics was that of control over space, and control, moreover, in a competitive situation in which conflict was natural.

Moreover, this approach permitted Kjellén to measure states by the same criteria and thus to put aside what he presented as subjective approaches and views such as those centred on ethical standards. His was an international order or system in which all were to be judged as one, and to be understood and ranked accordingly. In his *Stormakterna (The Great Powers*, 1905), Kjellén pressed the value of superstates and also a larger Germany. At the same time, Kjellén advocated particular Swedish goals, notably the maintenance of the 1814–1905 union with Norway and the containment of Russia, which had destroyed Sweden's empire in the eastern Baltic in 1709–13, finally annexing Finland in 1809 after the third Russian conquest of the territory.

This process of applying geopolitical perspectives to particular national interests (as well as of such interests to geopolitics) was a widespread feature of a period in which politicians, military planners, diplomats and commentators sought to respond to international problems and opportunities by creating alliance systems and devising military strategies accordingly.[3] Thus, at one level, geopolitics was an aspect of the pre-First World War period of strategic concern and planning. It was also related to a rise in industrial, commercial and agrarian protectionism that reflected both economic nationalism and the strains and anxieties arising from global competition in a world that seemed smaller and more interdependent. Indeed, the idea that the world would be dominated by large and competitive geopolitical blocs that sought strategic and economic self-sufficiency was one that lent itself to geopolitical discussion. This idea appeared to pose a major challenge to the European states and empires as, in a changing environment, they needed to retain a competitiveness, both to outside powers and to each other.

A Swede writing in Swedish is unlikely to make a major impact, but Kjellén's *Staten som Lifsform* (*States as Living*

Organisms, 1916) was published in Leipzig in 1917 as *Der Staat als Lebensform*.[4] Germans scarcely needed to read this in order to consider the possibility for a geographical reordering of Eastern Europe in the wake of the collapse of the Romanov dynasty, the latest version of a reordering of parts of Europe that they had been pursuing from 1914, but the emphasis on the now was particularly appropriate.

So also for Japan. At the time of the Sino-Japanese (1894–5) and Russo-Japanese (1904–5) Wars, the Japanese political and military leadership of the 1890s–1900s had a specific world view, one convinced of the Social Darwinist interpretation of geopolitics. Their translation of 'survival of the fittest' was 'jaku niku kyoo shoku', literally 'weak meat, strong eat'. Moreover, a recurring phrase about their own situation in the world was that Japan was like 'a piece of meat before tigers'.

Meanwhile, a global dimension had been added from London. On 25 January 1904, at a meeting of the Royal Geographical Society, Halford Mackinder (1861–1947), an influential Oxford geographer, presented a paper entitled 'The Geographical Pivot of History'.[5] In this, he focused on the largest landmass on Earth and developed his notion of a Eurasian Heartland. This Heartland was impregnable to attack by sea and, whoever controlled it threatened to overrun the whole of Eurasia. Mackinder argued that, in the heart of Eurasia, there was a 'geographical pivot of history', control over which would threaten other powers. Mackinder saw 'Europe and European history . . . subordinate to Asia and Asiatic history, for European civilisation is . . . the outcome of the secular struggle against Asiatic invasions . . . for a thousand years a series of horse-riding peoples emerged from Asia.'[6] Taking conflict as normal, Mackinder also claimed that, thanks in part to technology, the nature of the military challenge in Eurasia had altered:

> Russia replaces the Mongol Empire. Her pressure on Finland, on Scandinavia, on Poland, on Turkey, on Persia, on India, and on China, replaces the centrifugal raids of the steppeman . . . the camel-men

> and horse-men are going . . . railways will take their place, and then you will be able to fling power from side to side of this area.[7]

Thanks to railways, Mackinder saw a Heartland power in Eurasia, able to deploy its strength more effectively than the nomads had done. In this case, the emergence of the Geographical Pivot of History, as a strategic entity, was seen as a result of technological change. Mackinder was interested in the Trans-Siberian Railway and its implications for the unity of the Heartland. The economic potential was presented as vast: the 'potentialities in population, wheat, fuel, and metals [are] so incalculably great, that it is inevitable that a vast economic world, more or less apart, will develop there'.[8] Indeed, rail links were seen as key demonstrations and enablers of power and in particular spatial contexts,[9] rather as, today, there is interest in the implications of new oil and gas pipelines.

Technology thus enhanced, indeed created, geopolitical forces and axes; thus geopolitics was, in large part, a function of technology. In the 'Pivot' paper, Mackinder argued that the greater powers were playing on a global board with a great ocean in which the size and arrangement of continents presented opportunities to the players. Yet, Mackinder was no environmental determinist[10] and stepped back from predicting which state would be successful, although he mentioned those that might dominate the Pivot.

At the meeting, Mackinder's interpretation was challenged by the young Leo Amery, then a *Times* journalist, who emphasised the onward rush of technology and the role of industrial capacity. He told the gathering that sea and rail links and power would be supplemented by air, a remarkably prescient remark given that the Wright Brothers had only had their first flight the previous year. Amery added that, once air power played a role, then:

> a great deal of this geographical distribution must lose its importance, and the successful powers will be those who have the greatest industrial basis. It

> will not matter whether they are in the centre of a continent or on an island; those people who have the industrial power and the power of invention and of science will be able to defeat all others.[11]

The USA, where manned flight had just begun, was an obvious candidate for this role. Thus, geopolitics was being challenged even as it was advanced as a concept. From a different direction, Spencer Wilkinson criticised Mackinder at the meeting for using a Mercator projection, and thus exaggerating the size of the British Empire, as well, more pertinently given the map employed in Mackinder's article, as the Eurasian Heartland.

At a time of growing concern in British political circles about both overreach and a deteriorating global position, Mackinder's survey was, in effect, a call for vigilance, and for a united British empire able to resist whichever of Germany or Russia dominated the 'Pivot'. British imperial moves, which, in 1904, included the occupation of Lhasa, the capital of Tibet, were made in a context of pronounced international competition. Two years earlier, in his *Britain and the British Seas,* Mackinder argued forcefully that the development of rail technology and systems altered the paradigm of economic potential away from maritime power, a view that seemed borne out by the economic growth of the USA and Germany. To respond to the crisis of British power, Mackinder, a Liberal imperialist who in 1903 moved to the Conservative Party, turned to protectionism and social reform, and to the Dominion status of the former settlement colonies – Australia, Canada and New Zealand:

> The whole course of future history depends on whether the Old Britain besides the Narrow Seas have enough of virility and imagination to withstand the challenge of her naval supremacy, until such time as the daughter nations shall have grown to maturity, and the British Navy shall have expanded into the Navy of the Britains.[12]

Mackinder, indeed, was an advocate of imperial federation, pressing for emigration only within the Empire: 'In all these lands they will remain the subjects of our king, Edward VII; the same flag will be theirs and they will not be among foreigners'.[13]

Mackinder's was a geography and geopolitics of challenge and threat, one that gave depth to, but otherwise reflected, much of the contemporary writing about Britain's position. Although he disliked the words 'geopolitics' and 'geopolitician', and wrote extensively on geographical topics, Mackinder is generally considered the leading British geopolitician.[14] Geopolitics as an analytical approach was clearly not incompatible with the definition of geography he offered in 1904: 'It answers two questions. It answers the question Where? and it then proceeds to answer the question Why there?'[15]

Mackinder was certainly more influential and engaged than most academics. From 1903 to 1908, Mackinder was the second Director of the London School of Economics, while he was a Conservative MP from 1910 to 1922; Kjellén was also a member of the Swedish Parliament for six years. Mackinder's roles included British High Commissioner to South Russia in 1919–20 and Chairman of the Imperial Shipping Committee in 1920–39.

Mackinder's views and role were affected by the strains in Britain's imperial position and, subsequently, by the First World War. As such, there was a parallel with other commentators of the period, for example J. A. (John Atkinson) Hobson, the author of *The Physiology of Industry* (1889), a critique of *laissez-faire* economics, and of *Imperialism: A Study* (1902), which ascribed the formative role to the tendency of these economies to overproduce capital and goods. Whereas Mackinder was important in the development of Conservative thought on international relations, Hobson was involved in the New Liberalism of the same decade. Whereas Mackinder came to favour imperial protection, Hobson moved away from this remedy. Indeed, Hobson argued against imperialism and, instead, in favour of a peaceful democracy seeking to widen social prosperity. He also came to favour an internationalism linked to free trade. In his *Democracy after the War* (1917), Hobson returned to his critique of imperialism and protectionism as anti-democratic and anti-liberal.[16]

During Mackinder's career, geographers continued to serve the cause of British imperialism, not least because the First World War added extensive German and Ottoman (Turkish) possessions to the British empire, while the pressure for development of existing colonies gathered pace. These were not the limit of British interest. For example, an Imperial Conference that met in 1926 decided to assert British and Dominion title to parts of Antarctica. To support these claims, the Committee on British Policy in the Antarctic commissioned a revision of the Hydrographic Office's South Polar Chart, one that emphasised the role of British explorers.

Mackinder himself responded to the European situation at the close of the First World War, not least German success against Russia in 1917–18 and Russia's move to Communism, by proposing a new order in Eastern Europe, namely a group of 'buffer states' backed by Britain and France, in order to restrain both Germany and Russia.[17] He argued that 'we must see to it that East Europe, like West Europe, is divided into self-contained nations.'[18] In many respects, his proposal of 'buffer states' was a rationale of Anglo-French policy, both the post-war settlement in Eastern Europe, in particular the support for the creation and expansion of Czechoslovakia, Poland, Romania and Yugoslavia, and the intervention in the Russian Civil War, which indeed personally involved Mackinder in 1919–20. Moreover, the Anglo-French military and political support in 1919–20 for the new states resisting Russian expansionism, notably the Baltic Republics and Poland, was a key aspect of the new order advocated by Mackinder.

Mackinder's work at this juncture was also intended as a response to the internationalism offered by proponents of the League of Nations. He felt that Wilsonianism, the democratic internationalism, ideas and policies associated with President Woodrow Wilson, was naive and that it was necessary for commentators to distinguish between reality, in the shape of geopolitical realities, and democratic ideals. Indeed, Mackinder argued that it was important to understand the fundamental geographical inequalities of nations. This alleged tension between reality and idealism was to be one of the binary divides that geopoliticians regarded as a defining characteristic of the situation and a rationale for their subject.

Geopolitical discussion also responded to strategic issues and notions, and to related spatial awareness and assumptions. Thus the geopolitics of navalism advanced in works such as *The Influence of Sea Power upon History, 1660–1783* (1890) by Alfred Thayer Mahan, an American naval commander and lecturer at Naval War College, can be seen as responding not only to the potential of naval power but also to the immensity of the oceans in the Mercator projection. At the same time, Mahan's call for America to develop its naval strength as a strategic tool allowed for the specific maritime requirements of particular states as a consequence of their geographical position and their strength vis-à-vis the other naval powers. In short, there was a two-way relationship between state and system, a relationship in which geopolitics seemed to have particular weight. Mahan's theories encouraged the USA into playing a role in international relations.

In some respects, the geopolitics of navalism described a system in which major differences in strategic culture and tasking affected powers that had access to similar weaponry, a situation that was to be more generally true of geopolitical writings. Thus, Britain had to protect maritime routes that provided her with food, raw materials and links to export markets, a case argued by navalist interests funded by the City of London, for example the Navy League;[19] while challengers sought a doctrine, force structure, strategy and operational practice that could contest these routes. Navalists argued that greater force would enable them to change power relations. Mahan, for example, was influenced by the German historian Theodor Mommsen (1817–1903), who, in his *History of Rome,* presented Roman naval power as playing a crucial role against Carthage in the Second Punic

War (218–201 BCE). Reading this in Lima in 1884, while on naval duty protecting American interests, Mahan was struck by 'how different things might have been could Hannibal have invaded Italy by sea . . . instead of by the long land route, or could he, after arrival, have been in free communication [with Carthage] by land.'[20]

Building on the relationship between geopolitical arguments and particular political requirements, navalism as a thesis for strategic strength can also be linked to the particular nature of British and American societies. Neither had a large army nor employed conscription, and this situation was a reflection of political norms that favoured freedom and liberty (at least for their citizens as opposed to their imperial subjects) over the authoritarian political cultures of states with large armies such as Germany and Russia in the late nineteenth century.

For Britain, as for the USA, the key question was how best to pursue a strategy that made optimal use of its resources without requiring a change in strategic culture. The USA wished to use its navy to become a great power, and Britain to do so to stop itself losing this status; and each therefore required a geopolitical prospectus that made sense of this position or could limit challenge to it. Yet, that suggests an instrumentalism for which direct evidence is scanty. Moreover, in both Britain and the USA, as in France, Germany, Russia and Japan, there was a tension between maritime and territorial, naval and army, priorities; and discussion of national interest and geopolitics has to be seen in terms of this tension.

This point underlines the controversial nature of geopolitical works, whether they are explicitly geopolitical or, more commonly, implicitly so. Thus, Mahan sought a naval power to effect national destiny of international power expressed through naval strength, while Mackinder, in the early 1900s, came to support the new imperialism of the Liberal Unionists, as he saw territorial control as a key to economic strength. Indeed, while growing overseas trade underlined the importance of sea power, not least with its power to blockade and thus interrupt this trade; on the other hand, the industrialisation and political coherence of large land powers – the USA, Germany and Russia – appeared to challenge the value of sea power.[21]

Mackinder told his audience in 1904 that sea power was coming to an end as a result of the reassertion of land power made possible by the railway. Alongside that technology of transport came the importance of that of communications, notably telegraphy and the onset of radio.[22] These technologies were important to military command and control, as well as to imperial governance and to economic activity, especially maritime trade. The geopolitics of the communication routes were strategic in intent, although the costs stemming from the specifications arising from that rationale considerably affected their profitability. The strategic nature of these routes was seen in British action against German radio posts and submarine cables after the outbreak of the First World War in 1914.

More generally, the development of geopolitics reflected not only the impact of strategic issues but also the environmental determinism that was so influential from the 1890s. Although not all geographers accepted the idea of such determinism, geography was a central aspect of an intellectual world that linked humans and the physical environment and helped explain these linkages. Thus, distribution maps played an increasing role in scientific investigation and exposition, whether with the science of mankind or with biological and physical sciences.[23] Furthermore, the very notion of environmental determinism helped to politicise the physical environment and geographical relationships, because this environment, and these relationships, were seen as directly affecting the strength and policies of states.

Environmental causation was particularly attractive to geographers because it emphasised their importance: they could best explain the present and suggest the future. In addition, environmental causation made geographers seem better interpreters of the past than historians, as well as facilitating the understanding of change by archaeologists.

The rise of environmentalism looked back to eighteenth-century notions of the role of geography and nineteenth-century interest in nationalism and evolution, concepts that combined to suggest an agenda of political history in which environmentally moulded nation-states played a crucial role, displacing dynastic interest in favour of what were styled national interests. In the eighteenth century, the notion that objective national interests existed developed rapidly. In large part, it was a product of the Enlightenment proposition that humans live in a universe governed by natural laws which proclaim, among other things, the existence of 'nations', defined through a mixture of geography, language, culture, physical features, even traits of personality; and that the 'interests of nations', essentially, are to be understood in terms of protecting their geographical, cultural and physical (i.e. security) integrity.

Such ideas became more prominent in the nineteenth century as states were increasingly defined in nationalist terms, a process that led to greater interest in ethnic and environmental factors: it was environmental influence that apparently could best explain the differing political trajectories of various ethnic groups, the processes by which they had become nations and states with particular characteristics and interests. Far from being an alternative to nationalism, environmentalism could make these processes appear natural and necessary. In terms of the relations between nations, this situation led to an emphasis on 'natural frontiers', a theme found in the writings of the geopolitical school associated with Ratzel and his disciples.

Trained mostly in the natural sciences, nineteenth-century geographers assumed a close relationship between humanity and the biophysical environment and sought to probe it in terms of the environmental control that they took for granted. Mackinder, who took a degree in history after a first one in animal morphology, wrote in his 1887 paper 'The Scope and Methods of Geography' of 'an interaction between man and environment'.[24] Environmentalism was an attractive method for the geographers and historians of successful and expanding states,[25] such as Germany and the USA. Aside from justifying a place in the sun for these states, acting as a physical dimension of notions of Manifest Destiny about ineluctable expansionism, environmentalism played a crucial role in the organic theory of the state and in the treatment of culture as defined by the integration of nature and society.

Thus, in the USA, there was a treatment of the country's territorial expansion which could be made to seem inevitable, and thus necessary, an academic counterpart to providential notions of American Manifest Destiny. Key works included Albert Perry Brigham's *Geographic Influences in American History* (1903) and two by Ellen Churchill Semple, a geographer at the University of Chicago: *American History and its Geographic Conditions* (1903) and *Influences of Geographic Environment on the Basis of Ratzel's System of Anthropo-Geography* (1911). Semple had studied under Ratzel in Leipzig in 1891–2 and 1895, and she popularised the idea of anthropogeography, the geography of environmental influences. In contrast to the more cautious and less determinist Brigham, Semple argued the relationship between the physical environment and historical movements.[26]

The political implications of such works were readily apparent. Thus, Semple claimed that Africa was inert and attributed this in part to the lack of the fructifying variety of geographical conditions. Moreover, the inevitable triumph of the 'civilised' was a theme of the Oxford geographer Hereford B. George, author of *Relations of Geography and History* (1901).[27]

George, whose book appeared in new editions in 1903, 1907, 1910 and 1924, the last of which was reprinted in 1930, stressed the role of geographical influences but also argued that human action could affect the environment, an emphasis that was different to that of Semple, and, instead, accorded more with that of Mackinder. The analytical tension over the placing of emphasis in this relationship was an important theme in human geography in the early twentieth century and one that coincided with the rise of geopolitics as a distinctive discourse. In part, discussion by geographers underlined the idea of inevitable clear-cut interests for particular states flowing from their geographical nature; yet, in addition, geographers' discussion of the autonomous part of human action undercut this idea and also left much role for intellectual assessment of these interests and the related political debate and contention. Thus, geopolitics, understood as the debate over national interests, appeared more necessary.

A shift of emphasis, from the environment as a determining force, towards its interaction with human society was particularly associated with Paul Vidal de la Blache (1845–1918). Trained as a historian, Vidal de la Blache played a major role in the development of French geography and was appointed to the chair of geography at the Sorbonne in 1899. Geographical and historical studies were closely associated, a key unlocking of the potential for geopolitics, and indeed, until 1942, the *agrégation,* the major competitive examination for admission to teaching posts in French universities and high schools, entailed a joint examination in history and geography. As a result, the two subjects were each more open to the influence of the other than in Britain or the USA.

Vidal de la Blache argued that the environment created a context for human development rather than determining it. The environment thus set the parameters for socio-cultural developments, rather than being the central issue in history. The emphasis was therefore shifted back to humanity and to the varieties of human activity, to cultural geography, and to the complexities of nation-building.[28] Vidal de la Blache also argued that political geography had to be seen as an aspect of human geography as a whole.

Vidal de la Blache's work was taken up by Lucien Febvre. Opposed to determinism and the work of Ratzel, Febvre was suspicious of the use of the notion of influences and, instead, preferred the idea of an interaction between man and environment. In an argument with instructive implications for geopolitical writing, Febvre also directed attention to the problematic nature of the sources of environmental determinism that were all too often presented in simplistic terms, referring for example to the 'complexity of the idea of climate'. Although not published until 1925, Febvre conceived of his critique in 1912–13, and it can therefore be placed alongside American criticism of Ratzelian notions, most obviously these notions as expounded by Semple, who referred to Ratzel as her master.[29] In opposition to determinism, Febvre advanced what he termed 'possibilisme'.

Febvre also directed attention to the study of human regions. This approach was geographical, but one that implicitly challenged the geopolitical emphasis on imperial nation-states. Febvre indeed argued that states were man-made, whereas the sole geopolitical entities that were 'givens' were natural regions. Thus, states could be remade or could be subsumed by civilisations based on these regions, for example, Rhenish civilisation, which he saw as spanning France and Germany.[30]

To Febvre, distinctive *genres de vie* existed in human regions, which were specific and distinct physical units, and he argued that study of them became the obvious way to understand the relationship between humans and environment. A study at the regional level offered the possibility of a more detailed assessment of the relationship, and directed attention to human activity, because, although the physical geography of the French regions was far from uniform, the differences, for example in climate, were not sufficient to explain regional variations in human geography. More generally, the path-breaking *Annales* school of French historians, among whom Febvre was prominent, deliberately set out to fuse history and geography. They stressed regional characteristics that gave places an identity that was historical as well as geographical, but devoted little attention to geopolitics, and certainly not at the national level.[31]

It would be very convenient to play forward from the start of the twentieth century to the present day, fitting the major elements of geopolitics and the analysis of the subject throughout the intervening period into the theories and arguments advanced at the time. Nicholas Spykman, indeed, used the term 'Rimland', taking over Mackinder's 'Inner Crescent' (albeit with significant differences), and the Heartland–

Rimland contrast provided (and provides) a convenient one to consider not only the two world wars but also the Cold War. All three can be seen in terms of a struggle to dominate the Eurasian Heartland, notably between Russia/Soviet Union and German/NATO, and the consequent pressure by Russia/Soviet Union on the Rimland.

For example, during the Cold War, British strategic thinking, which consciously owed much to Mackinder's ideas, discerned a tension between Heartland and Rimland and thus saw the stability of South Asia as closely linked with that of the Indian Ocean, in which Britain was the leading naval power until the 1970s. China's easy victory over India in their border war of 1962 could be seen in this context, as could the Soviet invasion of Afghanistan in 1979, each representing both an expansion by the Heartland and a threat to Western interests. Looking to the future, the combination of a weak Heartland and a rising China has been seen as providing a new geopolitical situation.[32] With its emphasis on long-term strategic issues based on geographical consideration, the Heartland–Rimland analysis employed geopolitics and apparently demonstrated its applicability.

However, leaving aside the serious problems with the applicability of that approach, notably its tendency to underrate the specificity of particular episodes; there is also the difficulty posed by the relatively limited conceptual armoury of the classical geopolitician and thus the recurrence of particular concepts. Indeed, instead of emphasising continuity, it is as pertinent to follow Amery's intervention in 1904 and to note fundamental discontinuities in context. These can be provided by technology, most pertinently the rise, first, of air power and then of the use of space.

In addition, as a challenge to geopolitical continuity, there were the key shifts stemming from major changes in public culture, whether structural, notably the rise of democratisation, or ideological, the latter indeed looking towards Samuel Huntington's 'clash of civilisations', although requiring a more sophisticated approach than that work. These changes were downplayed in the classic accounts of geopolitics, as those accounts subordinated everything to the spatial character and interests of the state, understood in terms of conventional power politics, and, indeed, as Kjellén did, put the state as an entity above its population. Without neglecting the role of this character and interests of states, a different geopolitics, however, was offered by the changes in public culture, a process that had already been prefigured in the rise of public politics in selected countries in the West in the late eighteenth century, notably Britain, America and France.

The need to consider wider perspectives in geopolitics and related fields was also indicated, from a totally different direction, by the limitations of strategy as generally conceived in the early twentieth century. In the decades prior to the outbreak of the First World War in 1914, the development of general staffs on the model of that of Prussia/Germany encouraged a process of continuous military planning and preparation that placed new demands on cartographers. Specifically, aside from planning for war, the regular summer manoeuvres that armies undertook to maintain their fighting capacity created a need for maps that integrated topography and transport routes. Yet, this heavy staff emphasis on operational factors also proved to be a key instance of the way in which militaries lost sight of the need to relate planned operations to wider issues of strategic viability, not least the relationship between output and outcome. The resulting failure was very much to be demonstrated with German war-making during 1914, because proficiency in moving units and whole armies did not equate with an understanding of the wider political context of the war.[33] Geopolitical discussion needed (and needs) to take account of this context.

At the same time, alongside the weaknesses of classical geopolitical writing, it is instructive to note the limitations in discussions of power politics in Eurasia that make no reference to geopolitical writers. For an example of such a discussion, Alfred J. Rieber, in offering a borderland perspective on the origins of the Cold War, saw the latter as 'a phase in a prolonged struggle over the Eurasian borderlands that stretches back to the early modern period, when the great polyethnic, bureaucratic conquest empires . . . began to reverse a thousand years of nomadic military hegemony over sedentary cultures.'[34] This argument was related to the social dimension offered by the interaction between conquered borderland populations and imperial authorities.[35] At one level, such arguments indicated the centrality of geopolitical analysis, as well as the limitations arising from a reluctance to discuss new perspectives in terms of this geopolitical literature;[36] and yet this issue also highlights the failure of much of this literature to advance with reference to such new perspectives, many of which arose (and arise) from outside the often self-referential approach of the subject specialists.

Returning to the point about major changes in public culture, the contrast between German policy in the two world wars made the role of ideological suppositions in geopolitics (or to be modish in the construction of space), readily apparent. There was a treatment of Eastern Europe in the First World War as uncivilised,[37] but this treatment lacked the genocidal character and objective of German policy in the Second World War.[38] Indeed, the Nazi propagation of a racist geopolitics organised round the notion of racial purity was a highly distinctive form of geopolitics, although also possibly one that has later, generally less-genocidal, echoes, in 'ethnic cleansing' in Eastern Europe and, even more, in ethnic violence in much of Africa after the Second World War.

Moreover, this policy was scarcely extraneous to the geopolitics and strategy of Nazi international relations. Instead, there was an intensely racist inflection to the latter, one that led directly to the genocidal anti-Semitism that was central to German policy. Rather than seeing this situation as a marked contrast to Kjellén's argument about the primacy of the state, the latter was conceptualised by the Nazis as a racial space, with governance a matter of enforcing this character internally and extending it externally.

Nazi geopolitics is a vexed topic for those who work on geopolitics, because Karl Haushofer, one of the leading geopoliticians, was closely associated with the regime. In practice, this association was more ambiguous than was to be suggested, notably in the latter years of the Second World War, but, earlier, there were strong links between German expansionism, Nazi propaganda and many German geographers. These links with geographers were as much the result of widespread compliance with Nazi thinking as of a coherent propaganda offensive. The major theme was ethnographical – pressing hard the cause of the German people, many of them under foreign rule, for example the Sudetan Germans in Czechoslovakia – and this theme drew on the development of right-wing German geopolitics in the 1920s.

Moreover, this geopolitics was adversarial. For example, German geopoliticians strongly criticised Isaiah Bowman (1878–1950), the leading American political geographer of the age, and indeed Haushofer claimed that the science of geopolitics had been perverted by the Anglo-Saxons.

Director of the American Geographical Society from 1915 and Chief Territorial Specialist of the American Commission to Negotiate the Peace, at the close of the First World War, Bowman took maps from Mark Jefferson to President Woodrow Wilson at Paris. Bowman relished behaving as a kind of Wilsonian arbiter when dissecting the national claims of Europeans and, as a cartographer of ethnicity, played a key role in charting post-war territorial losses by Austria and Germany as part of the Versailles settlement. As a consequence, he became the academic nemesis against which the concepts of German geopolitics were fashioned. Ironically from the German perspective, Bowman, who was offered the executive secretaryship of the League of Nations in 1919, was himself very depressed by the failure of Wilson, Versailles and the League to bring order out of chaos, and indeed reflected 'The whole world has fallen into disorder.'[39]

Geopolitics became more important as a self-conscious discourse in Germany in the 1920s and 1930s, and also influenced Nazi ideas from early in the party's history. At the same time, objective geographic standards and values were abandoned in favour of tendentious presentation, in response to the aggressive and racist conservatism of German geopolitical circles in this period.[40] For example, skin, hair and eye colour in *Mitteleuropa* (itself very much a German concept) were mapped in Hans F. K. Günther's *Rassenkunde des deutschen Volkes* (1935), reflecting Nazi concerns with racial characteristics. The blondish character of the Sudetenland in Czechoslovakia would have underlined its German character to the map's German readers.

Mitteleuropa in this map was defined as including Alsace and Lorraine, although these regions had been returned to France after the First World War, as well as incorporating the territories lost to Poland, including the Polish Corridor, and the South Tyrol, which had been transferred from Austria to Italy after that war. In 1938, however, as a reflection of the care taken not to risk offending Mussolini's Fascist regime in Italy, Hitler ordered the withdrawal of a map of German culture showing the German ethnic areas in the South Tyrol. More generally, German cartographers sought not freedom of choice but rather clear directives that ensured continued favour.[41]

The Nazis also encouraged maps in public displays. These emphasised areas where Germans lived under foreign rule – in 1933 a cartographic play on this theme was staged in Berlin; and maps were also used in German films. A map displayed at the 1938 Nazi Party convention showed the danger of Soviet attack on Germany by indicating the routes that could be used. The polemics of the Nazi use of space were matched in Fascist Italy but were also more generally a characteristic of the propagandist stance of the new ideologies of the period. The result was very much a geopolitics of commitment, with the assumption that the control over space was inherently political. For example, the British writer J. F. (Frank) Horrabin employed maps to advance his left-wing agenda, as in 'The New Map of Europe' published in his *The Plebs Atlas* (1926), a work designed for use by working-class students at the National Council of Labour Colleges. This map presented Europe as subject to imperialism, with nominally independent states in fact 'colonies' of the major powers. Thus, Portugal, Greece, the Netherlands, Denmark,

Norway, Finland and the Baltic states were all depicted as British colonies. The primacy of foreign policy in the Soviet state owed much to a sense of spatial threat arising from anxiety about just such imperialism. Stalin's perceptions of encirclement, capitalist crisis and inevitable, imminent war generated his policies of breakneck modernisation, as well as the internal repressions, although his chosen course also had to do with domestic political struggles.

German geopolitics was to affect Nazi foreign policy.[42] There were, however, tensions in the relationship, not least between the Nazi desire for a geopolitics of untrammelled expansion, with space a measure of the stages or impact of expansion, and, on the other hand, the attempt by geopoliticians to provide a consistent rationale of what would be an extensive, but limited, expansion, notably in terms of the distribution of German populations outside Germany.[43] There was also a tension in understanding the dynamic forces: between geopolitical emphasis on the formative role of the environment and that of the Nazis on such a role for the German people, although the geopoliticians were also committed to the latter.

The geopoliticians looked to the theories advanced by Ratzel and Kjellén, seeing German identity and interest very much in geographical terms, and supporting expansionism accordingly. Moreover, it was argued that an understanding of Germany's geographical position and context was necessary in order to enable the state to realise its potential. The key figure was Karl Haushofer, who had been a general during the First World War, directing the artillery against the British attack on the Somme in 1916. After the war, angry at Germany's defeat, like many right-wingers, he gave a particular political slant to the political geography he lectured on at Munich.

From 1924, Haushofer was editor of the *Zeitschrift für Geopolitik,* which he founded as the mouthpiece for the *Geopolitik* he advocated. Influenced by Kjellén's writings on the state, and Mackinder's paper of 1904, Haushofer sought to adapt the latter to German interests, by defining a German sphere of influence in terms of his own ideas on pan-regions. Subsequently, Haushofer extended this idea to the benefit of Germany's allies, Italy and Japan, which were pursuing geopolitical ambitions of their own.[44] Haushofer had visited Japan from 1908 to 1910 as a military adviser and was much impressed by the culture of the society and its strong militarism. In turn, Haushofer took part in negotiations between Germany and Japan and was influential in the move in Japan to a greater endorsement of geopolitics from the mid-1930s.

Haushofer developed and led a group of geopoliticians at Munich, and they argued in favour of great powers defined by control of large spaces, which provided these powers with security. Such control was seen as the basis for the expansionism that served the interests of their struggle for independent endeavour. Laying claim to what was presented as an appropriately committed objectivity, geopolitics was seen by Haushofer as an applied science that permitted the pursuit of national policy. As a variant on Mackinder, whose 1904 essay he greatly praised, Haushofer saw the leading pan-regions as PanEuropa, PanAsien and PanAmerika. The second was designated for Germany's ally, Japan, but Germany's region was to include expansion into Russia.

Rudolf Hess was his personal assistant and Haushofer's favourite pupil. Haushofer visited Hess in Landsberg prison after Hitler's failed *putsch* in 1923, and Hitler took up some of his ideas. In power as Hitler's deputy, Hess in 1934 appointed Haushofer the president of a council for those of German origin living outside Germany, while the sales of the *Zeitschrift für Geopolitik* shot up. In 1939, Haushofer was to receive the Order of the Eagle of the German Reich from Hitler in recognition of his services to geopolitics. His ideas also circulated widely outside Germany.

Haushofer's geopolitics were strongly attacked by French political geographers, not least because of the tendency in German geopolitics to adopt a determinism of space and earth (the Nazis emphasised race as well), and thus to diminish the role of human society and free will. Albert Demangeon, a key

French human geographer of the inter-war period, explicitly criticised German *Geopolitik*, not least for lacking academic rigour and for placing geography very much at the service of the state.[45] Ironically, if the last phrase is altered to 'at the service of criticism of the state', similar points can be made today about some of the literature.

By 1939, Haushofer's earlier calls for the revision of Germany's loss of territory and prestige in the 1919 Versailles peace settlement had been fully realised, and Germany was in the ascendant. By the end of 1939, it was allied with Japan, Russia and Italy, and, by the end of 1940, France and much of Western Europe was conquered, while the USA remained neutral. Haushofer had pressed the case for geopolitics as a striving for survival and primacy between competing powers. This vision appeared to have been implemented in full.

Yet, with his construction of politics in terms of races not states, and of races supposedly engaged in an existential struggle, Hitler had no time for any limitation of, or on, German expansion. Redressing Versailles was at best a tactic, as was cooperation with Poland in 1935–8 or Russia in 1939–41. This refusal to consider limits was linked to a central flaw in much geopolitical thought, an inability to understand the inner workings of other states and societies. Thus, the Nazis did not appreciate the strength of Britain, the USA and the Soviet Union, while, similarly, the USA failed to understand German and Japanese motivations or at least to incorporate such an understanding into their pre-war military planning.

Global war from 1941, as Germany attacked the Soviet Union and also declared war on the USA after the latter had been attacked by Japan, brought forward the millenarian strain in Nazism and encouraged Hitler to give deadly effect to his aspirations and fears. The removal of Jews from a German-dominated Europe became a key aspect of geopolitics, and an extreme instance of the extent to which, across history, space was, at least in part, often an expression of racial or ethnic interest. From the outset, the Nazis had presented German nationalism very much in terms of the *Volk* (people), treating Jews as a threat to the organic, ethnic concept of Germanness and as automatically antithetical to the *Volksgemeinschaft* (people's or national community) that was the Nazi goal. In one respect, this ideology was a perverted consequence of the advent of Western-style nation-states in multi-ethnic Central Europe. The Nazis were convinced of the elemental characteristics of race and overlooked the extent to which their definitions were an aspect of racial construction.

A stress on the *Volk* also challenged alternative readings of the internal geopolitics of Germany. Aside from denying a role for individualism, the focus on the Aryans ensured that serious regional, political, religious, social and economic distinctions and divisions within Germany were deliberately downplayed. This process was an extreme accentuation of that by which the state created in 1871 overlaid earlier identities and loyalties and was a crucial aspect of the internal depoliticisation associated with dictatorships.

The Nazi leadership planned a 'New Order', with an enlarged Germany central to a new European system, and with the Germans at the top of a racial hierarchy. The economy of Europe, both conquered and allied, was to be made subservient to German interests, with the rest of Europe providing Germany with labour (both *in situ* and in Germany), raw materials and food, and, in turn, taking German industrial products on German terms. Industrial plant in occupied areas was to be taken over. New rail and, in particular, road routes were to provide the transport links. The unusually harsh winter of 1941–2 revealed the inadequacies of the road system in the western Soviet Union, which the Germans had conquered; and these inadequacies led the Germans in the spring of 1942 to decide to build a series of strategic roads to supply their forces and link their territories. DG IV, designed to link Lvov and Stalino, was the most important, and Himmler's personal involvement led to the road being called the 'Highway of the SS'. Such roads were also seen as a way to kill Jews through very cruel forced labour. Mass graves marked the route. The road was also seen as a setting for new model towns. A spur of the DG IV was to cross the Crimea and to be linked to a bridge across the Straits of Kerch, a span of 4.5 kilometres. From there, the road would continue into the Caucasus, to serve German strategic interests in the area, notably oil and the possibility of deploying forces near the Turkish border and advancing against the British in the Middle East. Hitler took a personal interest in the bridge, which was seen as a symbol of German control and engineering prowess. The DG IV and the bridge were never completed, however, as the Red Army advanced back into Ukraine in 1943. Instead, the sections stockpiled at Kerch enabled the Soviets to finish the bridge as a railway bridge, and, from October 1944 to February 1945 (when it broke up under the pressure of ice), the bridge supported the Soviet advance.

The Crimea was seen by the Nazis as a German Gibraltar, a German Riviera, or, for Hitler, a Gotengau, the land of the ancient Goths, in which South Tyroleans, displaced to satisfy Mussolini, were to replace the native population, while Ukraine was to be devoted to SS *latifundia* (estates) supported by subjugated peasants. A settler colony of ethnic Germans in Ukraine was planned by Himmler under the name of Hegewald. The slaughter of Jews and the killing of Russians were far more comprehensive than that of native Africans by the Germans earlier in their colonies of modern Namibia and Tanzania, as this slaughter drew on a determination to restructure totally both peoples and space.[46] The Nazi discussion in 1940 of sending Jews to Madagascar, where it was presumed that they would die in the hostile environment, also drew on an ethnic geopolitics.

Much of the former Soviet Union was designated for German occupation (with small sections for some of Germany's allies), but, to the east, Siberia was to be maintained as a rump state to which those deemed undesirables, appropriate neither for Germanisation nor for extermination, were to be forcibly transferred. What was presented as a spatial purification was a key aspect of Nazi population policy;[47] and the latter, as so often with geopolitics, was a theme in state policy and ideology, as well as a product of control over territory.

The Holocaust, indeed, was a distinctly geopolitical process, not only at the strategic level, in terms of ensuring the 'biological eradication of the entire *Jewry* of Europe', which Alfred Rosenberg, the Minister of the Eastern Territories, promised a press briefing on 18 November 1941. Indeed, Germany was declared '*judenfrei*' in June 1943. The geopolitical nature of the Holocaust was also apparent at the operational and tactical levels. The former involved the large-scale movements necessary to ensure a concentration of Jews in Poland, and then in the extermination camps, while the latter related to the organisation of killing in the camps. Detailed research has indicated that this situation was made more complex by the relationship between central direction and local initiatives,[48] but the movement of Jews was fundamental to the Holocaust, and this movement reflected spatial assumptions, including where best to slaughter and from where first to deport Jews. 'Evacuation to the East' was employed by the Germans as a euphemism for slaughter, and communication routes, in the shape of railways, were crucial to the process. Thus, the rail spur constructed to ensure that trains could go directly to Auschwitz II helped reflect and also ensure the preponderant role of this camp in the killing.[49]

In 1934, Haushofer's son Albrecht became a personal adviser to Hess, but, having angered Ribbentrop, the German Foreign Minister, in 1938 by arguing that any attack on Czechoslovakia would only unite Britain against Germany, Albrecht even more than Karl wished to end war with Britain in 1940 and was closely linked to Hess's unsanctioned peace overture to Britain in 1941. Hess's flight to Britain led to the disgracing of the Haushofers, although they were kept in play as possible intermediaries in any future negotiations with Britain. Relations with Britain were not the sole reason for a breach between the Nazi regime and the Haushofers. In addition, to Karl, Germany had succeeded with the overthrow of the balance of power in 1940 and the dictates of geopolitics did not require further invasion. To him, the invasion of the Soviet Union was mistaken.

The presentation of geopolitics was brought more under Nazi control and made more racialist in intent. Going into hiding after the July Bomb Plot, Albrecht was captured, imprisoned and, finally, shot the following spring. Karl was imprisoned in Dachau but survived the war. He argued then that his works had been misunderstood by the Nazis, but, dismayed by Germany's defeat and his own failure, Karl and his wife took poison in March 1946.[50]

Life Magazine, in November 1939, devoted an article to the Haushofers, presenting Karl as the 'philosopher of Nazism' and the 'inexhaustible Ideas Man for Hitler', while Albrecht was depicted looking at a globe. Readers were assured that in 'Haushofer's German Academy in Munich . . . the world is remade every day between breakfast and dinner.'

This article was a key work in the charge against Haushofer and German geopolitics that characterised American popular discussion of geopolitics during the war, a discussion that looked forward to hostile post-war consideration of geopolitics. Geopolitics was seen as a militaristic outlook, a view Mackinder noted as also prevalent in Britain. Nazi aggression was traced in part to the impact of geopolitical thought, and these charges were repeated in popular works such as *Readers' Digest*. The same charge was made on film, with the American army's film unit under the Hollywood director Frank Capra producing *Why We Fight*, a series of films intended to ensure motivation. *Prelude to War* (1943) depicted a hemisphere of light and another of dark dictatorship, while the maps of Germany, Italy and Japan were transformed into menacing symbols. The film *The Nazis Strike* (1943) presented Haushofer's institute as part of an account of geopolitics explained as the 'military control of space'. In this film, a Mackinder sequence, reprising his dictum of 1919 ('Who rules East Europe commands the Heartland; / Who rules the Heartland commands the World-Island; / Who rules the World-Island commands the World'[51]) is presented as the German geopolitical intention: 'Conquer Eastern Europe and you dominate the Heartland. Conquer the Heartland and you dominate the World Island. Conquer the World Island and you dominate the World.'

Indeed, in a speech at the American Embassy in 1944, Mackinder noted, 'It has, I am told, been rumoured that I have inspired Haushofer, who inspired Hess, who in turn suggested to Hitler while he was writing "Mein Kampf" certain geo-political ideas which are said to have originated from me.'[52] This thesis was to be propagated by Hugh Trevor-Roper: 'That Hess was a channel whereby Haushofer's geopolitical ideas (derived from Mackinder) were conveyed to Hitler's mind, there to be transformed into the doctrine of Eastern *Lebensraum*, seems to me almost certain.'[53]

The MGM film *Plan for Destruction* (dir. Edward L. Cahn, 1943), an account of Haushofer, depicted him as advising Hitler and coordinating German intelligence-gathering around the world. This information is presented as helping the Germans achieve victory, and Haushofer as having a master plan to dominate the Heartland and then to join the Japanese in attacking the Americas. Such a presentation made President Franklin Delano Roosevelt's 'Germany First' policy appear necessary. The German naval staff indeed had well-developed plans for a forward policy in the Atlantic.[54]

More sophisticated commentators also linked German expansionism with German geopolitics and, specifically, Haushofer, but did so in a way that called for the USA to have an explicit geopolitics in keeping with its own interests and divorced from the German *Geopolitik* that was held to represent a perversion of the subject as well as a nationalist ideology. This distinction was powerfully argued by Isaiah Bowman in his essay 'Geography versus Geopolitics', published in *The Geographical Review* of 1942.[55] The last paragraph of this essay offers a powerful critique of quasi-scientific certainty, one that drew on Robert Strausz-Hupé's *Geopolitics: The Struggle for Space and Power* (1942): 'Geopolitics is simple and sure, but, as disclosed in German writings and policy, it is also illusion, mummery, an apology for theft. Scientific geography deepens the understanding. But, like history or chemistry, it has no ready-made formulas for national salvation through scientifically "demonstrated" laws.'[56]

This distinction has been challenged by those concerned to argue the 'essentially contested and political nature of all geopolitical discourse'.[57] While accepting that there was not a moral equivalence between German and American geopoliticians, these later, self-styled 'critical geopoliticians' suggested elements of equivalence. Neil Smith and Gearóid Ó Tuathail have referred to 'American lebensraum'.[58] While such remarks are arresting, and, correctly, serve to underline the extent to which geopolitical arguments could be employed to serve many interests and ideologies, these remarks also reflect an inability to make clear distinctions, an inability that rests on a disinclination to accept notions of objectivity, or judgements other than that of the writer.

The argument in this book is that such an approach is flawed. Objectivity may not be realisable, certainly as a complete state, but objectivity is the appropriate goal for scholarship. Moreover, informed analysis would suggest that the use of geopolitical ideas in the 1930s and early 1940s by the USA and Britain did not equate with that by Germany, a point that also could be made about the employment of cartographic conventions.

The combination of the war with the German use of geopolitics led American political scientists and geographers to an explicit interest in geopolitics as well as to its application to American foreign policies. German developments were commented on by George Kiss[59] as well as Bowman. Bowman brought Strausz-Hupé forward as a commentator (and understudy) able to discuss the German geopolitical school. Strausz-Hupé did not believe in a science of politics, the argument that geopolitics was a scientific school of politics, nor in the view, associated with Henry Morgenthau, Secretary of the Treasury, of immutable national interests and thus the permanence of the German question.[60] Instead, Strausz-Hupé saw Mahan and Mackinder as recruiting the immutables of geography towards the goal of understanding how to work the balance of power. Strausz-Hupé argued that earlier geopolitics had been used to encourage this balance whereas the German geopolitical school was employing geopolitics to try to overthrow the balance, an argument also advanced by Bowman.

In turn, the development of the discipline of geopolitics in North America encouraged analysis.[61] Nicholas Spykman (1893–1943), a Dutch emigrant and former journalist, who was head of the Department of International Relations at Yale, sought to apply geopolitics to explain America's position and to advance her interests. Rebutting the powerful isolationism of the inter-war years, he argued that interventionism was a key American interest as if any one power dominated Eurasia it would threaten the New World.[62]

During the Second World War, American geographers played a role in the war effort, with over 100 of them employed in the Office for Strategic Studies, while Bowman advised Roosevelt and the State Department, usually on the refugee question. Bowman was a key figure in what might be termed the bloodline of American geopolitics. Beginning with Mahan, this was initially limited mostly to military circles but entered political circles with Theodore Roosevelt. His admiring cousin, Franklin Delano Roosevelt, was impressed by this example and hired Bowman as, in effect, his own personal geographer. In the meanwhile, however, Wilson had repudiated the active American role in international relations encouraged by Mahan and represented by Theodore Roosevelt. Instead, Wilson had returned to the earlier American tradition of neutrality, albeit changing it into an idealism that justified, first, the intervention into the First World War in 1917 that Wilson had long opposed and, subsequently, the support for the League of Nations, for which he unsuccessfully pressed. Franklin Delano Roosevelt tried to combine the geopolitics of both Theodore Roosevelt and Wilson. This was seen in the plans for the United Nations, the collective security of which were to be dependent on the great powers represented in the Security Council.

Attempts to organise an intellectual response to Haushofer led to discussion about an American Institute of Political Geography or of Geopolitics, which, in fact, did not come to fruition, but, in June 1942, a Geopolitical Section was organised inside the Military Intelligence Service. This section drew on civilian interest in geopolitics, although its public role helped ensure criticism from within the military and it was abolished the following year.

Meanwhile, American involvement in the Second World War both expanded the logistical possibilities and needs that were key elements of geopolitics and also led to a sustained need to explain the conflict to what was very much a mass democracy at war, and in a more wide-ranging conflict than any of its previous wars. In particular, in response to the potent isolationism of the inter-war years, it was necessary to defend American interest in distant regions. The explanation addressed not only popular concerns but also the governmental perception that, under the shadow of air power, the oceans no longer offered security while Japanese and German capabilities posed direct threats to the USA.[63]

The government also sought to explain why the Japanese attack on Pearl Harbor in December 1941 had led to the 'Germany First' policy, in which the USA determined to focus its military on war with Germany, leading, for example, to the invasion of Vichy-ruled Morocco and Algeria in late 1942, a goal that appeared to have little to do with Japanese attack. The explanation involved both an account of Axis geopolitics, specifically an interconnectedness of threads and advances, and a propagation of a rival American one. President Roosevelt's radio speech to the nation on 23 February 1942 made reference to a map of the world in order to explain American strategy. He had earlier suggested that potential listeners obtain such a map, which led to massive demand and also to increased newspaper publication of maps. Roosevelt also created a map room in the White House.

The task of explaining engagement with distant regions posed a problem but also produced opportunities for innovation in both conception and presentation. Thus, the film *Plan for Destruction* depicted the actor playing Haushofer explaining global geopolitics in front of a map centred on the North Pole, an exposition of a threat which suggested that such a map helped explain what the American response should be. The innovative mapmaker Richard Edes Harrison used orthographic projections and aerial perspectives to bring together the USA and distant regions. The preface to his *Look at the World: The Fortune Atlas for World Strategy* (1944) explained that it was intended 'to show *why* Americans are fighting in strange places and *why* trade follows its various routes. They [the maps] emphasise the geographical basis of world strategy.'

The reporting and presentation of war, notably the dynamic appearance of many war maps, for example those in *Life* and *Time*, with their arrows and general sense of movement, also helped to make geopolitics present and urgent. Far from the war appearing as a static entity, and at a distance, it was seen as in flux. The maps also made the war seem able to encompass the spectator both visually, through images of movement, and also, in practice, by spreading in his or her direction.[64]

Thus, the role of air power, dramatised most powerfully first by the Japanese attack on the American Pacific Fleet in Pearl Harbor in 1941, and then by the American dropping of atom bombs on Hiroshima and Nagasaki in 1945, led to a new sense of space.[65] In part, this new sense was linked to a reduced emphasis on physical geography, in geopolitical discussion, geographical study (at least at the global level), and maps. Yet, this reduced emphasis also reflected the analytical shift away from materialistic explanations, and notably those based on the physical environment. The unintentional net effect was that there was a decline in the ability to explain, and notably with reference to the physical environment, as opposed simply to describe.

The new sense of space reflected both vulnerability to air attack and the awareness of new geopolitical relationships. In terms of maps, the Mercator projection was unhelpful in the depiction of air routes because great circle routes and distances were poorly presented in this projection, as distances in northern and southern latitudes were exaggerated. More profoundly, the Second World War suggested that Leo Amery's prediction of 1904 had been vindicated, at least in so far as the means of waging war and projecting power were concerned.

Underlying, however, the theme of rival geopolitical analyses, the extent to which Germany's armies had primarily been defeated on the Eastern Front (where two-thirds of the Wehrmacht's divisions were engaged from the summer of 1941) also appeared to demonstrate the thesis of the salience of the Heartland. Without this Soviet success, Anglo-American forces would only have been able to defeat Germany by the use of the atomic bomb to decapitate the Nazi regime, which, indeed, was the original intended goal of the Manhattan Project. The salience of the Heartland was also demonstrated by the rapid transfer of victorious Soviet forces to the Far East and their successful attack on the Japanese empire, particularly Manchuria, in August 1945, an attack motivated by a drive for influence and territory.[66]

This conclusion to the Second World War looked towards the geopolitics of the Cold War, for the combination of Soviet strength with Communist successes in Eastern Europe in 1945–8 and in China in 1949 ensured that the Heartland appeared more as one bloc, under one driving force, than ever before in history. By 1949, Russia–China could be seen as replacing Russia–Germany as the key relationship in the Eurasian Heartland, one displaying aggressive energy with the Berlin Blockade and Chinese intervention in 1950 in the Korean War. If it was unclear what the ideological aspect of Communist victory would mean for the validity of geopolitical analysis, the territorial dimension of international competition seemed as apparent as the ideological one.

CHAPTER 6

GEOPOLITICS AND THE COLD WAR

The Cold War was presented in geopolitical terms, both for analysis and for rhetoric. As during the Second World War, a sense of geopolitical challenge was used to encourage support for a posture of readiness. The sense of threat was expressed in map form, with both the USA and the Soviet Union presenting themselves as surrounded and threatened by the alliance systems, military plans and subversive activities of their opponents.

These themes could be seen clearly not only in government publications but also in those of other organisations. The dominant role of the state helps to explain this close alignment in the case of the Soviet Union and its Communist allies, but in the USA there was also a close correspondence between governmental views and those propagated in the private sector, not least in the print media.

News magazines offered an important illustration of the situation and served actively to propagate such governmental themes as the need for the containment of Communism. Thus, in the 1 April 1946 issue of *Time,* R. M. Chapin produced a map, entitled 'Communist Contagion', which emphasised the nature of the threat and the strength of the Soviet Union. The latter was enhanced by a split-spherical presentation of Europe and Asia, making the Soviet Union more potent as a result of the break in the centre of the map. Communist expansion was emphasised in the map by presenting the Soviet Union as a vivid red, the colour of danger, and by categorising neighbouring states with regard to the risk of contagion employing the language of disease: states were referred to as quarantined, infected or exposed.

Such terminology underlines the politicised nature of some of the use of geography during the Cold War; but, before using this instance to decry American views then, it is necessary to point out that Soviet expansionism was indeed a threat and that the geopolitical challenge from the Soviet Union was particularly acute due to its being both a European and an Asian power.

Carrying forward Franklin Roosevelt's use of maps to support his fireside chats, President John F. Kennedy, in a press conference on 23 March 1961, employed maps when he focused on the situation in Laos, where the Soviet and North Vietnamese-backed Pathet Lao were advancing:

> These three maps show the area of effective Communist domination as it was last August, with the colored portions up on the right-hand corner being the areas held and dominated by the Communists at that time. And now next, in December of 1960, three months ago, the red area having expanded – and now from December 20 now to the present date, near the end of March, the Communists control a much wider section of the country.

The use of the colour red dramatised the threat, as did the depiction on the map of Laos' neighbours: Thailand, Cambodia, South Vietnam and Burma. Thus, the Domino Theory was in play, and was used to support the deployment of 10,000 American Marines based in Okinawa. The threat of a graver conflict encouraged the negotiation of a ceasefire agreement ten months after the press conference.

The Domino Theory was an instance of the degree to which, compared to the classical European geopolitics of the early twentieth century, a relatively vague, less theoretically grounded and generic sense of geopolitics helped to shape the mental maps of American leaders during the Second World War and the Cold War. This approach focused on whose camp other states were placed in: the West, the Axis or the Communist bloc. There was an added ideological dimension compared to the early twentieth century but, otherwise, this set of geopolitical perceptions did not differ greatly from traditional concepts of spheres of influence.

Geopolitical discussion during the Cold War faced a number of problems that can be regarded as objective. First, it was unclear how best to assess the likely impact of strategic nuclear power and, subsequently, of rocketry. The high-spectrum military technology was never used and therefore it was difficult to gauge its probable effectiveness. This point, which did not exhaust the imponderables of possible conflict between the great powers, meant that it was very unclear how to measure strength and, therefore, respective capability. In terms of geopolitics, more specifically, the likely equations of power that might lead to the discussion of posture and policy as aggressive or defensive, this situation created serious difficulties.

These equations were not restricted to the high-spectrum end of the capability of the great powers. There were also conceptual and methodological issues arising from the processes of anti-imperialism and decolonisation. These processes involved the shifting meaning of control, influence and effectiveness. More particularly, the nature and frontier of control in anti-insurgency struggles were difficult to assess as a result of a reliance on air power, which proved less effective than its exponents had hoped and than initially seemed the case.

To a certain extent geopolitics seemed redundant. Indeed, the rise of nuclear power in conjunction with the later development of intercontinental ballistic missiles appeared to make conventional geopolitical assumptions obsolete as the entire world could be actualised as a target. As such, the world had become an isotropic surface, one that was equal in every point. A different form of simplification was provided by ideological readings of the world in terms of West or East.

Neither account appeared to leave much room for geopolitics, and, indeed, its reputation as a subject declined in the post-war years. In large part, this decline was because geopolitics was associated with the Nazis and was differentiated from the American discussion of the spatial aspects of power which was described as political geography. The latter was presented as different in both content and method because it was American and apparently objective, and the term 'geopolitics' was avoided. Moreover, the conceptualisation of the subject was not pursued.

Indeed, geography was in decline in American education. Harvard, a key opinion-leader, dismantled its Department of Geology and Geography in 1948, in part because geography was not a university subject. There is no proof that the alleged homosexuality of Derwent Whittlesey, who headed the programme, was a key issue.[1] Harvard's example was followed by other prominent institutions such as Stanford. With such a lead, it was not surprising that many state and local education systems also dropped a subject now held to be irrelevant. The teaching of geography was largely relegated to the elementary level, and this was to affect geopolitical understanding.

Political and intellectual currents interacted. Political geography no longer seemed acceptable in the USA,[2] and was anyway largely separated from geopolitics by scholars such as Jean Gottmann, Richard Hartshorne and Stephen Jones;[3] although some geopolitical work continued, in part by being presented as a different subject.[4] Geography as a subject was also affected by criticism of environmental determinism. The attacks on the mono-causal character of environmentalism by the anthropologist Franz Boas (1858–1942) influenced Carl Sauer (1889–1975), a geographer interested in anthropology. Sauer had taught determinist-type courses at the University of Michigan to at least 1918, but he came to repudiate determinism and to criticise American geographers who drew on Ratzel. Instead, in *The Morphology of Landscape*, Sauer advanced a possibilist interpretation of the role of environment.[5]

In Britain, political geography was distinguished from geopolitics. The former aspired to impartiality and generality: the nationality or ethnicity of a political geographer should be no more deducible from his writings than that of a palaeontologist or quantum physicist. Political geography, however, lacked intellectual drive and worked mainly by classification.[6] The subject lost impetus in Britain and largely died out in about 1970. In Germany, geopolitics ceased to be a major subject, although, after a gap beginning in 1945, the publication of the *Zeitschrift für Geopolitik* resumed in 1951, only to end again in 1968.

An intellectual pursuit of geopolitics from the perspective of the academic conceptions of the time can only go so far, however, notably because the contemporary pressure of the Cold War was in many respects acutely spatial. Indeed, the possibility of nuclear conflict initially played out very much in a territorial fashion as the early atomic weapons were free-fall bombs, to be dropped from aircraft. Thus, the geography of power-projection took on considerable weight. For example, in the event of the Third World War breaking out, it was assumed that the Red Army would be able to invade Continental Europe, but that the Soviet Union, in turn, could be bombed by British and American bombers from East Anglia, as well as from air bases in Cyprus and northern Iraq. For example, Canberras could fly from Cyprus, over the Black Sea, to attack industrial cities in Ukraine.

Once long-range bombers had been replaced by a new nuclear geography of ground- and submarine-based intercontinental missiles, such considerations ceased to be pertinent, but, already, a strongly spatial sense of international politics had arisen in the development and application of Cold War ideas of containment, with the perception of threats and opportunities shaping these ideas. More was involved than the prospect of Soviet advances into particular areas, for the avoidance of large-scale conflict in the late 1940s combined with the Soviet acquisition of nuclear weaponry in 1949 to ensure a need to rethink American strategy. This need was driven not only by a sense of Soviet expansionism but also by a belief that periods of peace and war alike served Soviet interests. Indeed, as far as Stalin was concerned, geostrategic and geopolitical issues shaped both foreign policy and internal political developments. These issues included incipient East–West antagonisms and the ambition for territorial expansion into or political control over Eastern Europe, which was seen as ideological bridgehead, strategic glacis and economic resource.

At the same time that the concept of legitimacy became more important, or at least newly institutionalised, with the formation of the United Nations; containment as a concept that was to be applied in American political and military strategy received its intellectual rationale in 1946 from George Kennan. This concept was followed by the Truman government advancing the idea of America's perimeter of vital interests, and the perimeter was to be consolidated by the creation of regional security pacts, foremost of which was to be the North Atlantic Treaty Organisation (NATO), created in 1949. In 1950, the National Security Council's NSC-68 document reflected the strong geopolitical sense of American strategy in the face of what was presented as a threat from the Soviet Union and China to American civilisation.

The call to defend Western Europe accorded with the geopolitical stress by Spykman on the Rimland, notably Western Europe and South-East Asia, but other areas could be pushed into prominence by the application of the essentially malleable concept of containment. Indeed, Europe could be taken to mean Western Europe, but could also be extended to comprehend the eastern approaches of the Mediterranean. Thus, Soviet pressure on Greece and Turkey were key occasions of American engagement in the late 1940s, and both powers were to become members of NATO, despite an Anglo-Canadian preference for a focus on Western Europe and the North Atlantic.

The American emphasis was on a global struggle because, for those concerned with opposition to Communism, individual states, such as Poland, took on meaning in these terms, rather than having important issues of their own. While this approach indeed captured a key aspect of the international situation, it underplayed the role of separate interests within blocs and, notably, the extent to which allies and supporters have agency, as, for example, with the role of North and South Koreans in the run-up to the Korean War,[7] or the independence towards the USA displayed by Israel, and still displayed, notably over settlements in the West Bank.

At the same time, the primacy of geostrategic concerns meant that the geopolitics of containment was more concerned with territory and strength than with values. The USA and NATO were ready to ally with autocratic states, as in Turkey, Spain, Greece and Latin America, rather than to focus on liberal democracies. Moreover, this geostrategic approach was to lead to a failure to appreciate the difference between Communism and Third World populist nationalism.

A number of writers developed the idea of containment but did so in a difficult context to geopolitics because German *Geopolitik* had not only discredited the subject and language of geopolitics at university level[8] but also affected its more general public profile. Because of their connotations of Nazi thought and practice, formalised theories of the interrelationship or interdetermination of geography and politics, let alone explicit geopolitics, had limited purchase in the Soviet Union[9] and indeed Europe, where, moreover, large-scale post-war forced population displacements and resettlements undermined established linkages of space and people. Soviet historical geography has also been presented as underdeveloped.[10]

In the USA, however, there was the attempt to define and apply a geopolitics based on containment, with 'defence intellectuals' playing a role of which geographers fought shy. A key figure was Robert Strausz-Hupé (1903–2002), a Viennese-born American political scientist who had criticised Haushofer. Strausz-Hupé argued the need for a geopolitics directed against the Soviet Union which he correctly saw as combining the expansionism of imperial Russia with the revolutionary threat of Marxist-Leninism.[11] Strausz-Hupé supported a European federalism anchored in an Atlantic Alliance as a crucial bar to Soviet expansion, and he very much backed NATO. His *The Estrangement of Western Man* (1952) presented a robust Western civilisation, now headed by the USA, as a key component in the geopolitical equation, one that must limit Communism.

Strausz-Hupé argued that the crisis he had lived through reflected more than short-term problems and, instead, focused on larger problems in Western culture, specifically an absence of social values that rested on philosophical and moral confusion and failure. Thus, the geopolitical response he advocated – Britain and France joining in the cause of European unity, which he saw as likely to cooperate with the USA in bearing the burden of Western defence – could, to Strausz-Hupé, only be part of the remedy. In his thesis, cultural and intellectual clarity, coherence and values, in short a metaphysical rearmament, was crucial to the defence of the West.

Five years later, he followed with 'The Balance of Tomorrow', an essay published in the opening issue of *Orbis,* a quarterly he had founded:

> The issue before the United States is the unification of the globe under its leadership within this generation . . . The mission of the American people is to bury the nation-states, lead their bereaved peoples into larger unions and overcome with its might the would-be saboteurs of the new order who have nothing to offer mankind but putrefying ideology and brute force.[12]

In *Protracted Conflict* (1959), Strausz-Hupé and the others who helped him write his books argued that the Soviet Union were waging such a war, one that employed the Islamic idea of a bloc that was immune to democratic influence opposed to another that was to be worn down, the West. Convinced that the Soviets were out to sap the West through means short of large-scale conflict, Strausz-Hupé argued that détentes would simply be short-term periods in which the Soviets would pursue their interests by different goals. In short, *Protracted Conflict* was a call both to vigilance and to a more robust approach to containment.

As with other geopolitical works, that by Strausz-Hupé was very much located in terms of the politics of the age, or, more specifically, in terms of the domestic politics and foreign policy of the state in question: classic geopolitics might be binary, but it was rarely bilateral; in other words, the national perspective on international relations encouraged views of the international situation in terms of binary divides. Criticising the containment practised by the Eisenhower administration (1953–61) for passively waiting to respond to Soviet attacks, and therefore failing to be proactive, Strausz-Hupé was, in part, responding to the concern that Eisenhower's strategy, both military and diplomatic, was lessening American options. In order to reduce the costs of a military build-up and to prevent the deleterious political consequences that he assumed would follow, Eisenhower had put the emphasis on nuclear strength, arguing that the threat of nuclear destruction would prevent Soviet attack. Thus, limited wars were not to be an option, both as they would likely lead to total war and because the USA would not be prepared from them.

This approach was challenged by writers and politicians who favoured the creation of a force-structure and doctrine able to fight limited war as an alternative to (and as well as) those designed for a nuclear total war. In some respects, geopolitical arguments were an aspect of this pressure for a limited war capability, as writers such as Strausz-Hupé and Henry Kissinger sought to define goals and parameters that made sense of limited war. Limited nuclear war was part of the equation, and the possibility of this outcome underlay John Kennedy's presidential campaign in 1960, notably his critique of Eisenhower for supposedly allowing a 'missile gap' to develop. However, in office, faced with the Berlin (1961) and Cuban (1962) crises, Kennedy found that such strategies ran the risk of a full-scale nuclear conflict. In short, the apparent precision of strategic planning proved unstable under the pressure of international crisis.[13]

Protracted Conflict was endorsed by Kissinger, a historian of nineteenth-century international relations who became a 'defence intellectual', publishing *Nuclear Weapons and Foreign Policy* (1957). Kissinger was a member of Strausz-

Hupé's Foreign Policy Research Institute, as well as playing a role in the Council on Foreign Relations and being a frequent contributor to *Foreign Affairs*. *Protracted Conflict* was taken forward by Strausz-Hupé in *A Forward Strategy for America* (1961), which pressed for a solidification of the West, so as to thwart the Soviet advance, combined with pressure on the Soviet bloc. Thus, containment was to be made a problem for the Soviet Union. *In Building the Atlantic World* (1963), a transformed and robust NATO was seen by Strausz-Hupé as the basis for a powerful West able to prevail over the Soviets in the balance of power. Strausz-Hupé regarded American military superiority over the Soviets as fundamental to containment, and he treated the Vietnam War as an unnecessary entanglement,[14] an emphasis that, itself, can be given a geopolitical slant by drawing attention to his European origins and East Coast career. More generally, Strausz-Hupé argued that geography gave you a basic understanding of geopolitics, and that geographical influences were sometimes negated and at other times confirmed by technological change. He was also convinced that geopolitics would be abused in both the political sphere and the academy (the academic world) by being pushed beyond what the geopolitical means of analysis could really explain.

Meanwhile, breaking from the unwillingness of most academic geographers in the world's leading power to discuss international power politics, Saul Cohen, a Whittlesey pupil, in his *Geography and Politics in a Divided World* (1963), provided a wider Eurasian scope than Strausz-Hupé's focus on NATO, albeit one that largely reprised Mackinder by discerning two geostrategic regions. Focusing on what he termed the shatterbelts between these regions, Cohen saw them as crucial zones of confrontation and conflict between the major powers, zones, moreover, whose instability was likely to draw in these powers. Cohen was subsequently to revise his account in order to take note of changes in power politics.[15]

Although much Cold War thinking focused on Europe, it was in East Asia that geopolitical ideas and American strategy were placed under particular pressure as a consequence of concern about Communist expansionism. Whereas the Soviet Union appeared to threaten such a course in Europe, Communist expansionism actually seemed to be in progress in East Asia. There, a theme of continued threat could be used to link Chinese intervention in the Korean War in 1950, Chinese pressure on Taiwan, China's victory over India in 1962, and Chinese and Soviet support for North Vietnam. These anxieties conflated American concern about the ideological challenge from Communism with the long-standing instability of the region that looked back to the 1890s.

The Domino Theory, of incremental Communist advance, a geopolitical concept that enjoyed powerful traction in the USA in the 1960s, not least because it could be readily explained in public, appeared to require the vigorous containment seen in the Vietnam War to which the USA decided to commit ground troops in July 1965. However, at the same time, the stress in Vietnam for the USA, as earlier with the Korean War of 1950–3, was on intervention in a secondary theatre and the avoidance of full-scale main force conflict with the Soviet Union and China.

America was to lose in Vietnam, but the subordination of the operational military level to the strategic geopolitical, one just glanced at, was further indicated by the wider success in benefiting from the Sino-Soviet rift and in developing a form of strategic partnership with China. In a 1962 article in *Orbis*, 'The Sino-Soviet Tangle and U.S. Policy', Strausz-Hupé had argued that Marxist-Leninism was weakened by its failure to rate nationalism, and that this nationalism led to tensions in Sino-Soviet relations. This situation was seen as an opportunity for the USA, which, he argued, should put aside ideological preferences and seek to ally with China as the weaker power of the two. Strausz-Hupé also regarded the Soviet Union as the key threat to the USA.

Richard Nixon, then a failed Republican politician, was interested in the argument, and he drew on it in his article 'Asia After Vietnam', published in *Foreign Affairs* in October 1967. Nixon saw the possibility of China taking an independent role as useful to the USA. Winning the 1968 presidential election, Nixon moved self-proclaimed pragmatic geopoliticians to the fore. Kissinger became National Security Adviser, and Strausz-Hupé, who had wanted that job, began a diplomatic career as an ambassador. Kissinger found geopolitics a pertinent term in trying to conceptualise his view of international relations. This view was one in which the emphasis was on national interests, rather than ideological drive, and the former interests were traced to long-term geographical commitments within a multi-polar and competitive international system. Thus, geopolitics was linked to *Realpolitik,* indeed, in part, becoming the assessment of the international consequences of the latter. A refugee from the anti-Semitism of Nazi Germany, Kissinger associated ideology, emotionalism and ostentatious moralising in foreign policy with the Germany he had fled, and, instead, favoured a statesmanship based on rational calculations of national self-interest in which the stress was on order and security.[16] Kissinger, moreover, had an 'avowedly conceptual approach to international relations', one given to grand designs.[17] He argued that states were largely motivated by concern for their national security, which was therefore the key component of geopolitics. To Kissinger, the foreign policies of states reflected their physical environment, natural resources and historical experience, the last leading him to emphasise the impact of time more than that of space.

For Kissinger, such views were important to the understanding both of American policy and of that of the other great powers. In supporting disengagement from South-East Asia within a context of continued adherence to a robust containment of the Soviet Union, Kissinger had to provide a defence of what appeared militarily necessary. This defence was made more difficult in light of pressures on American interests elsewhere, particularly the Middle East, as well as of the consequences of serious economic and fiscal problems. Alongside these realist pressures came the crucial matter of political location. The Republican charge in the late 1940s, one then stated vociferously by Nixon, had been that the Truman administration had 'lost' China to Communism, and this charge had proved a way subsequently to berate the Democrats. Similarly, Kennedy had run for President in 1960 in part on the claim that the Eisenhower administration, in which Nixon was Vice-President for both terms, had failed to be sufficiently robust, not least in maintaining American defences.

Although, as President (1969–74), Nixon was helped by Democrat divisions and the leftward move of the Democratic Party, he also had to consider potential criticism from within the Republican Party. As a consequence, Kissinger's rationalisation of American policy has to be understood at least in part as a political defence, a point more generally true of other rationalisations of policy. In producing this defence, Kissinger had to argue not only that the USA could align with a Communist power but also that such an alignment could be regarded as worthwhile (rather than a form of Communist deception of a duped USA) because China and the Soviet Union had clashing geopolitical interests. Thus, realism in international relations was seen as conducive to American goals.

This approach built on Kissinger's own background as a Harvard scholar of European international relations in the nineteenth century, when powers of a similar political system had nevertheless been rivals. Far more intellectually self-conscious than most politicians, Kissinger naturally looked for similarities between past and present, and found them in the concepts and language of national interests, balance of power, geopolitics and the pressure of Russian expansionism. Indeed, he provided a key instance of the historicised nature of geopolitics, as opposed to the tendency of ideologies to treat the world in terms of a gradient of ideological congruence or rivalry. Thus, the USA reaching out to China, a policy advocated by both Nixon and Kissinger, had a geopolitical logic directed against the Soviet Union, rather as Britain had allied with Japan in 1902 as a response to Russian expansionism.

Kissinger's theme was *Realpolitik*. He sought to use Sino-American cooperation to isolate and put pressure on the

Soviet Union in order to get the latter to persuade North Vietnam, which was seen as a Soviet client, to reach an accommodation with South Vietnam. In turn, Nixon and Kissinger reminded China that the American alliance with Japan would enable the USA to restrain Japan if its growing economy was to lead it back to expansionism. To Kissinger, mutual interests were essentially variable but the pursuit of interest was fixed, so that he advised Nixon in February 1972:

> I think in 20 years your successor, if he's as wise as you, will wind up leaning towards the Russians against the Chinese. For the next 15 years we have to lean towards the Chinese against the Russians. We have to play the balance of power game totally unemotionally. Right now, we need the Chinese to correct the Russians and to discipline the Russians.[18]

As far as China itself was concerned, the Chinese started from a separate but comparable tradition of geopolitics, but since the early twentieth century this tradition has been inflected by modernity while also drawing on past Chinese precedent, for example in the use of tributary states, an attitude attempted towards neighbours such as North Korea and Vietnam.

Kissinger also appealed beyond ideological rivalries when trying to ease relations between Israel and its Arab neighbours. These relations were of considerable international importance not least because of the close relationship between regional conflict and superpower tensions, notably from the Six Days' War of 1967. The Middle East was also of rising significance because the Arab response to defeat by Israel in the Yom Kippur War in 1973 was a major increase in the price of oil.

The consequences of the OPEC price hike spelled out the significance of the geopolitics of resources, one that had already encouraged strong American interest in the Middle East from the 1940s, notably by the development of links with Saudi Arabia, and, from the 1950s, with Iran. This process also entailed a deliberate lessening of British influence. The background to this American interest was an understanding of the strategic importance of oil, one that the Second World War had demonstrated and an understanding that was encouraged by fears about the future scale of American oil production.[19]

The general issue of oil availability was permeated with specific political concerns and events, as is still the case today. The price of oil per barrel rose from $3 in 1972 to $12 at the close of 1974. The prosperity, and thus politics, of the USA ultimately depended on unfettered access to large quantities of inexpensive oil. The price of oil was raised again in 1979, from $14 to $25, as a consequence of the Iranian revolution against the Shah. In 1971, aided by rising oil imports, the USA had run the first trade deficit of the century. This deficit greatly affected confidence in the dollar and in the architecture of the international economic order.

Kissinger's approach to China and his frequent use of 'geopolitics' as a term helped revive interest in the subject and, more generally, in strategy as a flexible tool rather than a fixed product of ideological rivalry. A personal engagement with the outside world assisted in this process. Thus, after the German-born Kissinger, who served as National Security Adviser from 1969 to 1973 and as Secretary of State from 1973 to 1977, came Zbigniew Brzezinski. Polish-born and educated, he served as President Carter's National Security Adviser and later taught at Georgetown University, as also did Kissinger. Kissinger was subsequently to establish Kissinger Associates, a source of geopolitical advice that also served as a network of power or at least influence.[20]

Brzezinski and others employed the term 'geopolitics' in order to present themselves as realists unswayed by emotional considerations.[21] This antithetical juxtaposition of geopolitics and sentiment was part of the self-image of those who saw themselves as geopoliticians, but it also demonstrated their need to justify the commitments they deemed necessary. Geopolitics as a self-conscious rhetoric, as well as policy, thus became an aspect of the reaction to American failure and weakness in the early 1970s and, indeed, part of the 'culture wars' of that era. In particular, geopolitical discourse could be seen as a way for Democrats to distance themselves from their McGovern-era predecessors, consequently it was unsurprising that Brzezinski was a keen advocate of such thinking.

At the same time, Kissinger, Carter and détente were criticised as weakening the West by a group of conservative Democrats led by Henry (Scoop) Jackson, as well as by key Republicans who were influential in the Ford administration (1974–7), notably his Chief of Staff, Richard Cheney, and the Secretary of Defense, Donald Rumsfeld. They drew on advice from commentators such as Richard Pipes and Paul Wolfowitz who warned about Soviet intentions. The continuity of this group, through 1990s' opposition to Clintonian liberal internationalism, to the neo-conservatism activism of the early 2000s is notable.

Returning to the 1970s, but from an overlapping, yet different, perspective, geopolitical discussion also offered an alternative to détente and was therefore part of the movement, towards the close of the Carter presidency, to a firmer response to the Soviet Union, a situation that replicated that seen with the movement towards confrontation in the early 2000s.[22] The combination of the overthrow of the Shah in January 1979 with the Soviet invasion of Afghanistan that December suggested a general deterioration in America's position, gave it a regional focus, and seemed to call for action. The response included the Carter Doctrine, the declaration that any attempt to gain control of the Persian Gulf would be resisted as an attack on American interests, and the establishment of the Rapid Deployment Task Force, which was to become the basis of Central Command.

That Iran and Afghanistan were the points of concern helped give the crisis a geopolitical resonance, one that drew on the old Heartland–Rimland concept. Indeed, in 1907, Britain and Russia had defined spheres of influence in Persia (Iran), a classic geopolitical scenario. In 1979–80, there was talk of the Soviet Union seeking a warm-water port, and of the possibility of the Soviets advancing from Afghanistan to the Indian Ocean across the Baluchistan region of Pakistan, the theme of a former Conservative cabinet minister with whom I was staying at the time. Small-scale maps on television and in newspapers appeared to demonstrate the feasibility of such moves, although there was a failure to consider their practicability; which provided another instance of the Marquess of Salisbury's dictum about using a map with the right scale.

The notion of the search for a warm-water port reflected the determination to put realist considerations first, as well as the historicised resonance that many of those who saw themselves as geopoliticians liked, and indeed required. History became a data set that apparently provided a correction to the ideological formulations of those who offered alternative views. While laudable as an aspiration, this reading of history was usually somewhat simplistic, not least as it generally underplayed ministerial and governmental agency in favour of the environmental determinism of state interest.

There was continuity from the later Carter presidency to the Reagan years of 1981–9, although the latter saw more risk-taking and a greater emphasis on a more active approach. This policy was designed to roll back the Soviet system, most obviously by firm opposition to Soviet allies in Africa and Central America, notably Angola and Nicaragua, an approach that frequently underplayed the complexity of the relevant regional struggles by focusing on the global dimension. There was also a robust commitment to the defence of NATO, notably the deployment of new missiles, especially in Europe, to give new force to containment. Although elderly, Strausz-Hupé was brought back to serve as ambassador to Ankara during the Reagan years.

Geopolitics in this context was an aspect of a self-conscious realism in international relations that focused on active confrontation with the Soviet bloc. Great-power rivalries made an understanding of this world in terms of long-term geographical drives seem particularly appropriate. In turn, to geopoliticians, Western victory in the Cold War in 1989–91 came because Soviet expansionism had been thwarted by Western robustness and also weakened by the need to cope with the opposition of China which was still aligned with the USA. These views did not preclude the argument that Soviet weaknesses were a key element in the collapse of the Soviet bloc, but these weaknesses were linked by geopoliticians to the strains arising from international competition, and these strains were seen in geopolitical terms.

The fall of the Soviet Union also appeared to resolve the theory of dual state types that had been so important to Mackinder's geopolitics, and, indeed, had taken forward a long-standing Western discourse, seen in the early modern Netherlands and Britain, and then in the USA and Britain, directed against autocratic states and their large armies. Navies, trade and liberty had been joined in what could be modishly referred to as a discourse of power.[23] In practice, they served as aspects of a different politics of force to that of autocratic states and large armies; one, moreover, in which assumptions about how best to organise a state militarily were linked to an analysis of relative capability on this basis. Mackinder had suggested that what he termed the Columbian epoch, that of maritime dominance, was over, brought to an end by the new effectiveness of land routes and powers; but the conflicts of 1914–18, 1939–45 and 1946–89 indicated otherwise. Germany was defeated in both world wars, while Britain was victorious, and the USA played a key role in the Second World War, and an important one in the First. The defeat of Japan in the Second World War, alongside the victory of the Soviet Union, nevertheless, suggested that naval empires could fail and land powers be victorious, but the situation in the Cold War was very different. The Soviet Union collapsed when the USA was not acting as a land power, not least with no conscription, and when China had turned to capitalism.

This shift away from land power was given an arresting military-technological perspective by Peter Hugill, in an account that took forward Amery's critique of Mackinder.

Hugill argued that precision bombing had become a reality by the late twentieth century and continued by seeing the relevant technology, of GPS and computers, as a characteristic of modern trading states. He concluded:

> As long as the trading states have no desire to occupy territory, merely to control flows and nodes, the air power developed in the trading states in the late twentieth century and now being deployed has restored the global geopolitical balance of power in favour of the trading states. Just as sea power did at the height of the Columbian epoch, aerospace power today allows weak control at great, now planetary distances.[24]

This argument may appear less secure in the aftermath of the wars of the 2000s: the American 'surge' that made a major difference in Iraq in 2008 was of ground troops, especially infantry, and not of air power.[25] There is also a more general need to distinguish between output and outcome when considering military capability. Nevertheless, Hugill took forward Mackinder's ability to discuss global politics in terms of different types of power and gave it a continuing technological resonance. The extent to which technology and type of power were linked in a causal fashion is possibly more complex than was argued by navalists, and, by descent, by air-power enthusiasts, but the issue is an important one. A similar point about technology can be made with reference to communications technology, which has economic, organisational and military consequences.

The understanding of geopolitics in realist terms of national self-interest and international competition was to be challenged in the 1990s and 2000s by advocates of a global order based on cooperation as well as part of the postmodern project that provided a left-wing critique to intellectual analyses and strategies laying claim to objectivity. Maps, for example, were re-examined, being presented either as a means for appropriation or as works that inherently lacked objectivity due to the subjective nature of knowledge and perception. A painterly approach to the latter was Jasper Johns' *Map* (1963) in which a map of the USA was remodelled as a painting.

The drive for a different approach to the spatial dimension of power was already present in the 1980s, for example in the world-economy thesis of Immanuel Wallerstein,[26] while a left-wing geopolitics had been developed in France with the journal *Hérodote,* which appeared in January 1976. The first issue of what set out to be an analysis of current issues from a radical geographical viewpoint included an interview with Michel Foucault and an article on the Vietnam War.[27] Its author, Yves Lacoste, a professor of geography at the University of Vincennes, subsequently published a dictionary of geopolitics.[28]

Lacoste argued that geography and geographers had usually served the cause of war, which was seen in itself as a cause for complaint, and he attacked not only the *Geopolitik* of Haushofer but also the traditional French political geography associated with Vidal de la Blache, which was also seen as serving the cause of the state. *Hérodote* engaged with a different range of issues including ecology, global poverty and the attempt to advance values and groupings different from those of the Cold War. All this was presented by Lacoste as serving his goal of moving geography from being a servile discipline, focused on the state, into, instead, an engaged and objective science. The tension between engagement and objectivity was not fully addressed.

This French development played a key role in that of Anglo-American 'critical geopolitics', but the latter had other sources as well. They included a somewhat delayed case of 1960s radicalism, the delay reflecting the culture of the academic subject of geography. At the same time, there was a reaction against the quantitative turn that had been so important to 1970s academic geography, indeed helping persuade me to take history rather than geography at university: I was put off by the idea of measuring interquartile ranges. This emphasis on quantification was closely related to a stress on human beings as economic beings primarily concerned to maximise their benefit and to locate their activities accordingly; and that at a time when locational analysis played a central role in the academic discipline.

Thus, the turn to a very different human geography, one that engaged directly with political issues, was part of a reaction against quantification, and this turn was crucial to the development of 'critical geopolitics'. So also was the interest in commitment as a means of validating scholar, student and subject. The emphasis on commitment owed something to a sense of guilt about the major role of geographers in supporting Western imperialism in the nineteenth and early twentieth century. This potent mix resulted eventually in a situation in which commitment became not so much a concluding add-on as a measure of quality and, indeed, a definition of 'critical geopolitics'.

The value of this approach is problematic, not least because it does not really admit of and to critical analysis except within the parameter of 'critical geopolitics'. Moreover, because of the postmodern roots of 'critical geopolitics', it cannot construct anything for fear of becoming akin to the 'meta-narratives' it spends its time deconstructing. Hence, without a meta-narrative, there is no basis for a long-term view, so that what is done is to critique documents as if they were abstracted from broader events. In turn, the broader events were seen as some evil American plan, as 'critical geopoliticians' found it difficult to adopt a theoretical framework to provide a more grounded perspective.

Other approaches would indeed be more fruitful. A more pertinent development of the standard geopolitical approach would be an emphasis on the geopolitics of states other than the great powers, as well as of political movements that did not correspond with Cold War alignments. These levels of geopolitical interest, analysis and rhetoric are commonly neglected due to the understandable focus on the great powers, as well as the misleading tendency to emphasise a systemic perspective. A stress on the international system generally entails treating it as an entity in its own right (and not as the derivative of its members), and indeed regards its members, the states, as dependants of the system.[29] Such an approach encourages a focus on the dynamics of the system, notably its interaction with and through the great powers. Unfortunately, this approach implies dependency and subordination for the other powers, which is inaccurate. This error arises in part from academic strategies with their stress on salience, significance and comprehension – only so many words, and why spend any on Denmark? – but also from the rhetorical identity of geopolitics with its particular focus, almost obsession, with the world scale and global threats. Indeed, this is a subject that often has a preference for hyperbole.

Britain is an instance of a state that has geopolitical interests which are more than regional but which cannot be simplified in terms of a subordination, in a geopolitical bloc, to the USA, however much critics might advance that analysis. British geopolitical interests spanned (and span) a number of traditional concerns and commitments, many dating from the period of imperial expansion, while also seeking to respond to assumptions about relations within the US-dominated West and in Europe.

An instance of traditional concern was that of the British presence in Antarctica and the South Atlantic over the past century, a presence that led in 1982 to Britain fighting a conventional war without allies. This presence was no mere footnote to empire but rather a manifestation of a continued desire to act as an imperial power, and one that has attracted scholarly attention from the geopolitical angle. The creation of the Falkland Islands Dependencies Survey in 1945 signalled a determination to use scientists to consolidate influence, and the battleship HMS *Nigeria* was dispatched to Antarctic waters in 1948. The mapping of the Antarctic Peninsula and nearby areas carried out by the Survey was designed to underline Britain's title to the area. Mapping was linked to naming. In 1932, the British had established the Antarctic Place Names Committee in order to ensure that British maps at least reflected official views. The categories excluded included names of existing territories, towns or islands, names in any foreign language, names of sledge dogs, 'names in low taste', and 'names with obscure origins'. British maps omitted names found on Argentine and Chilean maps of the Antarctic Peninsula. Mapping and naming were seen as crucial to sovereignty claims, and thus of justifying the costs of surveys. In addition, the Churchill government (1951–5) funded expeditions to consolidate territorial claims, while the cost and time taken by ground surveying led to greater support in the 1950s for aerial photography, leading to the taking of 10,000 photographs in parallel traverses in the summer seasons of 1955–6 and 1956–7. The 1959 Antarctic Treaty led to an increase in the geopolitical profile of the Falkland Isles and South Georgia, but the British government, however, did not wish to provoke Argentina by developing an airfield in Stanley, and this left the Falklands vulnerable. The 1982 Argentinean invasion provoked a major shift in the awareness of the South Atlantic empire.[30]

The notion of geopolitical direction for British policy, while yet also a degree of flexibility, was recently captured by Colin Gray:

> our freedom of choice for broad policy and strategy is really rather narrow . . . compelled by the national geography, Britain's overall military strategy must be maritime in the Corbettian sense, and the national security policy that the strategy must serve has to remain within reach of, though not always in lock-step with, that of Britain's giant ally, the United States. This blessedly likely permanent geopolitical reality of the British condition is not easy to explain domestically to a nationally prideful public undereducated in strategic activities. Necessity rules![31]

Gray's account suffered from the overly convinced character (and assertive tone) of most geopolitical writing. The notion of permanence appears questionable given the possible changes over the next half-century, and still more the next century, in Britain itself, including Scottish separatism, as well as in Britain's relations within the EU. Like most geopoliticians, Gray took his wishes and endowed them with normative force. Yet, he also valuably captured, in his phrase 'not always in lock-step', a degree of autonomy that challenges the account in terms of blocs.

Whereas British commerce and pretensions ensure a far-flung range of interest, the geopolitics of most states were (and are) regional in that global pressures and opportunities tended to have regional consequences. Thus, the Cold War played out in the Horn of Africa in terms of the geopolitics of Somalia, Ethiopia and Eritrean separatists. Such relationships also involved a degree of autonomy for second-rank powers, for example South Africa in Angola, Israel in the Middle East, and France in Africa and, to a considerable degree, in Europe.[32]

Geopolitical concepts played an explicit role for some of these powers. For example, classical European geopolitics was a core component of right-wing authoritarian-nationalist philosophy in Latin America from the 1920s to the 1980s. The conduits ranged from Iberian Falangist influences in the 1920s and 1930s to German and French military missions in the 1940s, 1950s and 1960s, and these concepts were still influential in the 1980s, notably with Augusto Pinochet's book *Geopolítica* (1968) as well as with the ideas underpinning the Argentine 'Dirty War'. Geopolitics was seen as a way to understand the development of national power. Pinochet was a professor of geopolitics at the Chilean Army War College when he published his book.[33]

To treat geopolitics as the global dimension would be misleading, not least because there is no inherent reason why geopolitical elements at other levels should be ignored. This challenge was to become more apparent in the 2000s, as the narrative and analysis of global strength based on great powers, and, primarily, the great power, the USA, was qualified by the resistance of a number of other world views. The latter had a strong spatial element, notably in particular sites of opposition to American power but also in proposing large areas in which this power should be resisted and displaced.

The ability of the USA to devise a new realist geopolitics to comprehend and counter this resistance remains unclear.

The notion of environmental determinism as a key to human development, and thus to geopolitics, was challenged in mid-century by a stress on human activity. Combined with technological advances, this emphasis led to a strong sense that humanity could mould the environment and could transform or transcend the limits of physical geography and environmental influence. Human action, rather than natural features, particularly rivers and mountains, came increasingly to locate routes and boundaries, both in the mind and in maps. The world appeared as a terrain to shape and a commodity to be used. There was a focus on the pursuit of power and on its use for ends, and in a fashion, that assumed that environmental considerations were not a problem and, indeed, that the world's resources could be readily commodified and consumed without difficulty. Environmental determinism was thus denied during the years of the long post-war boom that lasted until the early 1970s.

These assumptions were pushed particularly hard in the Communist bloc. In China, Mao Zedong rejected the traditional Chinese notion of 'Harmony between the Heavens and Humankind' and, instead, proclaimed 'Man Must Conquer Nature'. In 1958, Mao declared 'Make the high mountain bow its head; make the river yield the way', and, soon after, in a critique of an essay by Stalin stating that men could not affect natural processes such as geology, Mao claimed, 'This argument is incorrect. Man's ability to know and change Nature is unlimited.' Indeed, for Mao, nature, like humankind, was there to be forcibly mobilised in pursuit of an idea, an idea pushed with scant regard for human cost, scientific knowledge, rational analysis or environmental damage. Although not generally stated so bluntly, nor linked so clearly to an authoritarian policy of modernisation, these ideas were widespread across the world, and major projects such as the building of dams suggested that nature and physical geography could be readily tamed and that this was a noble goal.

A key aspect of geopolitics was an emphasis on the state and ideological struggles of the Cold War because, at that time, environmental constraints and influences on human geography, specifically political geography, appeared weak. Looked at differently, geopolitics in part became a matter of human impact on the environment, rather than vice versa. The end result of planned and unplanned expansion, however, was seen to be not only particular drawbacks, such as dams lessening the ability of rivers to 'flush out' deltas and estuaries and also to replenish them with soil, but, more generally, a pernicious assault on an interdependent global environment. Thus, the environmental movement that became prominent in the 1960s and 1970s can be seen as a critique of what were then recent and current geopolitics.

This conclusion serves as a reminder of the degree to which the idea of geopolitics extends to cover a variety of spheres. Usage at the time, as Chapters 2, 3 and 4 suggest, is as significant as the formal development of an explicit geopolitical theory.

CHAPTER 7

GEOPOLITICS SINCE 1990

The closer a historian comes to the present, the greater the danger that the benefit of long-term reflection will be lost. This point is certainly true of the geopolitics of the 2000s, as the struggle with radical Islam came to the fore with the attacks on New York and Washington on 11 September 2001, leading to the subordination of other themes, such as growing American estrangement from both China and, subsequently, from post-Communist Russia. Moreover, if the assessment of significance within an agreed analytical structure was unclear, with, for example, debate about the respective importance for the USA of the Middle East and the Far East, the fracturing of geopolitical analysis with the prominence, from the 1990s, of a self-conscious 'critical geopolitics' made the situation even more problematic.

Of course, geopolitics, like other disciplines, has generally not displayed a consistent approach.[1] Moreover, as a reminder of the need to be cautious before dividing the past into neat chronological periods, with their own themes and analysts, such that 1990, for example, becomes a turning point, there was, in practice, considerable continuity in the literature. For example, just as Mackinder spanned the First World War, publishing important works both before and after and, indeed, lived on until the 1940s, so Saul Cohen, whose first major work appeared in 1963, published an important article forty years later,[2] with a second edition of his *Geopolitics of the World System* following in 2008.

Alongside continuity by individuals, the end of the Cold War encouraged a rethinking of geopolitics in some academic circles, not least with an interest in new states and also in Europe as a continent of new relationships, notably the European Community,[3] indeed with East versus West replaced by Eastern and Western Europe. In turn, the power of NATO and the European Union was exerted in Eastern Europe and, subsequently, membership in both was extended, in return for acceptance of their norms.[4] More generally, there was a degree of optimism, if not naivety, in some of the literature, with the hope that geopolitics, like the longer-established peace studies, could be a force for a more benign world order as well as a description of it. The pressure for commitment was a notable feature of much of the geopolitical literature.[5]

At the same time, American hegemony and the apparent inception of a unipolar world system posed an issue not only for those offering an explicitly politicised geopolitical analysis but also for scholars looking for long-term patterns. Thus, William Thompson, a political scientist, having discerned a pattern over 13,000 years, in which 'one state gained enough coercive advantage over its rivals – based on relative endowment deriving from the organizational-technological-political-economic-war co-evolutionary spiral [sic] – to encourage an attempt at regional hegemony', noted that the USA had gone on from being the leading global sea power to becoming also the leading global power, which led him to wonder whether this was a temporary phenomenon or the harbinger of a new era in world politics.[6]

Turning to the present, there were a number of theories on offer by international-relations specialists and political geographers as they sought to conceptualise global power politics. The displacement of containment theory at a time of apparently unipolar power encouraged, for example, an emphasis on political economy, which apparently provided a way to link American/capitalist structuring of the global economy with competition at every scale over resources. Spatial issues could be incorporated into this approach.

One continued theme in the literature was the preference, on the part of those offering geopolitical analysis, to claim salience for their own particular analysis. Indeed, a rush of world visions were on offer, for the analyses presented by writers and commentators were as much prospectuses for the future as understandings of the present. This situation was very much the case for the two most prominent accounts of the 1990s: Francis Fukuyama's article 'The End of History?', published in *The National Interest,* a neo-conservative journal, in 1989, and Samuel P. Huntington's article 'Clash of Civilizations', published in *Foreign Affairs* four years later. Neither article put spatial considerations foremost, nor offered an equivalent response to an apparent spatial threat, as the varied understandings of containment had done during the Cold War, but each account had important implications for the operation of the international system and, therefore, for the relationship between particular struggles and the wider situation. Fukuyama's approach was influential, or at least highly newsworthy, in the 1990s, and Huntington's in the 2000s.

In one sense, Fukuyama, a former pupil of Huntington and the Deputy Director of Policy Planning under President George H. W. Bush, proposed the end of geopolitics when he wrote of 'the universalization of Western liberal democracy as the final form of human government', notably thanks to the acceptance of liberal economics by Asia, particularly China. Fukuyama, however, was frequently criticised by those who had not read him, and it tends to be forgotten that, towards the end of his article, he wrote 'clearly, the vast bulk of the Third World remains very much mired in history, and will be a terrain of conflict for many years to come', and, later, that 'terrorism and wars of national liberation will continue to be an important item on the national agenda.'[7]

Fukuyama went on to publish *The End of History and the Last Man* (1992), and, by then, his argument seemed especially prescient, as the collapse of the Soviet state in 1991 had followed that of Communism in Eastern Europe in 1989. Adopting a commonplace approach, for example that of the Enlightenment stadial writers, his account was not only spatial but also teleological, with certain states presented as more successful because they were post-historical in his terms.

Some critics presented Fukuyama as a triumphalist neo-conservative who failed to relativise his own position, criticism that, in practice, owed something to an opposition to the USA, or, at least, to American policies. More pertinent was the problem posed by Fukuyama's relative optimism about the prospect for a new world order, although his warning about the world of Islam as resistant to this new order was to be noted by those writing after 11 September 2001.[8] Already, bitter conflict in the former Yugoslavia in the 1990s had indicated the strength of ethnic, religious and regional animosities that had only been just contained during the Cold War by Communist rule.

At the same time, a new form of geo-power was employed in the attempt at Dayton in 1995 to broker a new order for Bosnia-Herzegovina by agreeing a new border between the warring communities in former Yugoslavia. The use of high-tech geographic information-processing systems speeded up the process of negotiation. Ironically, Powerscene, the prime system used, had been developed by the US Defense Mapping Agency for military purposes, notably the American air attack on the Bosnian Serbs in 1995. It is a computer-based terrain-visualisation system, in which digital cartographic data overlaid with remote sensing imagery permits users to explore the landscape as a three-dimensional reality.[9] Yet, the technology and doctrine of the so-called Revolution in Military Affairs was also misleading as it contributed to a downplaying of physical geography in the age of self-styled military transformation.

Huntington was less optimistic than Fukuyama. In 'Clash of Civilizations', which was expanded into a successful book, *The Clash of Civilizations and the Remaking of World Order* (1996), Huntington rebutted Fukuyama and predicted not the triumph of Western values but rather the rise of 'challenger civilisations', especially China and Islam. This rise would be as part of a relative decline of the West that, he argued, had to be addressed carefully. Thus, this was not a book about the threat from a Heartland but, instead, one that proposed a different geopolitical shaping of the Eurasian question, with the Rimland far more problematic than the Heartland.

Moreover, the emphasis on ideology, in the shape of Islam, was one that put the inner-city immigrant communities of places such as Paris at the front line of contention. Huntington drew on the analysis of Islam by another American scholar, Bernard Lewis, specifically his 1990 article 'The Roots of Muslim Rage'. Huntington argued that, in light of the rise of 'challenger civilisations', the established and rival concept of a global community of nation-states accepting a shared rule of international law and set of assumptions, a community that had been the aspiration of Wilsonian and Cold War American policies and that seemed achieved in the 1990s, could no longer be the answer to the world's problems and, thus, satisfy demands.

Terrorism was to drive this lesson home, and Huntington's book, which has been overshadowed during the triumphant globalisation of the late 1990s, now appeared prescient after the attacks on 11 September 2001, and, indeed, was to be translated into thirty-three languages. The focus was on relations with Islam, and Huntington was generally seen as an exponent of the likelihood of conflict between Christendom and Islam, and was praised or criticised accordingly. To some critics, Huntington, who was in fact a lifelong Democrat as well as a self-declared conservative, was a key neo-conservative who had sketched out the prospectus for the new ideological confrontation of the 2000s as well as for the assertive American policies that followed the 11 September attacks.[10]

The idea of a clash of civilisations, while arresting, also led to criticism on the grounds of a misplaced simplification. Thus, from the Left, Edward Said wrote an article 'The Clash of Ignorance', published in the *Nation* on 22 October 2001, arguing that there was a danger that the 11 September attacks would be misleadingly treated as an assault by a monolithic Islam. Indeed, subsequent violence within Iraq was to demonstrate the depths of animosity within Islam.

From the perspective of specialists in geopolitics, there was also scepticism, not least based on the highly problematic nature of geography in Huntington's work. In particular, there was an unresolved tension in his use of geography, between a Realist understanding of it as an objective and autonomous element in the political process, and, on the other hand, Huntington's emphasis on the 'primacy of subjective, non-geographical factors of social psychology'.[11]

It was far from ironic that the idea of a clash of civilisations was also pushed hard by Osama bin Laden and his supporters. This clash was given particular geographical force by al-Qaeda as they saw Islam as a civilisation with a spatial sway, and a converting and controlling faith, rather than a religion limited to the devotion of the faithful. Moreover, al-Qaeda treated Islam as having been driven back from spaces it should control, especially Palestine/Israel and southern Spain, while the presence of American troops in Saudi Arabia following the Gulf War of 1990–1 was seen by them as another instance of cultural spatial violation. The geopolitical imagination of al-Qaeda was one that ranged widely[12] and offered no prospect of peace nor of understanding of other cultures. This imagination also served as a reminder of the political consequences of psychological senses of space and alienation. In another disturbing parallel, Huntington's thesis of a clash of civilisations was also echoed in the emergence of ethno-geopolitics in post-Soviet Russia, although the latter explicitly imbued the civilisational entity with specific ethnic characteristics of its own.[13]

Although very different in his willingness to debate, Huntington also clearly found simplification conducive, as with his *Who Are We? The Challenges to America's National Identity* (2004), a work that warned about a change of consciousness and a challenge to Americanness as a consequence of large-scale immigration. In the book, Huntington expressed concern about the applause from Mexican-Americans for Mexican teams competing with Americans. As with the *Clash of Civilizations*, he seemed to find both multiple identities and interdependence as unwelcome concepts, and, as a result, was reduced to the notion of incompatible groups operating through rivalry. Such an attitude was crucial to the habit of presenting geopolitics in binary terms. Looked at differently, binary concepts lent themselves to geopolitics.

Despite being drawn by some critics, the path from Huntington to the policies of the George W. Bush administration of 2001–9 was in fact at best indirect. Huntington himself was critical of the neo-conservatives and of the 2003 invasion of Iraq. He was particularly unimpressed with the attempt to install a Western-style democracy, which he saw as misplaced cultural superiority leading to a flawed transference of ideas and structures. Huntington also told an interviewer that he voted for John Kerry rather than Bush in 2004.

Instead, neo-conservative geopolitics were linked more to the 'Project for a New American Century' (1997). This project, or rather prospectus, was the product of a movement which arose from a reaction against the policies of President Clinton (1993–2001) and from an attempt to revive the essential elements of the Reagan administration, or rather what were presented as these elements, and to reposition them for the post-Cold War era. As with earlier generations of American interventionists, this drive entailed a commitment to Eurasia: 'America has a vital role in maintaining peace and security in Europe, Asia, and the Middle East', and these responsibilities were seen as fundamental American interests. The specific policies that flowed from these assumptions were, in many respects, traditional, notably strong support for Israel and Taiwan, and, in some respects, the general suppositions can be seen as formulaic and trite hyperbole that seek to provide rationale and structure for a series of specific commitments.

That remark is not intended as a criticism of the neo-conservatives as it could be made about most attempts to offer a global geopolitics, including liberal and left-wing attempts. Looked at differently, the deductive processes of geopolitics at the global level are weak, and the specific goals that arise can best be understood as individual and lacking a general structure. Thus, geopolitics as a global analysis emerges as implausible as an inductive method, and as weak as a deductive one.

At the same time that thc fall of the Soviet Union and the anchoring of East Asia to the American economy had led to optimism in the 1990s, global politics also had been widely reshaped in a more challenging fashion. An imploding Soviet Union did not challenge American hegemony and, unlike revolutionary France in 1789–92 and, to a lesser extent, Russia in 1917–20, Russia in the 1990s did not swing from revolution to dangerous expansionism; which provided a background for the restatement of a classic geopolitics in Brzezinski's *The Grand Chessboard: American Primacy and Its Geostrategic Imperatives* (1997), a work not mentioned in Ó Tuathail et al.'s *Geopolitics Reader.*[14]

Across much of the world, identity and conflict were shaped and expressed in the 1990s in terms of ethnicity. Thus, although formalised 'theories' of the interrelationship, or interdetermination, of geography and politics had had little purchase in the Soviet Union because of their blood-and-soil connotations, these ideas came to enjoy widespread credence and popularity in post-Soviet Russia as a new territoriality was developed especially by Aleksandr Dugin, a polemical commentator, with an assertive account of national space and the supposed biological imperatives of the nation. Some of the Russian work, in contrast, has been better informed and not partisan.[15]

Although the results of expressing identity in ethnic terms were frequently very much defined in spatial terms, not least as the goal of many activists were ethnically homogenous territorial spaces, this emphasis on ethnicity was not a practice that was conducive to geopolitical theorising on the global scale, nor to American leadership. Furthermore, drawing together Fukuyama and Huntington, the internationalisms that had greatest impact in the 1990s and 2000s were consumerism and religion. These could be compatible, as in the USA, not that religion defines American civic identity; but in some countries, notably in the Middle East, hostility to globalisation meant opposition to modernism and modernisation, and thus could draw on powerful interests and deep fears.

The 2001 attacks led to this regional hostility becoming a key geopolitical issue for the USA, with resulting concerns in terms of possibilities for supporting force projection. These concerns entailed a different geopolitics, one focused on Central Asia and Pakistan, to that of the Cold War, when forward operating capabilities sought to meet different requirements. The end of the Cold War had led to a withdrawal of political support for America's overseas posture, which affected the geostrategic options facing its forces.[16] The War on Terror, in contrast, led to a revival of geopolitics at a number of levels. These included the focus on Area Commands by the Pentagon and also the extent to which conflict in Afghanistan and Iraq obliged newspapers and the television news to include maps. Most of these maps, however, were flat maps, devoid of information on such factors as terrain or religious affiliation.

Tensions over resources, notably oil, water, food and space, also played a major role in geopolitics, both local struggles and international concerns. This role was particularly sensitive in the Middle East and notably added a key strand in its relations with the USA. American oil imports – close to 2 per cent of GDP in 2005 – led to a dangerous dependence on the politics of the Middle East and the stability of particular regimes, such as those of the Shah in Iran in the 1970s and the Saud dynasty in Saudi Arabia. In 2003, Saudi Arabia held 25 per cent of the world's oil reserves, and Iraq another 10 per cent, with the Middle Eastern OPEC states having two-thirds of the world's reserves. Whatever the future development of American supplies, particularly in Alaska, the Middle East will dominate future supply.

Population growth drives resource issues alongside economic demands.[17] At the global level, population changes are also an important element in geopolitics. In particular, most of the expansion in the world's population is occurring, and will continue to occur, in East and South Asia. The population is due to increase from 6 to 8 or 9 billion, with the West still only providing 1 billion and thus proving a declining minority of the world's population. The 1999 UN Population Fund Study suggested a rise from 6 billion people in 1999 to 8.9 billion in 2050.

Although the role of oil in the American decision to attack Iraq in 2003 was exaggerated, in what was a reflection of the more general tendency to simplify motivation and causation, oil certainly played a major role in the geopolitics of American strategy. Indeed, this was an aspect of the cost that oil dependence forced on the USA, and thus the burden placed on its economy and consumers. In 2004, the USA imported 58 per cent of the oil it consumed, compared to 34 per cent in 1973. The American Energy Information Administration has predicted this percentage rising to 68 by 2025. The USA's dependence on energy and currency inflows are fundamental to its strategic position and to its geopolitical concerns.

Indeed, energy and financial dependency makes isolationism an implausible option for the USA, as indeed for China and the European Union (EU), each of which, albeit in different ways and for contrasting motives, display less of a willingness than the USA to intervene with force. This dependence ensures an American interest not only in the Middle East but also in Central Asia, West Africa and Venezuela, the last of which provided a seventh of America's oil imports by 2005. Similarly, the EU's concern about Russia owes much to its dependence on Russian gas. Yet, such supplies also increase the interdependence of supplier and consumer.[18]

The impact of the end of the age of cheap energy for the geopolitics of the next generation is unclear. Alongside issues linked to areas of the supply of oil and gas, there will be competition between importing countries, notably China and the USA. This may demonstrate Mackinder's point that the great wars of history arise from the unequal growth of nations, a point frequently made in literature about the cause of wars.

The attacks on 11 September 2001 led to a dramatic reconfiguration of American commitment, with a revival of Cold War ideas but now in a more proactive fashion. Moreover, the new direction of policy was seen as representing a revival of Cold War-style geopolitics after the anti-geopolitics of the Clinton years. This argument rested in particular on the new-found American determination not to be restrained by the need for international agreement and for working through international bodies. Instead, regional cooperation directed by the USA seemed a key way to pursue American policy, but the search for such cooperation was defined in part in terms of regional goals.

This practice was linked to a globalist account of the metaphysics of the new situation. Addressing a Joint Session of Congress on 20 September 2001, President George W. Bush stated 'Either you are with us, or you are with the terrorists.' In practice, the call for a 'War on Terror' was also a call for a more broad-based action to maintain order, or a vision of order, in the world. Both were universal missions, in which geographical limits were regarded as an irrelevance that was to yield to will. In short, there was an open-ended commitment in both time and space, one that was emphasised by the American leadership. The 'War on Terror' thus served as a concept to structure the complexities of world affairs and to help direct alliances. Conversely, al-Qaeda sought to use *jihad* as a call for action and an organising concept that could incorporate Islamic activism and disputes across the world, as in January 2009 when Osama bin Laden pressed for *jihad* over Gaza.

In September 2002, the National Security Strategy argued the need for pre-emptive strikes, a key policy innovation, in response to the dual threats of terrorism and of 'rogue states', such as Iran and North Korea, developing weapons of mass destruction, the latter seen as another variant on terrorism.

The global extension of American values was seen as the answer to the danger of either:

> The great struggles of the twentieth century between liberty and totalitarianism ended with a decisive victory for the forces of freedom . . . These values of freedom are right and true for every person, in every society – and the duty of protecting these values against their enemies is the common calling of freedom-loving people across the globe and across

> the ages . . . We will extend the peace by encouraging free and open societies on every continent.

To that end, Bush pressed for democracy in the Middle East and China, a call that appeared to ignore any suggestion of geographical limits. In many respects, and here emphasising the plasticity of the concept and placing of geopolitics, this call for not only democracy but also for modernisation was a denial of the geopolitics of *Realpolitik* advanced by Kissinger, as the assumption, under Bush, was that a change in the values of a society, as well as of the operations of its domestic politics, would alter the country's position in international relations. Thus, building on the oft-repeated claim that democracies do not declare war on democracies, the drive for democracy was a move away from the argument that particular nations were somehow fated to a malign political system. The latter argument was a form of political environmentalism that more readily lent itself to classic geopolitics and to the conventional understanding of international relations as a realist structure. Moreover, the call for democratisation was an aspect of a strategy seeking to maintain stability and prevent wars, as much as to win them. Opposition to weapons proliferation was part of the same policy.

Bush also argued, in a speech given at Tbilisi in Georgia in May 2005, that the peace settlement of 1945 had been flawed because it had left Eastern Europe under Communist control, again a remark that underplayed the suggestion of geopolitical limits, while also offering a comment on the Democratic administrations of the 1940s.

In practice, the American preference in the 2000s was for democracy in the Middle East, rather than in China, as that appeared a more practical goal, as well as one made more necessary by the challenge posed by Islamic fundamentalism. Whether it is helpful to view this prioritisation in a geopolitical light is unclear unless the latter is understood, as is so often the case, as a rationalisation of the obvious. For, in practice, despite the call for universal freedom, there was a cartography of concern and action, and one in which prudence and pragmatism about introducing democracy played a greater role than ideological rhetoric might suggest. This point is not intended as a criticism of policy but underlines the extent to which geopolitics can be seen as an exercise in prudence or rather in debating strategies of prudence in terms of international concerns. As such, there is a parallel with the early American republic in which the call for universal rights enunciated in the Declaration of Independence (1776) was very much compromised by the exigencies of power politics in the Americas, as well as by the racial politics of the USA itself.

Yet, if not a target for democratisation, China still focused American concern, with the 2006 Quadrennial Defense Review describing it as having 'the greatest potential to compete militarily with the United States and field disruptive military technologies that could over time offset traditional US military advantages'.[19] Confronting this challenge entails not only appropriate force structures and doctrine but also an understanding of the political dimension from the Chinese perspective and that of other Asian powers.[20] These needs are in a dynamic relationship such that, for example, 'a larger number of [American] submarines could be warranted, depending on how the geopolitical situation in the Pacific plays out.'[21]

However, after 2001, the China issue was overshadowed by the War on Terror, with the USA apparently able to employ its military preponderance to ensure a freedom of action.[22] While the Bush doctrine, which was reiterated in the version of the National Security Strategy issued in March 2006, was the opposite of isolationism (a point underlined in Bush's address to the United Nations in September 2005), at the same time, this was multilateralism in a War on Terror very much on American terms. Donald Rumsfeld's argument that 'The worst thing you can do is allow a coalition to determine what your mission is', was a call to reject the political counterpart to environmental determinism.

This rejection was perceived by critics as a departure from the existing constraints of the international order, a departure reflecting the weaknesses of the latter and the gravity of the American unilateral challenge. Yet, as this international order was legal and a matter of institutions and diplomacy, rather than geographical, so the rejection cannot be seen in geopolitical terms other than as a determined opposition to isolationism, but one on American terms.

The strategic counterpart for the USA in the 2000s was that deterrence no longer seemed effective when confronted by terrorism or states governed by fanatical rulers. Thus, pre-emption appeared necessary as a strategic means and goal, with the specific consequences that flowed in terms of the geopolitics constructed round particular challenges. The promotion of democratic governments appeared an aspect of this pre-emption. It was linked to the idea of 'draining the swamp', or removing the factors that made particular areas, such as Afghanistan, prone to serving as bases for terrorism. Looked at from the other perspective, terrorists, like guerrilla groups, required space as a base for operations, and what had been termed shatterbelts provided this. At the strategic level, control or dominance of these contested spaces was important in establishing the metropole's writ, and shatterbelts were the focus of concerns about the international order and the strength of individual states,[23] although strength was, and is, difficult to define. Moreover, definitions can in part be discussed with reference to particular national and regional political structures, a process that can be seen as an aspect of geopolitics.

The geopolitics of, and attributed to, the Bush administration (2001–9), in turn lent added force to the expression of the self-styled 'critical geopolitics'. This expression was as part of the more general critique of that administration, particularly of the War on Terror and of its unilateralism, reliance on force and alleged simplification of Islam. Much of this criticism was and is hyperbolic, with phrases such as 'rogue superpower',[24] and some of the criticism is explicitly political and also, in part, draws on the justification that geopolitical discourse is inherently contested and thereby political.

The last argument has a value, but all too much of the criticism is vitiated by resting on a fixed set of preferences and antagonisms. A difficulty in coming to terms with American power is one of the major issues. Moreover, adopting an inherently critical approach towards such overlapping categories as American public culture, consumerism, the West (an abstraction that tended not to include the critic in question), neo-conservatism, imperialist geopolitics and claims to objectivity is not only repetitive and somewhat exhausting but also suffers from the difficulties of then coming to terms with these forces and categories in subsequent analysis, other than in a crude fashion that relies on problematic theory, scant use of evidence and argument by assertion.

The *New Imperialism* (2003) by David Harvey provided an instructive example.[25] A former member of the Oxford School of Geography, who went on to teach at Johns Hopkins University before becoming Distinguished Professor of Anthropology at the Graduate Center of the City University of New York, Harvey based his book on the Clarendon Lectures he delivered in Oxford in 2003, and in the preface he acknowledges the help of Neil Smith in shaping his insight.[26] Seeking to expose 'deeper currents' in American policy, Harvey stressed 'All About Oil', the title of his first chapter, argued that Bush's foreign policy was designed 'to impose a new sense of social order at home',[27] established a binary divide between 'accumulation by dispossession', as a result of neo-liberal policies, and 'an even rising tide of global resistance',[28] and presented geopolitics as the product of economic forces:

> the really big issue is what happens to surplus capitals generated within sub-national regional economies when they cannot find profitable employment anywhere within the state. This is, of course, the heart of the problem that generates pressures for imperialist practices in the inter-state system. The evident corollary of all this is that geopolitical conflicts would almost certainly arise out of the molecular processes of capital accumulation no matter what the state powers thought they were about. . . . That the

> political state, in advanced capitalism, has to spend a good deal of effort and consideration on how to manage the molecular flows. . . . It will, in short, necessarily engage in geopolitical struggle and resort, when it can, to imperialist practices.[29]

In short, 'critical geopolitics' is apt to indulge (and that term is used deliberately) in the very Manichaeism for which it decried the Bush administration and also neo-conservative thought in general. Unless it ceases to indulge in this approach, the value of this 'critical geopolitics' will be less than its potential as a call for a new departure in the subject. Alongside Manichaeism comes the problem of projecting one's own frames of reference onto others. A historical account of geopolitical thought reveals a long tradition of doing so, one that predates 'critical geopolitics', but it is a practice that needs to be resisted. To do so is not to imply the possibility of objective perfection as an alternative, but, rather, to note that any argument, whether postmodern or not, for the universal practice of adopting particular points of view, is flawed as a prospectus for intellectual endeavour.

It would, of course, be totally misleading to imply a coherence for all the literature that could be referred to as 'critical geopolitics'. Indeed, the policies of the Bush government (and of its British ally) were debated (and criticised) across the political spectrum, including on the Right from those who would certainly not seem to share the views of the self-styled 'critical geopoliticians'. For example, the supposed nature of American policy as imperial was argued widely in a literature that brought together politics, geography and history, with some of this literature critical and part of it supportive. The extent to which these works had a geopolitical aspect varied, as there was often more of an interest in characterising the central ethos and thrust of policy than its spatial dynamic and manifestations, but the attempt to move beyond the analytical confines of the Cold War was valuable.

In an important work, *American Empire: The Realities and Consequences of US Diplomacy* (2002), Andrew Bacevich searched out themes and continuities that moved him away from turning points predicated on the start and end of the Cold War, as well as looking at the relationship between America's global power and her domestic political culture, a key geopolitical theme. He concluded:

> The question that urgently demands attention . . . is not whether the United States has become an imperial power. The question is what sort of empire they intend theirs to be. For policymakers to persist in pretending otherwise . . . is to increase the likelihood that the answers they come up with will be wrong. That way lies not just the demise of the American empire but great danger for what used to be known as the American republic.[30]

Bacevich looked at how American policy had developed with a pursuit of morality increasingly linked to the furtherance of what he saw as a potent imperium:

> the politicoeconomic concept to which the United States adheres today has not changed in a century: the familiar quest for an 'open world', the overriding imperative of commercial integration, confidence that technology endows the United States with a privileged position in that order, and the expectation that American military might will preserve order and enforce the rules . . . Those policies reflect a single-minded determination to extend and perpetuate American political, economic, and cultural hegemony – usually referred to as 'leadership' – on a global scale.[31]

Having thrown light on the extent to which the defenders of liberal internationalism had offered a mythic rendition of America's ascent to global power, specifically what he termed the myth of the reluctant superpower, Bacevich showed how, as the American imperium focused on globalisation, so those who resisted the latter were seen as opponents of the USA.

He argued that, inheriting British ideas from the nineteenth century, American writers and policy-makers focused after 1945 on free trade and the unfettered movement of money, as political as well as economic goods and goals, and thus as central goods and goals for government. The state thus became a protection system for an economic world view which, in turn, helped fund the state; but, rather than seeing this relationship in left-wing terms as the product of an economic conspiracy and class self-interest, Bacevich focused on the ideas that played a crucial role, specifically on the pursuit of a benign and mutually beneficial world order that reflected an imperium, rather than an empire of control, constraint and coercion. The democratic objective at the heart of American capitalism was seen by Bacevich as both cause and consequence of freedom. The American determination to overthrow the European colonial empires can be located more clearly in light of Bacevich's themes than in Cold War terms, as the Americans hoped that newly independent peoples would support democratic capitalism and thus look to the USA. This approach can be seen as a foolish aspiration, although the alternatives were not welcome, as any consideration of the American dilemma at the time of the Suez Crisis would indicate.

Bacevich underlined the degree to which this economic goal, seen at once as in America's and the world's interest, and as conducive to liberty as well as prosperity, provided a continuous theme that bridged the close of the Cold War. Democratic capitalism had to be supported and, if necessary, fought for. Yet, Bacevich argued that, in the 1990s, a greater reliance on coercion as an instrument of American policy, and the tendency of serving officers to displace civilians in implementing foreign policy, were manifestations of the increasing militarisation of American statecraft after the Cold War: 'Before the 1990s ended, evidence of civil-military dysfunction had become increasingly difficult to ignore. Meanwhile, events had exposed the limitations of the proconsular system – and of Americans' reliance on gunboats and Gurkhas to police the world.'[32]

The role of continuity and memory in framing responses to crises, not least highlighting perceptions of national interest, and thus the strategic nature of particular spaces, was another theme to emerge from recent scholarship. In *Making War, Thinking History: Munich, Vietnam, and Presidential Uses of Force from Korea to Kosovo* (2002), Jeffrey Record showed how historical lessons, particularly Munich and Vietnam, were misinterpreted, and suggested that 'the tendency to regard violent nationalism in the Third World as the product of a centrally directed international Communist conspiracy was a strategic error of the first magnitude.'[33] Record, in turn, was scathing about the failure of President George H. W. Bush and his advisers to respond adequately 'when confronting events without obvious parallel during the 1940s, 1950s, and 1960s'.[34] Thus, the geopolitics of time and memory play a key role, an element, moreover, that is emphasised if the stress is on the role of perception in assessing not only power but, more particularly, threats.

In part, the geopolitics of time and memory play a key role because commentators and politicians frequently continue writing for many decades. Thus, for example, Zbigniew Brzezinski, a National Security Adviser in the 1970s and a prominent user of the term 'geopolitics', published *The Choice: Global Domination or Global Leadership* in 2004, and, the previous winter, employed the concept as well as language of geopolitics.[35] Brzezinski referred to 'the crucial swathe of Eurasia between Europe and the Far East' as the 'new "Global Balkans"', a phrase intended

> to draw attention to the geopolitical similarity between the traditional European Balkans of the 19th and 20th centuries and the unstable region that currently extends from approximately the Suez Canal to Xinjiang . . . In the case of both areas, internal instability has served as a magnet for external major power intervention and rivalry . . . the ferment within the Muslim world must be viewed primarily as

> regional rather than a global perspective, and through a geopolitical rather than a theological prism.[36]

Subsequently, he referred in the article to 'the current geopolitical earthquake in the Persian Gulf'.[37]

In practice, this language served Brzezinski as a call for diplomatic action, and, in particular, for an active strategic partnership between a politically mobilised USA and a determined and united EU. The extent to which the vocabulary of geopolitics really advanced the argument in this or other cases is unclear although, in terms of rhetorical strategy, whether it did so in part was a matter of the assumptions of the likely audience, and their likely perception of the use of this vocabulary. As a reminder, moreover, of the malleability of geopolitical perspectives, the power politics of this 'crucial swathe' were to be re-examined by Robert Kaplan in 2009, but this time from the perspective of power centred on the Indian Ocean.[38]

Current geopolitics pose analytical problems, not least because the long term is more than a series of short terms. Understandable as it is for conservatives (and others) to frame questions and answers in terms of immediate issues – the 9/11-isation of American policy, or at least to focus on post-Cold War paradigms, it is necessary to consider issues in international relations in the longer term. Traditional conservative values, such as prudence, have been unduly neglected as internationalism has become the theme of much of the Right. This tendency has implications not only for conservative positions on domestic politics, particularly low taxation and restricted public debt, but also for the notion of national sovereignty that has played a central role in conservative thought on international relations.

Internationalism challenges many traditional conservative assumptions, and the extraordinary growth of the American national debt under the George W. Bush government amply demonstrated this, while also altering the geopolitics of international finance, and notably the fiscal and political relationships within the dollar world. For the imperial power, the USA, the internationalism made necessary by global interdependence also poses the difficulty of responding to the expectations of allies and, more seriously, those whose alliance is sought; as well as the issue of how best to answer calls for decision-making, judgement and arbitration through international bodies that the USA both distrusts and yet finds it necessary to use.

Alongside these issues, there is the question of the concepts that can be employed in discussing international relations. For example, there are the ongoing problems of what geopolitics means and of the degree of agency involved. When Charles Kupchan wrote 'The North–South divide will become a geopolitical fault line only if America turns it into one',[39] there was the commonplace assumption that agency, and therefore responsibility and blame, rested essentially with the USA. This approach, taken by many critics outside the USA as well as by most American commentators, underplays the role of others and its interaction with American policy. More systematically, it is appropriate to ask how far geopolitical argument at the international level is overly dependent on the idea of a hegemonic power and the responses to it or, alternatively, the idea of a binary struggle.

For other powers in the early 2000s, there was the problem of how best to protect and further national goals, whether conceptualised or not as traditional, while, at the same time, reacting to the demands of the imperial power at a time that it was particularly assertive. This issue is a key geopolitical quandry but one that is generally underrated due to the tendency to focus on the leading power. For example, at a very different scale, geopolitics involves the formulating, shaping and sustaining of distinct local identities, for example the Padania of the Lega Nord in Italy, as part of a way in which local autonomies, possibilities and claims are advanced and given a geographic identity. This spatial politics of identity is important in the politics of managing more complex and larger-scale pressures and demands; and a key element of this spatial politics is an opposition to what is presented as globalisation. Frequently, this opposition to globalisation entails a transfer of earlier opposition to imperial structures and demands.

Returning to the 2000s, the ambivalent American response to conservative Arab regimes is indicative of a more general problem, for it is not only in autocratic regimes, such as Saudi Arabia, that conservatism is challenged by the global range and application of American policies and pretensions. This global range and application, as well as the regional implementation of American policy, clash with the particular geopolitical concerns of individual states. This clash plays a role in the American challenge to populist discourses, for example those of Chávez's Venezuela. That the latter regime, like many others that manipulate populism, for example Iran under Ahmadinejad, is irresponsible and politically highly problematic does not lessen the point that the regime has a distinct geopolitics, one that conflates a traditional left-wing Latin American opposition to the USA with the particular dynamics of Venezuela and Latin America in the 2000s, notably oil wealth and competition with Colombia.

A consideration of such issues underlines the emotional as well as pragmatic, political and military issues faced by an interventionist internationalism and reopens the case for a more measured stance towards the latter on the part of the West. In particular, it is valuable to consider the difference between internationalism and interventionism as goals or as methods, in other words strategically or operationally. Geopolitics is a valuable analytical tool in responding to this question, although it also has to be accepted that what are seen as means, or operational policies, can, in turn, become ends, or strategic goals, in themselves, by gaining symbolic and practical weight. Geopolitical discussion, moreover, can as much lead to this elision as it can help maintain a rigorous contrast between the two.

The extent to which classical geopolitical theory is still valid for the post-Cold War period is problematic. On the one hand, the concept of mobilising a nation's mass human resources to protect the 'organic state' from military or ideological conquest by alien aggressors seems better suited to periods when great imperial systems were competing for global primacy, and notably so if linked to rival ideologies, whether Liberal-Democratic, Fascist or Marxist. On the other hand, both real and perceived spatial considerations continue to play a role in power politics irrespective of the ideological dimension.

Yet they play a role within a dynamic context that is greatly affected by major changes in, for example, resource availability, trade routes and military capability. The last can be seen with Israel's military commitment to retaining land conquered in 1967. Geopolitical factors focused on security were the leading Israeli argument against the demand that Israel should return occupied land. The argument used to be that the Golan Heights should be kept because, from Mount Hermon, it was possible to look deep into Syria and Lebanon and keep an eye on Syrian preparations to attack, and also that, with the tank being the backbone of the army, the Golan had to be retained to provide space for concentrating forces and for manoeuvre.

These arguments are still made but they are now less valid as it is possible to look into Syria from space, while, with attack helicopters, Israel does not need the land for manoeuvring. Moreover, with the Israeli doctrine of warfare becoming more similar to the American concept of Rapid Dominance, and with firepower replacing concentration of forces, land appears less important in military terms.

The same is the case with the West Bank. Immediately after its occupation in 1967, the Israelis came up with the Allon Plan to keep much of the West Bank and to build settlements along the River Jordan in order to stop a potential attack by an Eastern Bloc of Syria, Iraq and Jordan. However, missiles do not really care much about such buffer zones, and the strategic, operational and tactical arguments for such a zone have been challenged, if not undermined, by the use of rocket attacks on Israeli cities, a policy that began with Iraqi Scud attacks in 1991. Moreover, Jordan has peaceful relations with Israel, and Iraq and Iran lack a common border with it. The changing validity of a military strategic rationale for continued Israeli occupation of the West Bank and the Golan Heights throws attention back onto domestic political debates focused on the need for and value of, settlements in the occupied territories, and also on the nature of peace that might be possible and the role of Israeli withdrawal in such a peace settlement.

These points serve as a reminder that the geopolitics of a particular question has a number of angles. So also for example does the current discussion of whether there is a 'geopolitical niche' that requires a British nuclear deterrent separate to that of American cover.[40] The current relevance of geopolitical issues and debates provides a point of departure for looking at the future in the next chapter because much of the current discussion hinges on the issue of future consequences.

CHAPTER 8

THE GEOPOLITICS OF THE FUTURE

Current debate over the character and value of geopolitics, including indeed criticism of its validity, can be seen as exemplifying what Harvey Sicherman termed in 2002 'the revival of geopolitics'.[1] The ambiguities of the term 'geopolitics', however, remain. The impact of particular theories about geopolitics have left the subject one that, conventionally understood, is heavily historicised, but these theories are not crucial to the central question of the impact of geography on the political character, interests and interaction of states.[2] Here, the key issue is not Mackinder, Haushofer or Bush, nor the body of literature that self-consciously employs the language of geopolitics or the critique of critical geopolitics, but, rather, the relationship between environmental factors and human action and intentions. The lines of debate in this relationship are essentially still those of the early twentieth century, namely that focused on the extent and nature of environmental determinism and influence. In terms of structure and agency, moreover, environmental determinism had a parallel with the continuing emphasis on the role of the system in accounts of international relations, and each offered an approach that lent particular character to the related geopolitics.

The past value of these accounts can be queried, but the issue here is the geopolitics of the future. Given the volatility of international relations, of environmental developments such as resource availability, global temperature change and pandemics, and of other aspects of the future, such discussion may appear very problematic. It is not necessary to go as far as an improbable possibility, the discovery of intelligent life elsewhere in the Solar System, oft-predicted but never yet realised, to appreciate that a new sphere of geopolitical relationship and analysis may arise and that present-day parameters may change. Rather than assuming an ability to predict the future, especially that beyond several decades, it is appropriate to ask what analytical approaches may well be useful and may well be employed.

At the level of public policy and public rhetoric, commentators will attempt to respond to issues and crises. In short, there will be a continuation of the reactive character to geopolitics seen, for example, with Mackinder conceptualising both the apparent Russian challenge to the British empire in 1904, and that from Communist Russia to the European system in 1919; and seen also with the geopolitics of Cold War containment. Indeed, much of the predictive use of geopolitics is in practice reactive. In that perspective, it is instructive to consider geopolitical literature as futurology, with all the issues that gives rise to when looking to past texts.[3]

For example, to take a book that appeared in 2002 to great attention, a work that conceptualised geopolitical relationships as dynamic, Philip Bobbitt's *The Shield of Achilles: War, Peace and the Course of History* argued that the fundamentals of the international system were changing, because the nation-state was no longer able to cope with the challenges of the modern world and, instead, that there had been a shift to what he termed the market-state.[4] Bobbitt saw the society of market states 'as dominated by three important actors', Europe, Japan and the USA,[5] although he also, correctly, pointed out the co-dependency that arose from investment and debt. Bobbitt suggested in his chapter on 'Possible Worlds' that, by 2020, 70 per cent of the world economy would be in the former Third World and China, although some of his other suggestions, such as Pakistan and India joining in a free trade area in 2010, appeared distinctly problematic.

As far as military projections were concerned, Bobbitt offered a number of scenarios, for example a successful North Korean invasion of South Korea in 2018, followed, in

2020, by the first pre-emptive strike by an ad-hoc coalition against a Central Asian state possessing a ballistic missile system. Alternatively, the earlier acquisition by South Korea of nuclear weapons was seen as preventing North Korean attack. Proliferation was presented as encouraging aggression, as in the possible Chinese use of neutron bombs to gain Taiwan, while, in contrast, the further proliferation, arising from states rushing to acquire defences, was seen as producing multiple regional standoffs:

> the Iron Triangles, a series of interlocking deterrence relationships around the world in which, it was believed, a mutual stability was achieved through nuclear proliferation among regional adversaries: China-Korea-Japan; Germany-Russia-Ukraine; India-Pakistan-China; Iran-Israel-Iraq; Australia-Indonesia-Malaysia; Chile-Argentina-Brazil: these were the main Iron triangles, with subsidiary triangles such as Singapore-China-Viet Nam, Germany-Poland-Russia, France-Germany-Great Britain.[6]

However much a state or a group of states might dominate the power stakes, and however much diplomacy might resolve many problems, the costs, as a result of proliferation, of trying and failing to coerce a 'rogue' state were likely to rise, Bobbitt claimed, to a point that encouraged caution. This would not only be a *Realpolitik* scenario; it would also be the politics of prudence that most military leaderships are apt to encourage. On the other hand, as the experience of the Vietnam and Gulf War II conflicts suggests, politicians, while inexperienced about military matters, generally listen only to the advice they wish to hear and engage in promotion politics to ensure they receive this advice, a tendency taken far further in ideological and/or authoritarian regimes such as Iraq under Saddam Hussein. Thus, the politics of prudence are countered by the imperatives of commitment.

Bobbitt was at pains to stress that he was writing not futurology but about current choices. He saw cataclysmic war as a real possibility in Asia, with China, India and Russia each risking a civil war that could be succeeded by aggression. Bobbitt also suggested that the rise of civil disobedience and civil strife would provide opportunities for powers to wage indirect war, an instructive approach to geopolitics that, for example, echoed the role of religion in early modern Europe. Furthermore, Bobbitt predicted endless, low-intensity conflicts with states and non-state groups whose plights are, and will be, the consequence of an evolving pluralist society of market-states. The opponents of globalisation were thus seen as a threat not only to themselves but also to global stability.

The net effect, Bobbitt argued, would be an overturning of accustomed notions of national stability: that it is national (and not international), public (and not private), and seeks victory (and not stalemate). Bobbitt also argued that 'a state without a strategy for war would be unable to maintain its domestic legitimacy and thus could not even guarantee its citizens' civil rights and liberties.'[7] Works such as Bobbitt's emphasised a theme of challenge, one that extended to the fundamentals of international and domestic politics.

Geopolitical arguments provided a means of advancing such arguments and also of debating them. Indeed, geopolitics as a type of analysis served as a form of rethinking past, present and future. Moreover, a grasp of geopolitics is important to a revival of the largely lost art of strategy.

In many respects, current debates over the value and context of geopolitics can be fitted into the model of geopolitics as a form of response, as there is felt to be a need to react conceptually, or at least polemically, to such challenges and developments as large-scale terrorism, nuclear proliferation, American interventionism, globalisation and the Rise of China. Thus, Niall Ferguson, in the September 2008 issue of *Standpoint,* wrote of 'The End of "Chimerica" [China-America]', with the sub-heading 'The delicate balance of power between China and America is unstable and the geopolitical consequences will affect us all.'[8] This account of the economic crisis and of China's rapid growth asked 'What are the geopolitical implications of all this?', concluding 'One is that the great reconvergence between East and West is speeding up . . . The second . . . is that the days when the dollar was the sole international reserve currency are coming to an end . . . A third . . . is that troublemakers get richer.'[9] There was then an attempt, in the article, to add geographical factors, notably China's scramble for African resources, and a continuing Asian challenge to the West that began with Japanese expansionism in the 1900s.

The extent to which this argument should be seen as geopolitical in any profound sense is unclear, for example because there is only a somewhat crude juxtaposing of West and East; but a critic might suggest that this point is true of most geopolitical work. Such an assessment would draw attention to the extent to which the earlier attempt at precision offered by accounts of environmental impact in particular countries (of the type that the mountains made the East difficult to control) has been lost with the replacement of such specificity. Moreover, taking a different tract, much of the use of geopolitics is as part of a commentary driven by political factors. As a specific point, Ferguson is correct in arguing that the pursuit of resources has a geographical dimension, in this case a focus on Africa by China.

Terminology is also an issue, and 'geopolitical' frequently serves as a term meaning the international dimension. Thus, an editorial in the *Times* of 28 January 2009 on Russia's position argued that, with the resource boom over, 'Mr Putin remains politically powerful, but geopolitically he is weakened.' In this context, geopolitics simply serves as a means to discuss non-ideological international relations.

Yet, returning to the general point, more is involved when considering geopolitics than a simple conceptual or polemical response mechanism to problems, or, rather, more critically, the combination of the cacophony of competing politicised responses with the academic need to input events into theory. There are also questions of intellectual strategy. These include how best to assess geographical influence at a time of large-scale environmental change, as well as the comparable impact, in political geography, of transnationalism and of the weakness of nation states.

To return to the example of China, the relationship between the geographical facts of place and the dynamics of human and political geography remain important, despite the ruthless Chinese determination to overcome the constraints of nature, both in China and overseas, in their struggle for resources and growth. Proximity as a key issue for international politics has been underlined by developments as varied as tensions over headwaters and river rights and the spreading use of medium-range rockets. Psychological impact is related to place but is not the sole issue. Thus, the potential impact of Middle Eastern politics on Europe is greater than on Canada due to the factor of proximity. Yet proximity is not the sole factor: that potential impact is magnified in the case of Europe by the high birth rate in Muslim immigrant communities, while, in the case of the USA, the fact of distance from the Middle East is altered by political geography due to the strong commitment to Israel.[10]

Such a point underlines the value of those maps that present a spatial distortion in order to capture mental perceptions, for example different scales in the individual map. Humorous instances are provided by maps of the world from the perspective of an inhabitant of Manhattan or Chelsea, but, more seriously, mental perceptions of spatial concern are of importance. At the same time, in the case of American attitudes to the Middle East, as in other examples, such perceptions need to be understood in terms of different views by particular constituencies within the USA, as also in other countries. Again, geopolitical arguments are, in part, a product of these differing perceptions. That point does not reduce their value, but, instead, underlines the need for careful scholarship in understanding this situation and its implications.

Another level of complexity will continue to be provided by the level of decision-maker and commentator under consideration, with issues of geography being more important, or even dominant, to regional, and even more local participants, than to great powers.[11] The West Bank provides a good example, not least with differences between Israeli and American sensitivity to Israeli security; and this factor of scale will go on being significant. At the same time, scale takes on different meanings and is also transformed by technology, as shown for example by the deployment of longer-range missiles by Hizbullah and Hamas in the late 2000s.

Thus, despite talk of globalisation, one of the key challenges in geopolitical analysis will continue to be not just the understanding of what globalisation entails (not least for different constituencies that can be seen as spatially encoded) but also the relationship between the differing influence of geography at both local and global levels. Writing about the latter level provides much of the literature noted as geopolitical, and this may continue to be the case given the emphasis on globalisation and on global environmental change, as well as the academic, popular and publishing claims bound up with the statement that a coverage is global. Yet, the local, understood as state and sub-state levels, is a prime area of geographical and spatial impact on politics.

Conceptualising the nature of this geographical and spatial impact is likely to continue to be an important challenge. At the same time, the very diffusiveness of this impact makes it difficult to reduce to the clear-cut clarity of theory, not least the apparent clarity offered by the use of binary opposites to evaluate international challenges. The nature of geopolitical discussion in the future may therefore reflect the tension between the preference of some commentators for engaging with the complexities of the particular, and, on the other hand, the seductive simplicities of broad-brush approaches. These simplicities will continue to engage most attention, but they not only offer less than the full map but also a scale and projection that are frequently misleading.

CHAPTER 9

CONCLUSIONS

Contrasting definitions of the subject pose a series of problems. The extent to which politics, both international and domestic, can be variously interpreted indicates the difficulties with any narrow definition of geopolitics and indeed with any overly didactic account of geographical determinism. Yet, returning to the point made in the Introduction, there are objective factors such as space, distance and resources; and it is pertinent to consider their impact on the formulation and execution of policy.

To take another approach, the tendency to treat geopolitics as a subject focused on international relations begs two questions. First, why should geopolitics not address other forms of politics that have a spatial dimension, including the dimension of activity on city streets[1] and the politics of urban development? This question is particularly valid given the more general issue of geographic perspectives on history.[2] Second, if attention in geopolitical studies is restricted to, or focuses on, international relations, how far is the treatment of the subject to depart from the classic political agenda, primarily of states but also of international institutions, agreements and attitudes seen as the accumulation of state views, or as an international system in which, aside from the system, states are the constituent parts?

The second question has engaged most attention, notably, but not only, from those advocating a 'critical geopolitics'. Indeed, their very approach qualifies the role and perspective of both state and nation. Instead, there is a preference in 'critical geopolitics' for alternative voices, as well as for transnational (comparative) approaches and concerns, although there is no need to adopt a self-critical position in order to follow either approach. While this shift is not without value, there is a tendency, as in historical scholarship, to underplay the place of the state, if not to treat it as malign, and each of these tendencies is questionable. It is far from clear that effective governance can be organised in alternative forms, while, liked or not, the state remains the key player in international and domestic politics, as well as a vital source of identity. This emphasis on the state as key player is likely to become more pronounced as a consequence of the recession that began in 2008, as that will probably encourage protectionism in both government policy and public attitudes.

Irrespective of these points, there is a distinction between an appreciation of the role of geography and geopolitics, and, on the other hand, grand geopolitical theories.[3] Key issues can be addressed as geopolitical, not least the availability of resources and the resulting sensitivity of particular regions. Geopolitics is definitely useful when discussing the influence of geography (for example distance) on interstate politics and also when considering specific regions with their particular regional characteristics, as opposed to other regions with different characteristics. Linked to this is the issue of communications, with geopolitical considerations providing a key measure of the importance of changes. Thus, just as the consequences of the opening of the Suez (1869) and Panama (1914) canals in the late nineteenth century and the building of the Trans-Siberian Railway (between 1891 and 1917) involved geopolitical and geostrategic elements, so also with the likely opening of sea passages through the Arctic, to the north of both North America and Russia.

The value of routes is also a matter of cultural expression for political goals, as with the Chinese welcoming of Gavin Menzies' tendentious theory that the Chinese circumnavigated the globe in 1421.[4] The *China Daily* was happy to claim in July 2004 that the Chinese did so well before Columbus and Magellan, and their great fifteenth-century admiral, Zheng He, was commemorated in 2005. Other uses of spatial elements in the past, such as patterns of settlement or territorial extent, constitute a geopolitics that is designed to be of political value in the present and the future.

Changes to communications and transport routes serve as a reminder of the spatial dimensions, not only of power but also of interest, specifically state interests and those of, for example, major companies, and of the interest of concern that accompanies them. Interests and interest lead to, and reflect, commitments and tasks, both of which are very important to geopolitics. Indeed, the focus, in discussion of changing military technology, on the impact of air and, even more, space power, with the shrinking of the world that this impact entails, and the apparent banishing of spatial distinctions, tells us more about these advanced capabilities than about the tasks that states and militaries pursue. These tasks relate to state interests, and these have a spatial component, internally and externally, which helps explain the importance of geopolitics.

Of course the spatial component of state interests is made dynamic not only by changes in particular states and in the means of state action, for example military technology, but also in relationships within and between regions. Thus, for example, the geostrategic interests of the great powers have been very important for the Baltic/Nordic region and have helped direct its geopolitics. This dynamic interaction has ranged across issues such as trade, notably in naval stores and iron, as well as the Danish Straits as a choke point into the Baltic, Finland as a threat to, or security zone for, St Petersburg, and the Norwegian fjords as bases for forces attacking transatlantic communications.

More generally, such points indicate the value of geopolitics. If it is seen along the line of Mackinder's 'he who controls the Eurasian Heartland controls the world' or similar adages, then geopolitics is too vague and of use largely for rhetorical purposes. Moreover, some of the concepts, such as that of a geopolitical centre,[5] are problematic. However, if what is meant by geopolitics is that geography is an essential factor in understanding a country's foreign policy, then geopolitics is very important. For example, it is near impossible to understand the history of British and Russian strategic foreign policies without taking into consideration their geographic circumstances.

Looked at differently, however, state interests should be seen in terms of the ability of groups to present their views in these terms. In this light, geopolitics emerges as a central part of the debate in which such views are advanced and are identified with those of states. Thus, geopolitics becomes an argument about power, rather than a discourse of power. Indeed, in considering the treatment of Mackinder's Heartland theory in post-Soviet geopolitical discourse, Mark Bassin and Konstantin Aksenov have emphasised the conceptual plasticity of the theory, going on to suggest that

> the popular appeal of geopolitics more generally rests significantly on its ability to generate what it calls 'objective' geographical models of political relations which in fact are open to reinterpretation and even realignment, in response precisely to those shifts in historical, political, and ideological context which it claims categorically to transcend.[6]

These responses provide an obvious subject for study by those interested in a historicised approach to geopolitics, including historians. Similarly, the changing use of particular arguments is best understood in terms of a discussion of the historical context.[7]

The self-styled 'critical geopolitics', with their emphasis on how material realities are inserted into discursive contexts, can be incorporated into an account of geopolitics as an argument about power, an aspect that is particularly effective in terms of the fashionable academic culture of recent decades. From this perspective, the aggressively left-wing nature of 'critical geopolitics' becomes an understandable factor in light of the dynamics of the debate and the determination to advance concepts of interest; rather than this left-wing nature being a feature of 'critical geopolitics' that necessarily vitiates its value. Gearóid Ó Tuathail closes his critical account of geopolitics, one in which the latter is seen as 'organically connected' to militarism, by claiming, 'Critical geopolitics is one of many cultures of resistance to Geography as imperial truth, state-capitalized knowledge, and military weapon. It is a small part of a much larger rainbow struggle to decolonize our inherited geographical imagination so that other geo-graphings and other worlds might be possible.'[8]

There is no attempt here, or elsewhere, to conceal the sense of political imperative that the critical geopoliticians espouse. One wonders what response is offered to students who disagree or who pursue realist ideas of geopolitics. At the same time, it is important to stress the diversity of 'critical geopolitics' literature with many different proponents, including feminist, post-colonial and post-structuralist wings.

In short, 'critical geopolitics' is an aspect of a politicised debate, rather than the product of an academic culture as classically understood. Such a distinction and the argument that 'critical geopolitics' would benefit from further historical engagement and contextualisation, however, might seem to beg all sorts of questions about the traditional academic culture, not least about the possibility of objectivity. Indeed, by challenging this possibility, the critical geopoliticians self-consciously elide politicised debate and academic discourse.

The overt nature of such a prejudging of issues scarcely needs underlining. In criticism of this (now establishment) 'critical geopolitics', I could point out a host of problematic arguments in the standard texts and, more generally, an apparent inability to separate substance from style. Quotations at length would drive home these points.

These are not the sole issues, but this book is not the place to discuss the epistemological and philosophical aspects of objectivity. Instead, reprising my argument in the discussion of cartographic accuracy, I would argue for objectivity as valid and possible as an aspiration, whatever the difficulty in execution; and I would also draw attention to the role of autonomous sub-cultures, for example cartographers. That geopolitical arguments (often in the form of maps) have been exploited for propaganda purposes, often brilliantly so, does not mean that they are without values, or simply systems to control territory, by allocating it, or by manipulating the understanding of spatial issues.

Instead, it is necessary to understand the nuances of perception, and therefore representation, and to 'unpick' texts at the same time as appreciating the inherent problems of geopolitical analysis and exposition. For example, a 'Map of the West Coast of Africa . . . Including the Colony of Liberia', published in Philadelphia in 1830 can readily be castigated for its assumptions and languages. Tribes are stereotyped, as with the Dey 'an indolent and inoffensive people', and the interior is presented as lost in benighted obscurity:

> At a distance of from 30 to 60 miles inland, a belt of dense and almost impassable forest occurs along the whole of the coast, of from one to two days journey in breadth, which nearly prevents all intercourse between the maritime and interior tribes, and some of the principal causes why the inland parts of this section of Africa are so entirely unknown to the civilized world.

The last remark now seems ridiculously Western-centric, but there was still the practical problem in 1830 of how best to depict Liberia with the information available, a problem that recurs today.

Geopoliticians could be seen as another group worthy of discussion in these terms, notably those of the inherent difficulty of the subject and the practical problems involved; but, as emerges from this book, there is no coherence to the group. The lack of coherence is not a matter of chronological change, nor of differing national cultures or understandings of geopolitics; although each of those factors are relevant. Instead, there are differing understandings and uses of geopolitics, not least, but not only, between political geographers and political scientists, and between scholars and those in the public sphere, whether as commentators or as planners.

Such a matrix, however, is overly fixed and fails to allow sufficiently for overlaps and mutual impacts. Moreover, categories shift and are capable of a variety of analysis. This point is particularly the case with political geographers, a group that can be taken to cover geopolitics in its varied manifestations. 'Critical geopoliticians' are prone to regard old-school political geographers as reactionaries. Thus, one aspect of the history of geopolitics is of the differing definition of geography and geographers and the changing use of political geography, a point that can be greatly amplified by considering the varied definition of geography and contrasting use of geographers around the world at present.

A further dynamic dimension is that of time. Space and distance seem fixed by the scale, but the very notion of both has changed over time. Moreover, the rate of change in perception is not constant. For example, journeys and concepts of space and time in 1780 were more similar to the situation 230 years earlier than 230 years later. Time is more generally significant because a lack of historical sense cripples any classic understanding of geopolitics.

Geography and politics are closely intertwined, although that no more means that all geography is political than that all politics is geographical. A key element in which geopolitics is useful is that of the global scale, but geopolitics is also of crucial value in the understanding of particular states and communities. If the interconnection of areas in a region is a key sphere for geopolitical consideration, then there is no reason why the region in question should solely be that of the globe. Indeed, more attention needs to be devoted to sub-global levels, rather than to the lure of the world question.

Moreover, the quest for a single explanatory factor, or indeed means of analysis, is unhelpful. Geopolitical writing would benefit greatly from a measure of scepticism in assessing influences and in drawing conclusions, and also from offering more questions than answers. It is a sphere of commentary that is badly in need of a dose of humility.

NOTES

1 INTRODUCTION

1. C. S. Gray, 'Inescapable Geography', *Journal of Strategic Studies*, 22 (1999), pp. 161–77; J. J. Grygiel, *Great Powers and Geopolitical Change* (Baltimore, Md., 2006).
2. For how 'generalising' and 'particularising' approaches in history and the social sciences interact, see J. R. Hall, *Cultures of Inquiry: From Epistemology in Sociohistorical Research* (Cambridge, 1999), chapters 6–8.
3. B. D. Palmer, *Descent into Discourse: The Reification of Language and the Writing of Social History* (Philadelphia, Pa., 1990); E. Fox-Genovese and E. Lasch-Quinn (eds), *Reconstructing History: The Emergence of a New Historical Society* (London, 1999).
4. S. Amin, *Beyond US Hegemony? Assessing the Prospects for a Multipolar World* (New York, 2006).
5. T. Snyder, *The Reconstruction of Nations: Poland, Ukraine, Lithuania, Belarus, 1569–1999* (New Haven, Conn., 2003).
6. N. Smith, *American Empire: Roosevelt's Geographer and the Prelude to Globalization* (Berkeley, Calif., 2003), p. 21.
7. For a perceptive critique, see J. H. Andrews, 'Introduction: Meaning, Knowledge, and Power in the Map Philosophy of J. B. Harley', in P. Laxton (ed.), *The New Nature of Maps: Essays in the History of Cartography by J. B. Harley* (Baltimore, Md., 2001), pp. 1–32. For an effective collection of essays, see J. R. Akerman and R. W. Carrow (eds), *Maps: Finding our Place in the World* (Chicago, Ill., 2007).
8. For a revisionist historian who has engaged in self-critical work on the Cold War and can be contrasted to Neil Smith, see J. L. Gaddis, *We Now Know* (Oxford, 1997).
9. Smith, *American Empire*, p. 22.
10. Smith, *American Empire*, p. 374.
11. For a comparison made by a UN representation, see http://www.presstv.ir/detail.aspx?id=83418&sectionid=351021701 (accessed 16 February 2009). In Britain, the Labour politician Ken Livingstone made the comparison.

12. Smith, *American Empire,* p. 373.
13. Smith, *American Empire,* p. 7.
14. N. Smith, 'Scales of Terror and the Resort to Geography: September 11, October 7', *Environment and Planning D: Society and Space,* 19 (2002), pp. 631–7.
15. G. Ó Tuathail, S. Dalby and P. Routledge (eds), *The Geopolitics Reader* (2nd edn, London, 2006), p. 216.
16. Ó Tuathail et al., *The Geopolitics Reader,* pp. 276, 279–80.
17. D. Gregory, *The Colonial Present: Afghanistan, Palestine, and Iraq* (Malden, Mass., 2004).
18. K. Dodds, *Pink Ice: Britain and the South Atlantic Empire* (London, 2002).
19. K. Dodds, *Geopolitics: A Very Short Introduction* (Oxford, c. 2007), p. 15.
20. For example, Dodds, *Geopolitics,* p. 55.
21. Dodds, *Geopolitics,* p. 75.
22. J. Agnew, *Geopolitics* (London, 2003), p. 132.
23. V. Mamadouh, 'Geography and War, Geographers and Peace', in C. Flint (ed.), *The Geography of War and Peace* (Oxford, 2005), p. 41.
24. C. Flint, *Introduction to Geopolitics* (London, 2007), p. 212.
25. Although see the valuable K. Takeuchi, 'Japanese Geopolitics in the 1930s and 1940s', in K. Dodds and D. Atkinson (eds), *Geopolitical Traditions: A Century of Geopolitical Thought* (London, 2000), pp. 72–92.
26. M. D. Lewis, 'Geographies of Power: The Tunisian Civic Order, Jurisdictional Politics, and Imperial Rivalry in the Mediterranean, 1881–1935', *Journal of Modern History,* 80 (2008), pp. 791–830.
27. M. Brückner, *The Geographic Revolution in Early America: Maps, Literacy and National Identity* (Chapel Hill, NC, 2006), pp. 115–16. (For an example of Smith's prose, see p. 5.)
28. H. Sicherman, 'The Revival of Geopolitics', *Intercollegiate Review* (spring 2002), p. 17.
29. Subjectivity over time points to the historian's role.
30. E. W. Fox, *History in Geographic Perspective: The Other France* (New York, 1971), pp. 21–3.
31. G. Sloan, 'Ireland and the Geopolitics of Anglo-Irish Relations', *Irish Studies Review,* 15 (2007), p. 165.
32. D. Buisseret (ed.), *Oxford Companion to World Exploration* (New York, 2007), plate 8.

33. M. Monmonier, *How to Lie with Maps* (Chicago, Ill., 1991).
34. J. Baylis and S. Smith, *The Globalization of World Politics: An Introduction to International Relations* (3rd edn, Oxford, 2005) offers a good instance of the general situation.
35. Brückner, *Geographic Revolution in Early America*.
36. See, for example, P. Kelly, 'A Critique of Critical Geopolitics', *Geopolitics*, 11, 1 (2006), pp. 24–53.
37. H. J. Mackinder, *Britain and the British Seas* (Oxford, 1902), p. 19.
38. M. Z. Ispahani, *Roads and Rivals: The Political Uses of Access in the Borderlands of Asia* (Ithaca, NY, 1989); J. J. Bukowczyk, N. Faires, D. R. Smith and R. W. Widdis, *Permeable Border: The Great Lakes Basin as Transnational Region, 1650–1990* (Pittsburgh, Pa., 2005).
39. M. Trachtenberg, *A Constructed Peace: The Making of the European Settlement, 1945–1963* (Princeton, NJ, 1999).
40. C. Dale Walton, *Geopolitics and the Great Powers in the Twenty-First Century: Multipolarity and the Revolution in Strategic Perspective* (New York, 2007); C. S. Gray, *After Iraq: The Search for a Sustainable National Security Strategy* (Carlisle, Pa., 2009), pp. 7–9.
41. N. Spykman, *The Geography of the Peace* (New York, 1944).
42. H.-T. Lin, 'From Rimland to Heartland: Nationalist China's Geopolitics and Ethnopolitics in Central Asia, 1937–1952', *International History Review*, 30 (2008), pp. 52–75.
43. J. Walsh, 'China and the New Geopolitics of Central Asia', *Asian Survey*, 23 (1993), pp. 272–84; A. Banuazizi and M. Weiner (eds), *The New Geopolitics of Central Asia And Its Borderlands* (Bloomington, Ind., 1994).
44. 'Central Asia and the Caucasus: On the Centenary of Halford Mackinder's Geographical Pivot of History', special issue, *Journal of Social and Political Studies*, 4 (2005).
45. G. Parker, *The Grand Strategy of Philip II* (New Haven, Conn., 1998). For the similar application of the term 'Realpolitik' to earlier periods, see, for example, H. M. Scott, 'Religion and Realpolitik: The Duc of Choiseul, the Bourbon Family Compact, and the Attack on the Society of Jesus, 1758–1775', *International History Review*, 25 (2003), pp. 37–62.
46. T. Claydon, *Europe and the Making of England, 1660–1760* (Cambridge, 2007), pp. 13–66.

47. C. S. Gray, *National Security Dilemmas. Challenges and Opportunities* (Washington, DC, 2009), p. 107.
48. M. Heffernan, '*Fin De Siècle, Fin Du Monde?* On the Origins of European Geopolitics, 1890–1920', in K. Dodds and D. Atkinson (eds), *Geopolitical Traditions* (London, 2000), pp. 27–51; F. Driver, *Geography Militant: Cultures of Exploration and Empire* (Oxford, 2001).
49. M. Geyer and C. Bright, 'Global Violence and Nationalizing Wars in Eurasia and America: The Geopolitics of War in the Mid-Nineteenth Century', *Comparative Studies in Society and History*, 38 (1996), p. 651.
50. Geyer and Bright, 'Global Violence and Nationalizing Wars', p. 652.
51. Geyer and Bright, 'Global Violence and Nationalizing Wars', p. 652.
52. Geyer and Bright, 'Global Violence and Nationalizing Wars', p. 652.
53. Geyer and Bright, 'Global Violence and Nationalizing Wars', p. 653.

2 GEOPOLITICS BEFORE THE TERM: SPATIALITY AND FRONTIERS

1. L. B. Cormack, 'Flat Earth or Round Sphere: Misconceptions of the Shape of the Earth and the Fifteenth-Century Transformation of the World', *Ecumene,* 1 (1994), p. 379.
2. I have benefited from reading unpublished work by Timothy May. I am grateful to him for sending it.
3. J. B. Harley and D. Woodward (eds), *The History of Cartography,* II, 1 *Cartography in the Traditional Islamic and South Asian Societies* (Chicago, Ill., 1992).
4. J. Rickard, *The Castle Community: The Personnel of English and Welsh Castles, 1272–1422* (Woodbridge, 2002), p. 25.
5. J. Gommans, *Mughal Warfare: Indian Frontiers and High Roads to Empire, 1500–1700* (London, 2002).
6. S. P. Huntington, *The Clash of Civilizations and the Remaking of World Order* (New York, 1996).
7. T. J. Barfield, *The Perilous Frontier: Nomadic Empires and China* (Oxford, 1989); S. Jagehild and V. J. Symons, *Peace, War, and Trade along the Great Wall: Nomadic-Chinese Interaction through Two Millennia* (Bloomington, Ind., 1989); A. M. Khazanov, 'Muhammad and Jenghiz Khan

Compared: The Religious Factor in World Empire Building', *Comparative Studies in History and Society,* 35 (1993), pp. 474–5; C. Halperin, *Russia and the Golden Horde* (London, 1987). For the earlier period, N. di Cosmo, *Ancient China and Its Enemies* (Cambridge, 2004).

8. C. R. Whittaker, *Les Frontières de l'Empire Romain* (Besançon, 1989), p. 32; B. Isaac, *The Limits of Empire: The Roman Army in the East* (2nd edn, Oxford, 1992), pp. 3, 417, 419, 426.
9. C. Nicolet, *Space, Geography and Politics in the Early Roman Empire* (Ann Arbor, Mich., 1991).
10. J. Thornton, *Africa and Africans in the Making of the Atlantic World, 1400–1800* (2nd edn, Cambridge, 1998) and *Warfare in Atlantic Africa, 1500–1800* (London, 1999).
11. E. Luttwak, *The Grand Strategy of the Roman Empire from the First Century* AD *to the Third* (Baltimore, Md., 1976); *The Grand Strategy of the Byzantine Empire* (Cambridge, Mass., 2008). I would like to thank Edward Luttwak for sending a pre-publication copy of part of the book.
12. A. Ferrill, *Roman Imperial Grand Strategy* (Lanham, Md., 1991); E. Wheeler, 'Methodological Limits and the Mirage of Roman Strategy', *Journal of Military History,* 57 (1993), pp. 71–4, 215–40.
13. H. J. Mackinder, 'Man-Power as a Measure of National and Imperial Strength', *National and English Review,* 45 (1905), pp. 136–43.
14. J. Black, *The Curse of History* (London, 2008).
15. A. J. Bacevich (ed.), *The Imperial Tense: Prospects and Problems of American Empire* (Chicago, Ill., 2003); H. James, *The Roman Predicament: How the Rules of International Order Create the Politics of Empire* (Princeton, NJ, c. 2006); C. Murphy, *We Are Rome: The Fall of an Empire and the Fate of America* (Boston, Mass., 2007); A. Parchami, *Hegemonic Peace and Empire: The Pax Romana, Britannica and Americana* (London, 2009).
16. K. Kagan, 'Redefining Roman Grand Strategy', *Journal of Military History,* 70 (2006), pp. 333–62, esp. p. 362.
17. G. Parker, *The Grand Strategy of Philip II* (New Haven, Conn., 1998).
18. J. P. LeDonne, *The Russian Empire and the World, 1700–1917: The Geopolitics of Expansion and Containment*

(Oxford, 1997), *The Grand Strategy of the Russian Empire, 1650–1831* (Oxford, 2004), and 'Geopolitics, Logistics, and Grain: Russia's Ambitions in the Black Sea Basin, 1737–1834', *International History Review,* 28 (2006), pp. 1–41.
19. J. Black, *Why Wars Happen* (London, 1998).
20. Thornton, *Africa and Africans.*
21. J. Black, *The Slave Trade* (London, 2006).
22. M. Hendy, *Studies in the Byzantine Monetary Economy* (Cambridge, 1985), pp. 109–23.
23. D. Power and L. N. Standen (eds), *Frontiers in Question 700–1700* (Basingstoke, 1999); D. Power, *The Norman Frontier in the Twelfth and Early Thirteenth Centuries* (Cambridge, 2004).
24. R. R. Davies, *Lordship and Society in the March of Wales* (Oxford, 1978).
25. J. Riley-Smith, *Atlas of the Crusades* (London, 1991), p. 7.
26. R. Bartlett and A. Mackay, *Medieval Frontier Societies* (Oxford, 1990).
27. E. Edson, *The World Map, 1300–1492: The Persistence of Tradition and Transformation* (Baltimore, Md., 2007).
28. J. Marino, 'Administrative Mapping in the Italian States', in D. Buisseret (ed.), *Monarch, Ministers and Maps: The Emergence of Cartography as a Tool of Government in Early Modern Europe* (Chicago, Ill., 1992), p. 5. See also P. D. A. Harvey, *The History of Topographical Maps: Symbols, Pictures, and Surveys* (London, 1980), p. 86.
29. Quotation supplied by David Cohen.
30. Quotation supplied by David Cohen.
31. This section is heavily dependent on advice from David Cohen.
32. This theme was probed in the discussions at a conference 'The Limits of Empire in the Early Modern World' at which I spoke at Ohio State University in February 2009.
33. P. Cozzo, *La geografia celeste dei duchi di Savoia: Religione, devozioni e sacralità in uno Stato di età moderna, secoli XVI–XVII* (Bologna, 2006).
34. H. H. Rowen, *The King's State: Proprietary Dynasticism in Early Modern France* (New Brunswick, NJ, 1980); D. Potter, *War and Government in the French Provinces: Picardy, 1470–1560* (Cambridge, 1993).
35. J. Konvitz, *Cartography in France, 1660–1848* (Chicago, Ill.,

1987). See also D. Buisseret, 'Monarchs, Ministers, and Maps in France before the Accession of Louis XIV', in D. Buisseret (ed.), *Monarch, Ministers and Maps: The Emergence of Cartography as a Tool of Government in Early Modern Europe* (Chicago, Ill., 1992), pp. 99–123, especially pp. 99–101.

36. O. Subtelny, *Domination of Eastern Europe: Native Nobilities and Foreign Absolutism, 1500–1715* (Kingston, Ontario, 1986).
37. A. Bitis, *Russia and the Eastern Question: Army, Government, and Society, 1815–1833* (Oxford, 2006).
38. G. Parker, *The Army of Flanders and the Spanish Road, 1567–1659: The Logistics of Spanish Victory and Defeat in the Low Countries' Wars* (Cambridge, 1972).
39. V. Aksan, 'Whose Territory and Whose Peasants? Ottoman Boundaries on the Danube in the 1760s', in F. F. Anscombe (ed.), *The Ottoman Balkans, 1750–1830* (Princeton, NJ, 2006), pp. 61–86.
40. B. L. Davies, *Warfare, State and Society on the Black Sea Steppe, 1500–1700* (London, 2007), p. 205.
41. B. Downing, *The Military Revolution and Political Change: Origins of Democracy and Autocracy in Early Modern Europe* (Princeton, NJ, 1992); T. Ertman, *Birth of the Leviathan* (Cambridge, 1997).
42. J. Lukowski, *The Partitions of Poland, 1772, 1793, 1795* (London, 1999).

3 GEOPOLITICS BEFORE THE TERM: MAPS

1. P. J. Speelman (ed.), *War, Society and Enlightenment: The Works of General Lloyd* (Leiden, 2005), pp. 23, 27.
2. For an attempt to depict topography, in the case of the battle of Glenshiel of 1719 between British forces and Spanish invaders, British Library, Department of Manuscripts (hereafter BL. Add.) 613436.
3. J. R. Hale, 'Warfare and Cartography, ca. 1450 to ca. 1640', in D. Woodward, *The History of Cartography*, III: *Cartography in the European Renaissance* (Chicago, Ill., 2007), p. 723.
4. J. B. Harley, 'Contemporary Mapping of the American Revolutionary War', in J. B. Harley, B. B. Petchenik and L. W. Towner (eds), *Mapping the American Revolutionary War* (Chicago, Ill., 1978), p. 23.

5. J. C. Hosmer, *The Narrative of Gage's Spies, March 1775, with Notes* (Boston, 1912), pp. 9–11.
6. R. A. Durbin, 'Mapping the Wisconsin River', *Wisconsin Magazine of History,* 70 (1987), p. 257.
7. Hosmer, *The Narrative of Gage's Spies,* p. 35.
8. H. Rice and A. Brown, *The American Campaigns of Rochambeau's Army* (2 vols., Princeton, NJ, 1972), esp. Vol. II, Figs. 26–91.
9. G. Parker, *The Army of Flanders and the Spanish Road, 1567–1659: The Logistics of Spanish Victory and Defeat in the Low Countries' Wars* (Cambridge, 1972).
10. J. B. Harley and D. Woodward (eds), *The History of Cartography,* II, 2, *Cartography in the Traditional East and Southeast Asian Societies* (Chicago, Ill., 1994), p. 700. For a Turkish military map, see J. B. Harley and D. Woodward (eds), *The History of Cartography,* II, 1, *Cartography in the Traditional Islamic and South Asian Societies* (Chicago, Ill., 1992), p. 211.
11. D. Kupisz, *Polock 1579* (Warsaw, 2003), p. 96; M. J. Mikos, 'The Polish Kings and Cartography', *Imago Mundi,* 41 (1989), pp. 76–86; A. V. Lavrent'ev, 'Zapiska gosudarevym mernym verstam I stanom togo krymskogo pokhodu po verstam mernogo kolesu, 1689, g.', in R. A. Simonov (ed.), *Estestvenno-nauchnye predstavleniia drevnei Rusi* (Moscow, 1988), pp. 208–19; J. Cracraft, *The Petrine Revolution in Russian Imagery* (Chicago, Ill., 1997) and *The Petrine Revolution in Russian Culture* (Boston, Mass., 2004); V. Kivelson, *Cartographies of Tsardom: The Land and Its Meanings in Seventeenth-Century Russia* (Ithaca, NY, 2006). I am most grateful to Brian Davies for his advice.
12. J. Konvitz, *Cartography in France, 1660–1848: Science, Engineering and Statecraft* (Chicago, Ill., 1987).
13. J. Black, 'Government, State, and Cartography: Mapping, Power, and Politics in Europe, 1650–1800', *Cartographica,* 43 (2008), pp. 98–9.
14. Harley, 'Contemporary Mapping of the American Revolutionary War', p. 27.
15. G. N. D. Evans, *Uncommon Obdurate: The Several Public Careers of J. F. W. DesBarres* (Peabody, Mass., 1969).
16. K. Zandvliet, *Mapping for Money: Maps, Plans and Topographic Paintings and their role in Dutch Overseas*

Expansion during the 16th and 17th Centuries (Amsterdam, 1998).
17. C. Verner, *Introduction, The English Pilot: The Fourth Book* (London, 1689). Facsimile of original (Amsterdam, 1967).
18. A. V. Postnikov, 'The Russian Navy as Chartmaker in the Eighteenth Century', *Imago Mundi,* 52 (2000), pp. 79–95.
19. D. Howse and N. J. W. Thrower, *A Buccaneer's Atlas: Basil Ringrose's South Sea Waggoner* (Berkeley, Calif., 1992).
20. G. Agoston, 'Information, Ideology, and Limits of Imperial Policy: Ottoman Grand Strategy in the Context of Ottoman-Habsburg Rivalry', in V. H. Aksan and D. Goffman (eds), *The Early Modern Ottomans: Remapping the Empire* (Cambridge, 2007), pp. 80–1.
21. J. F. Chance, *The Alliance of Hanover* (London, 1923), pp. 708–25.
22. Draft with views of Charles, 2nd Viscount Townshend, Secretary of State for the Northern Department, May 1727, BL. Add. 48981, fol. 214.
23. La Manche, c. 1762, BL. Add. 74751.
24. Accessible through the website of the Staatsarchiv in Marburg: www.digam.net.
25. BL. Royal M518. D. III. fols 82–3.
26. J. Harris, 3rd Earl of Malmesbury (ed.), *Diaries and Correspondence of James Harris, First Earl of Malmesbury* (4 vols., London, 1844), Vol. II, pp. 304–6.
27. Canning to John Hookham Frere, 20 June 1800, BL. Add. 38833. William Pitt the Younger was British Prime Minister.
28. T. C. W. Blanning, *The Culture of Power and the Power of Culture: Old Regime Europe 1660–1789* (Oxford, 2002).
29. J. A. Downie, 'Public and Private: The Myth of the Bourgeois Public Sphere', in C. Wall (ed.), *A Concise Companion to the Restoration and Eighteenth Century* (Oxford, 2005), pp. 58–79.
30. J. Black, *European Warfare in its Global Context, 1660–1815* (London, 2006).
31. BL. Add. 17740.
32. For a copy from c. 1720, BL. Maps cc. 6. a. 2.
33. William, Lord Auckland, envoy in The Hague, to William, Lord Grenville, Home Secretary, 29 January 1791, BL. Add. 58919 fol. 33; Auckland to James Bland Burges, Under-

Secretary in the Foreign Office, 1, 9 March 1791, Bodleian Library, Oxford, Bland Burges papers, vol. 30, fols. 129, 133.

34. M. H. Edney, 'John Mitchell's Map of North America (1755): A Study of the Use and Publication of Official Maps in Eighteenth-Century Britain', *Imago Mundi,* 60 (2008), pp. 63–85.
35. L. C. Wroth, *An American Bookshelf, 1755* (Philadelphia, Pa., 1934; reprinted New York, 1969), pp. 132–42.
36. Montresor to Amherst, 18 October 1760, London, National Archives (hereafter NA), War Office papers 34/83, fols. 120–1.
37. Montresor to Amherst, 18 October 1760.
38. The first edition was dated 1775, although printed in 1776, the edition dated 1776 was printed in 1777, and that dated 1778 possibly as late as 1782.
39. G. F. J. Frentzel, *Carte von dem Hafen und der Stad Boston* (Leipzig, 1776); A. Krieger and D. Cobb (eds), *Mapping Boston* (Cambridge, Mass., 2001), plate 27, p. 181.
40. *Plan of Boston and Its Environs, Showing the True Situation of His Majesty's Army and Also Those of the Rebels* (1776); K. Nebenzahl, *A Bibliography of Printed Battle Plans of the American Revolution, 1775–1795* (Chicago, Ill., 1975), map 5; *Map of the Seat of War in New England* (1776); Krieger and Cobb, *Mapping Boston,* p. 103.
41. G.-L. Le Rouge, *Plan de l'armée de Cornwallis attaqué et faite prisonnière dans York Town, Le 19 8bre par l'Armée Combinée Française et Americaine Dessinée sur les Lieux par les Ingénieurs de l'Armée* (Paris, 1781); K. Nebenzahl and D. Higginbotham, *Atlas of the American Revolution* (Chicago, Ill., 1974), map 47.
42. *Literary Magazine,* 15 October 1756.
43. Grenville, by then Foreign Secretary, to George III, 25 September; George III to Grenville, 26 September 1792, BL. Add. 58857.
44. M. Pedley, *The Commerce of Cartography: Making and Marketing Maps in Eighteenth-Century France and England* (Chicago, Ill., 2005).
45. M. Poovey, *A History of the Modern Fact: Problems of Knowledge in the Sciences of Wealth and Society* (Chicago, Ill., 1998); E. Higgs, *The Information State in England* (Basingstoke, 2004).
46. E. Lund, *War for the Every Day: Generals, Knowledge, and*

Warfare in Early Modern Europe, 1680–1740 (Westport, Conn., 1999); M. Jacob, *Scientific Culture and the Making of the Industrial West* (Oxford, 1997).

47. J. Pallière, 'Un grand réconnu du XVIIIe siècle: Pierre Bourçet, 1700–1780', *Revue Historique des Armées* (1979), pp. 51–66.
48. Y. O'Donaghue, *William Roy, 1726–1790: Pioneer of the Ordnance Survey* (London, 1997).
49. For a more positive situation, A. V. Postnikov, 'From Charting to Mapping: Russian Military Mapping of Corfu in the Early Nineteenth Century', *Imago Mundi,* 53 (2000), pp. 83–96.
50. T. Hutchins, *A New Map of the Western Parts of Virginia . . . Comprehending the River Ohio* (London, 1778); W. P. Cumming, *British Maps of Colonial America* (Chicago, Ill., 1974), p. 36.
51. E. I. O. von Odeleben, *A Circumstantial Narrative of the Campaign in Saxony* (London, 1820), vol. I, p. 145.
52. For Lieutenant-General August, Count Gneisenau, the key figure in the modernisation of the Prussian army, memorandum from Colonel Christian Ompteda, 1811, in *The Correspondence of George, Prince of Wales, 1770–1812,* Vol. VIII, ed. A. Aspinall (London, 1971), p. 167.
53. A. Wakefield, *The Disordered Police State: German Cameralism as Science and Practice* (Chicago, Ill., 2009).
54. R. J. W. Evans, 'Frontiers and National Identities in Central Europe', *International History Review,* 14 (1992), p. 492.
55. L. Stewart, *The Rise of Public Science: Rhetoric, Technology and Natural Philosophy in Newtonian Britain, 1660–1750* (Cambridge, 1992).
56. A. M. C. Waterman, *Revolution, Economics and Religion: Christian Political Economy, 1798–1833* (Cambridge, 1991), p. 4.
57. P. Dear, *Revolutionizing the Sciences: European Knowledge and its Ambitions, 1500–1700* (Basingstoke, 2001).
58. B. Stone, *Reinterpreting the French Revolution: A Global-Historical Perspective* (Cambridge, 2002), p. 165.
59. Stone, *Reinterpreting the French Revolution,* passim.
60. J. Black, *Rethinking Military History* (London, 2004).
61. W. A. McDougall, *Freedom Just Around the Corner: A New American History, 1585–1828* (New York, 2004), pp. 175–85.

62. For the multiplicity of factors involved, see J. Black, *Crisis of Empire: Britain and America in the Eighteenth Century* (London, 2008), pp. 89–154.
63. R. White, *The Middle Ground: Indians, Empires and Republics in the Great Lakes Region, 1651–1815* (Cambridge, 1991); E. Hinderaker, *Elusive Empires: Constructing Colonialism in the Ohio Valley, 1673–1800* (Cambridge, 1997); F. Cooper and A. L. Stoler, *Tensions of Empire: Colonial Cultures in a Bourgeois World* (Berkeley, Calif., 1997); K. DuVal, *The Native Ground: Indians and Colonists in the Heart of the Continent* (Philadelphia, Pa., 2006).
64. R. Kagan, *Dangerous Nation: America and the World, 1600–1898* (New York, 2006). See also D. Reynolds, *America, Empire of Liberty: A New History* (London, 2009).
65. P. Kennedy, *The Rise and Fall of the Great Powers: Economic Change and Military Conflict from 1500 to 2000* (London, 1988); G. Parker, *The Grand Strategy of Philip II* (New Haven, Conn., 1998).
66. J. Black, *Great Powers and the Quest for Hegemony: The World Order since 1500* (New York, 2008), pp. 37–51; J. J. Grygiel, *Great Powers and Geopolitical Change* (Baltimore, Md.), p. 121.
67. R. V. Kubicek, 'The Role of Shallow-Draft Steamboats in the Expansion of the British Empire, 1820–1914', *International Journal of Maritime History*, 6 (1994), pp. 86–106.
68. T. Winichakul, *Siam Mapped: A History of the Geo-Body of a Nation* (Honolulu, Hawaii, 1994).

4 THE GEOPOLITICS OF BRITISH POWER, 1500–1900

1. Paris, Archives du Ministère des Relations Extérieures, Correspondance Politique (hereafter AE. CP.), Angleterre 579, fol. 314.
2. D. A. Bell, *The Cult of the Nation in France: Inventing Nationalism, 1680–1800* (Cambridge, Mass., 2001).
3. H. Kearney, *The British Isles: A History of Four Nations* (Cambridge, 1989).
4. T. Tackett, *Religion, Revolution and Regional Culture in Eighteenth-Century France: The Ecclesiastical Oath of 1791* (Princeton, NJ, 1986); see, more generally, X. de Planhol, *An Historical Geography of France* (Cambridge, 1994).
5. D. Woodward (ed.), *The History of Cartography,* III:

Cartography in the European Renaissance (2 vols., Chicago, Ill., 2007).

6. D. Armitage, *The Ideological Origins of the British Empire* (Cambridge, 2000).
7. R. Jervis, *Perception and Misperception in International Politics* (Princeton, NJ, 1976); K. Booth, *Strategy and Ethnocentrism* (London, 1979); C. G. Reynolds, 'Reconsidering American Strategic History and Doctrines', in his *History of the Sea: Essays on Maritime Strategies* (Columbia, SC, 1989); A. I. Johnston, *Cultural Realism: Strategic Culture and Grand Strategy in Chinese History* (Princeton, NJ, 1995); C. S. Gray, 'Strategic Culture as Context: The First Generation of Theory Strikes Back', *Review of International Studies,* 25 (1999), pp. 49–70; L. Sondhaus, 'The Strategic Culture of the Habsburg Army', *Austrian History Yearbook,* 32 (2001), pp. 225–34; W. Murray, 'Does Military Culture Matter', in J. F. Lehman and H. Sicherman (eds), *America the Vulnerable: Our Military Problems and How to Fix Them* (Philadelphia, Pa., 2002), pp. 134–51. For valuable historical applications, E. Ringman, *Identity, Interest and Action: A Cultural Explanation of Sweden's Intervention in the Thirty Years War* (Cambridge, 1996) and G. Parker, *The Grand Strategy of Philip II* (New Haven, Conn., 1998).
8. For example, A. R. Lewis, *The American Culture of War* (New York, 2007).
9. T. Farrell, *The Norms of War: Cultural Beliefs and Modern Conflict* (Boulder, Col., 2005).
10. J. B. Hattendorf, *England in the War of the Spanish Succession: A Study of the English View and Conduct of Grand Strategy, 1701–1712* (New York, 1987); N. A. M. Rodger, 'The Idea of Naval Strategy in Britain in the Eighteenth and Nineteenth Centuries', in G. Till (ed.), *The Development of British Naval Thinking* (London, 2006), pp. 19–33. For the significance of strategic political economy in the context of competing empires, J. I. Israel, *Empires and Entrepôts: The Dutch, the Spanish Monarchy and the Jews, 1585–1713* (London, 1990); J. D. Tracy (ed.), *The Political Economy of Merchant Empires: State Power and World Trade, 1350–1750* (Cambridge, 1991).
11. H. Kleinschmidt, *The Nemesis of Power* (London, 2000), esp. pp. 114–70 and 'Systeme und Ordnungen in der

Geschicht der internationalen Beziehungen', *Archiv für kulturgeschichte,* 82 (2000), pp. 433–54; A. Osiander, *The States System of Europe, 1640–1990: Peacemaking and the Conditions of International Stability* (Oxford, 1994).

12. P. W. Schroeder, *The Transformation of European Politics 1763–1848* (Oxford, 1994), pp. 6–7.
13. M. Schlenke, *England und das friderizianische Preussen, 1740–1763* (Munich, 1963), pp. 171–225.
14. G. Yagi Jr., 'A Study of Britain's Military Failure During the Initial Stages of the Seven Years' War in North America, 1754–1758' (Exeter, Ph.D., 2007).
15. B. Harris, *Politics and the Nation: Britain in the Mid-Eighteenth Century* (Oxford, 2002).
16. For example, *Journals of the Board of Trade and Plantations*, 61, 14 November 1753, noting the Order of Council of 10 August 1753; as well as pre-war British interests in mapping British land claims.
17. K. Wilson, *The Sense of the People: Politics, Culture and Imperialism in England, 1715–1785* (Cambridge, 1995).
18. R. Lodge (ed.), *The Private Correspondence of Sir Benjamin Keene* (London, 1933); J. McLachlan, *Trade and Peace with Old Spain, 1667–1750* (Cambridge, 1940).
19. J. Black, 'Debating Britain and Europe, 1688–1815', *British Scholar*, 1 (2008), pp. 37–52.
20. M. Pedley, 'Map Wars: The Role of Maps in the Nova Scotia/Acadia Boundary Disputes of 1750', *Imago Mundi*, 50 (1998), pp. 96–104.
21. Bedford to Benjamin Keene, 6 July (os) 1749, NA. State Papers (hereafter SP), 94/136 fol. 1.
22. Cumberland to Henry Fox, 23 September 1757, Earl of Ilchester, *Letters to Henry Fox* (London, 1915), p. 120.
23. J. Black, *George III* (New Haven, Conn., 2006) and *George II* (Exeter, 2007).
24. On Pitt's attitudes, J. Black, 'Pitt the Elder and the Foundation of an Imperial Foreign Policy', in T. G. Otte (ed.), *The Makers of British Foreign Policy: From Pitt to Thatcher* (Basingstoke, 2002), pp. 35–51.
25. U. Dann, *Hanover and Great Britain, 1740–1760* (Leicester, 1991), pp. 94–8.
26. BL. Add. 32856, fol. 380.
27. BL. Add. 32996, fol. 79.

28. R. Koser (ed), *Politische Correspondenz Friedrichs des Grossen* (46 vols., Berlin, 1879–1939), Vol. X, p. 386.
29. AE. CP. Angleterre, 438, fol. 15.
30. AE. CP. Angleterre, 438, fol. 305; 439, fol. 169.
31. NA. SP. 80/196, fols. 56–7.
32. Dann, *Hanover and Great Britain*, pp. 107–9.
33. AE. CP. Espagne 517, fols 26–8, 192–3, 281–5; A. Bourquet, *Le Duc de Choiseul et l'Alliance Espagnole* (Paris, 1906), pp. 6–7, 25.
34. K. W. Schweizer (ed.), *Lord Bute: Essays in Reinterpretation* (Leicester, 1988).
35. S. J. Hornsby, *British Atlantic, Atlantic Frontier: Spaces of Power in Early Modern British America* (Lebanon, NH, 2005), p. 226.
36. Hornsby, *British Atlantic, Atlantic Frontier,* p. 7.
37. J. B. Harley, 'Maps, Knowledge and Power', in D. Cosgrove and S. Daniels (eds), *The Iconography of Landscape* (Cambridge, 1988), pp. 277–312, and 'Rereading the Maps of the Columbian Encounter', *Annals of the Association of American Geographers*, 82 (1992), pp. 522–42.
38. G. Ó Tuathail, *Critical Geopolitics* (London, 1996), pp. 1–2.
39. I. Griffiths, 'The Scramble for Africa: Inherited Political Boundaries', *Geographical Journal*, 152 (July 1986), pp. 204–16; J. C. Stone, 'Imperialism, Colonialism and Cartography', *Transactions of the Institute of British Geographers,* new series, 13 (1988), pp. 57–64; T. Bassett, 'Cartography and Empire Building in Nineteenth-Century West Africa', *Geographical Review,* 84 (1994), pp. 316–35.
40. M. M. Portuondo, *Secret Science: Spanish Cosmography and the New World* (Chicago, Ill., 2009).
41. L. Cormack, *Charting an Empire: Geography at the English Universities, 1580–1620* (Chicago, Ill., 1997).
42. K. Zandvliet, *Mapping for Money: Maps, Plans and Topographic Paintings and their role in Dutch Overseas Expansion during the 16th and 17th Centuries* (Amsterdam, 1998); D. Headrick, *When Information Came of Age: Technologies of Knowledge in the Age of Reason and Revolution, 1700–1850* (Oxford, 2001). J. R. Akerman (ed.), *The Imperial Map: Cartography and the Mastery of Empire* (Chicago, Ill., 2009).
43. B. L. Walker, 'Mamiya Rinzô and the Japanese Exploration

of Sakhalin Island: Cartography and Empire', *Journal of Historical Geography*, 33 (2007), pp. 283–313.

44. J. H. Casid, *Sowing Empire: Landscape and Colonization* (Minneapolis, Minn., 2005).
45. G. Huggan, 'Decolonising the Map: Post-colonialism, Post-structuralism and the Cartographic Connection', *Ariel*, 20, 4 (1989), p. 127.
46. C. R. Markham, *A Memoir on the Indian Surveys* (2nd edn, London, 1878), pp. 198–206.
47. M. H. Edney, *Mapping an Empire: The Geographic Construction of British India, 1765–1843* (Chicago, Ill., 1997).
48. G. Byrnes, *Boundary Markers: Land Surveying and the Colonisation of New Zealand* (Wellington, 2001).
49. R. Drayton, 'Science and the European Empires', *Journal of Imperial and Commonwealth History*, 23 (1995), pp. 503–11; and R. Macleod (ed.), 'Nature and Empire: Science and the Colonial Enterprise', *Osiris*, 2nd ser., 15 (2000); Akerman, *The Imperial Map*.
50. M. W. Lewis and K. E. Wigen, *The Myth of Continents: A Critique of Metageography* (Berkeley, Calif., 1997).
51. D. Headrick, *The Tools of Empire: Technology and European Imperialism in the Nineteenth Century* (New York, 1981), *The Tentacles of Progress: Technology Transfer in the Age of Imperialism, 1850–1940* (Oxford, 1988), and *The Invisible Weapon: Telecommunications and International Politics, 1851–1945* (Oxford, 1991).
52. D. S. A. Bell, 'Dissolving Distance: Technology, Space, and Empire in British Political Thought, 1770–1900', *Journal of Modern History*, 77 (2005), pp. 523–62, esp. pp. 529, 562.

5 GEOPOLITICS AND THE AGE OF IMPERIALISM, 1890–1945

1. M. Bassin, 'Imperialism and the Nation State in Friedrich Ratzel's Political Geography', *Progress in Human Geography*, 2 (1987), pp. 473–95; H. Wanklin, *Friedrich Ratzel: A Biographical Memoir and Bibliography* (Cambridge, 1961); D. Livingstone, *The Geographical Tradition* (Oxford, 1992), pp. 196–202.
2. M. Heffernan, '*Fin de siècle, fin du monde?* On the Origins of European Geopolitics, 1890–1920', in K. Dodds and

D. Atkinson (eds), *Geopolitical Traditions: A Century of Geopolitical Thought* (London, 2000), pp. 27–51.

3. P. M. Kennedy (ed.), *The War Plans of the Great Powers, 1880–1914* (London, 1979); S. E. Miller, S. M. Lynn-Jones and S. Van Evera (eds), *First World War* (2nd edn, Princeton, NJ, 1991); G. A. Tunstall, *Planning for War Against Russia and Serbia: Austro-Hungarian and German Military Strategies, 1871–1914* (Boulder, Col., 1993).
4. S. Holdar, 'The Ideal State and the Power of Geography: The Life and Work of Rudolf Kjellén', *Political Geography,* 2 (1992), pp. 307–23; B. Haggman, 'Rudolf Kjellén and Modern Swedish Geopolitics', *Geopolitics,* 3 (1998), pp. 99–112.
5. Published in *Geographical Journal,* 23 (1904), pp. 421–37.
6. P. Kennedy, 'Mahan *versus* Mackinder: Two Interpretations of British Sea Power', in P. Kennedy, *Strategy and Diplomacy* (London, 1993), pp. 43–85.
7. Kennedy, 'Mahan *versus* Mackinder'.
8. Kennedy, 'Mahan *versus* Mackinder'.
9. T. G. Otte and K. Neilson (eds), *Railways and International Politics: Paths of Empire, 1848–1945* (London, 2006).
10. For more critical views, H. and M. Sprout, 'Geography and International Politics in an Era of Revolutionary Change', *Journal of Conflict Resolution,* 4 (1960), p. 152; J. J. Grygiel, *Great Powers and Geopolitical Change* (Baltimore, Md., 2006), p. 181.
11. Kennedy, 'Mahan *versus* Mackinder'.
12. H. J. Mackinder, *Britain and the British Seas* (London, 1902), p. 358.
13. H. J. Mackinder, *Our Own Islands* (London, 1906).
14. W. H. Parker, *Mackinder: Geography as an Aid to Statecraft* (Oxford, 1982); B. Blouet, *Halford Mackinder: A Biography* (College Station, Tex., 1987) and B. Blouet (ed.), *Global Geostrategy: Mackinder and the Defence of the West* (London, 2005); G. Ó Tuathail, 'Putting Mackinder in His Place: Material Transformations and Myth', *Political Geographical Quarterly,* 11 (1992), pp. 100–18; A. B. Dugan, 'Mackinder and His Critics Reconsidered', *Journal of Politics,* 24 (1962), pp. 241–57.
15. H. J. Mackinder, 'The Development of Geographical Teaching Out of Nature Study', *Geographical Teacher,* 2 (1904), p. 192.

16. P. J. Cain, *Hobson and Imperialism: Radicalism, New Liberalism, and Finance, 1887–1938* (Oxford, 2002); G. Kearns, 'Fin-de-Siècle Geopolitics: Mackinder, Hobson and Theories of Global Closure', in P. J. Taylor (ed.), *Political Geography of the Twentieth Century: A Global Analysis* (Cambridge, Mass., 1993), pp. 9–30.
17. H. J. Mackinder, *Democratic Ideals and Reality: A Study in the Politics of Reconstruction* (London, 1919), pp. 207–9.
18. Mackinder, *Democratic Ideals and Reality,* p. 203.
19. R. Parkinson, *The Late Victorian Navy: The Pre-Dreadnought Era and the Origins of the First World War* (Woodbridge, 2008).
20. A. T. Mahan, *From Sail to Steam: Recollections of Naval Life* (New York, 1907), p. 277.
21. R. Hobson, *Imperialism at Sea: Naval Strategic Thought, the Ideology of Sea Power, and the Tirpitz Plan, 1875–1914* (Boston, Mass., 2002).
22. P. J. Hugill, *Global Communications since 1844: Geopolitics and Technology* (Baltimore, Md., 1999), and 'The Geopolitical Implications of Communication under the Seas', in B. Finn and D. Yang (eds), *Communications Under the Sea: A Twice-Rejuvenated Nineteenth Century Technology and its Social Implications* (Cambridge, Mass., 2007).
23. J. B. Camerini, 'The Physical Atlas of Heinrich Berghaus: Distribution Maps as Scientific Knowledge', in R. G. Mazzolini (ed.), *Non-Verbal Communication in Science Prior to 1900* (Florence, 1993), pp. 481–2.
24. H. J. Mackinder, 'On the Scope and Methods of Geography', *Proceedings of the Royal Geographical Society,* 9 (1887).
25. R. Peet, 'The Social Origins of Environmental Determinism', *Annals of the Association of American Geographers,* 75 (1985), pp. 309–33.
26. H. C. Darby, *The Relations of History and Geography* (Exeter, 2002), p. 191. Semple was not a full-time geographer at the University of Chicago: she insisted on time for herself and her writing.
27. R. A. Butlin, 'Historical Geographies of the British Empire, *c.* 1887–1925', in M. Bell, R. A. Butlin and M. Hefferman (eds), *Geography and Imperialism, 180–1940* (Manchester, 1995), pp. 169–72.

28. V. Berdoulay, *La Formation de l'école française de géographie, 1870–1914* (2nd edn, Paris, 1995).
29. L. Febvre, *A Geographical Introduction to History* (London, 1925); G. J. Martin, 'Paradigm Change: A History of Geography in the United States, 1892–1925', *National Geographic Research*, 1–2 (1985), pp. 229–31.
30. A. Demangeon and L. Febvre, *Le Rhin: Problèmes d'histoire et d'économie* (Paris, 1935).
31. A. R. H. Baker, 'Reflections on the Relations of Historical Geography and the Annales School of History', in A. R. H. Baker and D. Gregory (eds), *Explorations in Historical Geography* (Cambridge, 1984), pp. 1–27.
32. J. J. Grygiel, *Great Powers and Geopolitical Change* (Baltimore, Md., 2006), p. 168.
33. A. Mombauer, *Helmuth von Moltke and the Origins of the First World War* (Cambridge, 2001); D. Showalter, 'From Deterrence to Doomsday Machine: The German Way of War, 1890–1914', *Journal of Military History,* 64 (2000), pp. 679–710.
34. A. J. Rieber, 'The Origins of the Cold War in Eurasia: A Borderland Perspective', in K. H. Jarausch and T. Lindenberger (eds), *Conflicted Memories: Europeanizing Contemporary Histories* (Oxford, 2007), p. 117.
35. Rieber, 'The Origins of the Cold War in Eurasia', p. 117.
36. See, for example, D. S. A. Bell, 'Dissolving Distance: Technology, Space, and Empire in British Political Thought, 1770–1900', *Journal of Modern History,* 77 (2005), pp. 523–62.
37. V. Liulevicius, *War Land on the Eastern Front: Culture, National Identity and German Occupation in World War I* (Cambridge, 2000).
38. D. Showalter, '"The East Gives Nothing Back": The Great War and the German Army in Russia', *Journal of the Historical Society,* 2 (2002), pp. 1–19, esp. pp. 15–16.
39. G. J. Martin, *The Life and Thought of Isaiah Bowman* (Hamden, Conn., 1980) and *Mark Jefferson, Geographer* (Ypsilanti, Mich., 1968). Jefferson was Chief Cartographer for the USA at the Paris Peace Conference. Geoffrey Martin also edited *Mark Jefferson, Paris Peace Conference Diary* (Ann Arbor, Mich., 1968). N. Smith, *American Empire: Roosevelt's Geographer and the Prelude to Globalisation* (Berkeley, Calif., 2003), p. 173.

40. G. Herb, *Under the Map of Germany: Nationalism and Propaganda, 1918–1945* (London, 1997); D. T. Murphy, *The Heroic Earth: Geopolitical Thought in Weimar Germany, 1918–1933* (Kent, Ohio, 1997).
41. M. Monmonier, 'Mapping Under the Third Reich: Nazi Restrictions on Map Content and Distribution', available online (2004), p. 5.
42. K. Kost, *Die Einflüsse der Geopolitik auf Forschung und Theorie der Politischen Geograpie von ihren Anfängen bis 1945* (Bonn, 1988); M. Burleigh, *Germany Turns Eastwards: A Study of Ostforschung in the Third Reich* (Cambridge, 1988); M. Korinman, *Quand l'Allemagne pensait le monde: grandeur et décadence d'une géopolitique* (Paris, 1990); H. Frei, 'Japan and Australia in Karl Haushofer's Geopolitics of the Pacific Ocean', *Journal of International Studies*, 22 (1989), p. 84; J. Loughlin and H. van der Wusten, 'Political Geography of Panregions', *Geographical Review*, 80 (1990), pp. 2–9.
43. M. Bassin, 'Race contra Space: The Conflict between German *Geopolitik* and National Socialism', *Political Geography Quarterly*, 6 (1987), pp. 115–34.
44. D. Atkinson, 'Geopolitics, Cartography and Geographical Knowledge: Envisioning Africa from Fascist Italy', in M. Bell, R. Butlin and M. Heffernan (eds), *Geography and Imperialism* (Manchester, 1995), pp. 265–97; K. Takeuchi, 'Japanese Geopolitics in the 1930s and 1940s', in K. Dodds and D. Atkinson (eds), *Geopolitical Traditions: A Century of Geopolitical Thought* (London, 2000), pp. 72–92.
45. A. Demangeon, 'Géographie militaire et géographie politique, à propos d'ouvrages récents', *Anales de Géographie*, 31 (1922), 'Géographie politique', *Anales de Géographie,* 41 (1932), and 'Géographie politique, à propos de l'Allemagne', *Anales de Géographie*, 48 (1939).
46. W. Lower, *Nazi Empire-Building and the Holocaust in Ukraine* (Chapel Hill, NC, 2005).
47. S. Heim and G. Aly, 'The Holocaust and Population Policy', *Yad Vashem Studies*, 24 (1994), pp. 45–70; M. A. Doehl and D. B. Clarke, 'Figuring the Holocaust: Singularity and the Purification of Space', in G. Ó Tuathail and S. Dalby (eds), *Rethinking Geopolitics* (London, 1998), pp. 170–97; I. Heinemann, '"Another Type of Perception": The SS Racial

Experts and Forced Population Movements in the Occupied Regions', *Holocaust and Genocide Studies*, 15 (2001), pp. 387–411.

48. I. Kershaw, 'Improvised Genocide? The Emergence of the "Final Solution" in the "Warthegau"', *Transactions of the Royal Historical Society*, 6th ser., 2 (1992), pp. 51–78; C. R. Browning, 'German Killers: Orders from Above, Initiative from Below, and the Scope of Local Autonomy – the Case of Brest-Litovsk', in C. R. Browning, *Nazi Policy, Jewish Workers, German Killers* (Cambridge, 2000), pp. 116–42.
49. M. Mazower, *Hitler's Empire: How the Nazis Ruled Europe* (London, 2008), pp. 414–15.
50. A. Dorpalen, *The World of General Haushofer: Geopolitics in Action* (New York, 1942); K.-H. Harbeck, *Die Zeitschrift für Geopolitik 1924–44* (Kiel, 1963); H. Heske, 'Karl Haushofer: His Role in German Geopolitics and in Nazi Politics', *Political Geography Quarterly*, 6 (1987), pp. 135–44; J. Douglas-Hamilton, 'Hess and the Haushofers', in D. Stafford (ed.), *Flight from Reality: Rudolf Hess and His Mission to Scotland 1941* (London, 2002), pp. 78–103.
51. Mackinder, *Democratic Ideals*, p. 194.
52. H. J. Mackinder, 'Speech at the Presentation of the Medals at the American Embassy', *Geographical Journal,* 103 (1944), pp. 132–3.
53. H. R. Trevor-Roper, *Hitler's Secret Conversations, 1941–44* (New York, 1953), p. xxxii.
54. N. J. W. Goda, *Tomorrow the World: Hitler, Northwest Africa, and the Path Toward America* (College Station, Tex., 1998).
55. See also D. Whittlesey, *German Strategy of World Conquest* (New York, 1942) and D. Whittlesey, 'Haushofer: The Geopoliticians', in E. M. Earl (ed.), *Makers of Modern Strategy: Military Thought from Machiavelli to Hitler* (Princeton, NJ, 1943).
56. I. Bowman, 'Geography versus Geopolitics', *Geographical Review*, 32 (1942).
57. G. Ó Tuathail et al., *The Geopolitics Reader*, p. 30.
58. N. Smith, *American Empire: Roosevelt's Geographer and the Prelude to Globalization* (Berkeley, Calif., 2003); Ó Tuathail et al., *The Geopolitics Reader*, p. 29.
59. G. Kiss, 'Political Geography into Geopolitics: Recent Trends in Germany', *Geographical Review*, 32 (1942), pp. 632–45.

60. H. Morgenthau, *Germany Is Our Problem* (New York, 1945).
61. H. M. Clokie, 'Geopolitics – New Super-science or Old Art?', *Canadian Journal of Economics and Political Science*, 10 (1944), pp. 492–502.
62. N. Spykman, *America's Strategy in World Politics: The United States and the Balance of Power* (New York, 1942) and N. Spykman, *The Geography of the Peace* (New York, 1944). See also S. Van Valkenburg (ed.), *America at War: A Geographical Analysis* (New York, 1942).
63. D. Reynolds, *From Munich to Pearl Harbor: Roosevelt's America and the Origins of the Second World War* (Chicago, Ill., 2001).
64. S. Schulten, *The Geographical Imagination in America, 1880–1950* (Chicago, Ill., 2001).
65. A. P. de Seversky, *Victory Through Air Power* (New York, 1942).
66. T. Hasegawa, *Racing the Enemy: Stalin, Truman, and the Surrender of Japan* (Cambridge, Mass., 2005).

6 GEOPOLITICS AND THE COLD WAR

1. N. Smith, '"Academic War over the Field of Geography": The Elimination of Geography at Harvard, 1947–1951', *Annals of the Association of American Geographers,* 77 (1987), pp. 155–72. I have benefited from advice by Geoffrey Martin on this matter.
2. J. Minghi, '"Do Not Start a Journal on Political Geography": Bowman to Whittlesey – 1945', *Political Geography,* 21 (2002), pp. 731–44.
3. J. Gottmann, 'Geography and International Relations', *World Politics,* 3 (1951), pp. 153–73 and J. Gottmann, 'The Political Partitioning of Our World: An Attempt at Analysis', *World Politics,* 4 (1952), pp. 512–19; R. Hartshorne, 'The Functional Approach in Political Geography', *Annals of the Association of American Geographers,* 40 (1950), pp. 95–130; S. B. Jones, 'A Unified Field Theory of Political Geography', *Annals of the Association of American Geographers,* 44 (1954), pp. 111–23, and 'Global Strategic Views', *Geographical Review,* 45 (1955), pp. 492–508.
4. L. W. Hepple, 'The Revival of Geopolitics', *Political Geography Quarterly,* 5 (1986), supplement, pp. 21–36.

5. D. Livingstone, *The Geographical Tradition* (Oxford, 1992), pp. 290–1, 296. C. Sauer, *The Morphology of Landscape* (Berkeley, Calif., 1938).
6. For example, W. Fitzgerald, *The New Europe: An Introduction to Its Political Geography* (Westport, Conn., 1946); A. E. Moodie, *Geography behind Politics* (London, 1949); H. R. Wilkinson, *Maps and Politics: A Review of the Ethnographic Cartography of Macdonia* (Liverpool, 1951); Y. M. Goblet, *Political Geography and the World Map* (London, 1955).
7. A. R. Millett, *The War for Korea, 1945–1950: A House Burning* (Lawrence, Kans., 2005).
8. R. Hartshorne, 'Political Geography', in P. E. James and C. F. Jones (eds), *American Geography: Inventory and Prospect* (Syracuse, NY, 1954), pp. 211–14.
9. O. Vitovskiy, 'Political Geography and Geopolitics: A Recurrence of American Geopolitics', *Soviet Geography, Review and Translation*, 22 (1981), pp. 586–97.
10. K. Matsuzato, 'The Concept of "Space" in Russian History: Regionalization from the Late Imperial Period to the Present', in T. Hara and K. Matsuzato (eds), *Empire and Society: New Approaches to Russian History* (Sapporo, 1997), pp. 181–4.
11. For a subsequent account of continuities between imperial and Soviet drives, R. Pipes, *Russia Under the Old Regime* (Harmondsworth, 1982), pp. 1–24.
12. R. Strausz-Hupé, 'The Balance of Tomorrow', *Orbis*, 1 (April 1957), pp. 10, 27.
13. C. A. Preble, *John F. Kennedy and the Missile Gap* (DeKalb, Ill., 2004).
14. A. Crampton and G. Ó Tuathail, 'Intellectuals, Institutions and Ideology: The Case of Robert Strausz-Hupé and American Geopolitics', *Political Geography*, 15 (1996), pp. 553–6; H. Sicherman, 'Robert Strausz-Hupé: His Life and Times', *Orbis*, 47 (2003), pp. 195–216.
15. S. B. Cohen, *Geography and Politics in a World Divided* (2nd edn, New York, 1973), 'Global Geopolitical Change in the Post-Cold War Era', *Annals of the Association of American Geographers*, 81 (1991), pp. 551–80, *Geopolitics of the World System* (Lanham, Md., 2002).
16. E. Kurz, *The Kissinger Saga: Walter and Henry Kissinger – Two Brothers from Germany* (London, 2009).

17. T. G. Otte, 'Kissinger', in G. R. Berridge, M. Keens-Soper and T. G. Otte, *Diplomatic Theory from Machiavelli to Kissinger* (Basingstoke, 2001), p. 181.
18. M. Jones, 'Between the Bear and the Dragon: Nixon, Kissinger and U.S. Foreign Policy in the Era of Détente', *English Historical Review*, 123 (2008), p. 1283; J. Suri, *Henry Kissinger and the American Century* (Cambridge, Mass., 2007).
19. W. J. Levy, *Oil Strategy and Politics, 1941–1981* (Boulder, Col., 1982); P. T. Hart, *Saudi Arabia and the United States: Birth of a Security Partnership* (Bloomington, Ind., 1998); R. Bronson, *Thicker than Oil: America's Uneasy Partnership with Saudi Arabia* (New York, 2006).
20. D. Rothkopf, *Running the World: The Inside Story of the National Security Council and the Architects of American Power* (New York, 2005).
21. C. S. Gray, *The Geopolitics of the Nuclear Era: Heartlands, Rimlands, and the Technological Revolution* (New York, 1977). See, more generally, G. Sloan, *Geopolitics in United States Strategic Policy, 1890–1987* (Brighton, 1988).
22. H. Sicherman, 'The Revival of Geopolitics', *Intercollegiate Review* (spring 2002), pp. 16–23.
23. For recent versions, P. Padfield, *Maritime Dominion and the Triumph of the Free World: Naval Campaigns that Shaped the Modern World, 1852–2001* (London, 2008) and W. R. Meade, *God and Gold: Britain, America and the Making of the Modern World* (New York, 2007).
24. P. J. Hugill, 'Trading States, Territorial States, and Technology: Mackinder's Contribution to the Discourse on States and Politics', in B. W. Blouet (ed.), *Global Geostrategy: Mackinder and the Defence of the West* (London, 2005), p. 123.
25. T. E. Ricks, *The Gamble: General David Petraeus and the American Military Adventure in Iraq, 2006–2008* (London, 2009).
26. I. Wallerstein, *The Modern World-System,* I: *Capitalist Agriculture and the Origins of the European World-Economy in the Sixteenth Century* (New York, 1974); Vol. II: *Mercantilism and the Consolidation of the European World-Economy, 1600–1750* (New York, 1980).
27. Y. Lacoste, 'Enquête sur le bombardement des digues du fleuve rouge (Vietnam, été 1972): Méthode d'analyse et réflexions

d'ensemble', *Hérodote*, 1 (1976), pp. 86–117; Y. Lacoste, 'The Geography of Warfare: An Illustration of Geographical Warfare: Bombing of the Dikes on the Red River, North Vietnam', in R. Peet (ed.), *Radical Geography* (London, 1977), pp. 244–62; and Y. Lacoste, *La Géographie, ça sert, d'abord, à faire la guerre* (Paris, 1976); P. Claval, '*Hérodote* and the French Left', and L. W. Hepple, '*Géopolitiques* de Gauche: Yves Lacoste, *Hérodote* and French Radical Geopolitics', in K. Dodds and D. Atkinson (eds), *Geopolitical Traditions: A Century of Political Thought* (London, 2005), pp. 239–301.

28. Y. Lacoste (ed.), *Dictionnaire de géopolitique* (Paris, 1993).
29. H. Kleinschmidt, 'Systeme und Ordnungen in der Geschichte der internationalen Beziehungen', *Archiv für kulturgeschichte*, 82 (2000), pp. 433–54.
30. K. Dodds, *Geopolitics in Antarctica: Views from the Southern Oceanic Rim* (Chichester, 1997).
31. C. S. Gray, 'Britain's National Security: Compulsion and Discretion', *RUSI Journal*, 153 (2008), p. 17.
32. X. Fraudet, *France's Security Independence: Originality and Constraints in Europe, 1981–1995* (Bern, 2006).
33. G. Arriagada, 'Ideology and Politics in the South American Military, Argentina, Brazil, Chile, and Uruguay.' I would like to thank Michael Grow for providing me with a copy of this paper. See also K. Dodds, 'Geopolitics and the Geographical Imagination of Argentina', in K. Dodds and D. Atkinson (eds), *Geopolitical Traditions: A Century of Political Thought* (London, 2005), pp. 150–84.

7 GEOPOLITICS SINCE 1990

1. V. Mamadouh, 'Geopolitics in the Nineties: One Flag, Many Meanings', *Geo-Journal,* 46 (1998), pp. 237–53.
2. S. B. Cohen, 'Geopolitical Realities and United States Foreign Policy', *Political Geography,* 22 (2003), pp. 1–33.
3. N. Kliot and S. Waterman (eds), *The Political Geography of Conflict and Peace* (London, 1991).
4. A. Gheciu, *NATO in the 'New Europe': The Politics of International Socialization after the Cold War* (Palo Alto, Calif., 2005).
5. J. O'Loughlin and H. Henning, 'From 'Geopolitik" to "Geopolitique": Converting a Discipline for War to a Discipline for Peace', in N. Kliot and S. Waterman (eds), *The*

Political Geography of Conflict and Peace (London, 1991), pp. 37–59.

6. W. R. Thompson, 'A Test of a Theory of Co-evolution in War: Lengthening the Western Eurasian Military Trajectory', *International History Review,* 28 (2006), p. 502.
7. F. Fukuyama, 'The End of History?', *The National Interest,* 16 (1989).
8. For example, Gary Schmitt, Executive Director of the Project for the New American Century, 'A Case of Continuity', *The National Interest,* 69 (2002), p. 12.
9. M. W. Corson and J. V. Minghi, 'The Political Geography of the Dayton Accords', *Geopolitics and International Boundaries,* 1 (1996), pp. 82–3.
10. For a critique of the binary divide, see S. Chan, *Out of Evil: New International Politics and the Old Doctrines of War* (Ann Arbor, Mich., 2005).
11. M. Bassin, 'Civilisations and Their Discontents: Political Geography and Geopolitics in the Huntington Thesis', *Geopolitics,* 12 (2007), p. 370.
12. N. Cigar (ed.), *Al-Qa'ida's Doctrine for Insurgency: 'Abd Al-'Aziz Al-Muqrin's 'A Practical Course for Guerrilla War'* (Dulles, Virg., 2009), p. 89.
13. M. Bassin, 'The Emergence of Ethno-Geopolitics in Post-Soviet Russia', *Eurasian Geography and Economics,* 50 (2009), p. 15.
14. Z. Brzezinski, *The Grand Chessboard: American Primacy and its Geostrategic Imperatives* (New York, c. 1997). G. Ó Tuathail, S. Dalby and P. Routledge (eds), *The Geopolitics Reader* (London, 2006).
15. A. Dugin, *Osnovy Geopolitiki* (Moscow, 2000); A. Tsipko, 'In Defense of Russian Sovereignty', *International Affairs: A Russian Journal of World Politics, Diplomacy and International Relations,* 49 (2003), no. 5; M. Bassin, 'Classical Eurasianism and the Geopolitics of Russian Identity', *Ab Imperio,* 4 (2003), pp. 257–67 and 'The Two Faces of Contemporary Geopolitics', *Progress in Human Geography,* 28 (2004), pp. 620–6.
16. R. Henry, 'Transforming the US Global Defense Posture', in C. Lord (ed.), *Reposturing the Force: US Overseas Presence in the Twenty-First Century* (Newport, RI, 2006); A. F. Krepinevich and R. O. Wok, *A New US Global Defense*

Posture for the Second Transoceanic Era (Washington, DC, 2007).

17. T. M. Kane and L. W. Serewicz, 'China's Hunger: The Consequences of a Rising Demand for Food and Energy', *Parameters,* 31, 3 (2001), pp. 56–66.
18. S. A. Yetiv, *Crude Awakenings: Global Oil Security and American Foreign Policy* (Ithaca, NY, 2004).
19. *Quadrennial Defense Review Report* (Washington, DC, 2006), p. 29.
20. W. H. Overholt, *Asia, America, and the Transformation of Geopolitics* (Cambridge, 2008).
21. F. Hoffman, *From Preponderance to Partnership: American Maritime Power in the 21st Century* (Washington, DC, 2008), p. 21.
22. C. Layne, 'The Unipolar Illusion Revisited', *International Security* (autumn 2006), pp. 7–41; R. Haass, 'The Age of Nonpolarity', *Foreign Affairs* (May/June 2008), pp. 44–6.
23. F. Fukuyama, *State-Building: Governance and World Order in the 21st Century* (Ithaca, NY, 2004).
24. G. Ó Tuathail, Simon Dalby and Paul Routledge (eds), *The Geopolitics Reader* (2nd edn, London, 2006), p. 130.
25. D. Harvey, *The New Imperialism* (Oxford, 2003).
26. Harvey, *The New Imperialism*, p. viii.
27. Harvey, *The New Imperialism*, p. 7.
28. Harvey, *The New Imperialism*, p. 208.
29. Harvey, *The New Imperialism*, pp. 107–8.
30. A. Bacevich, *American Empire: The Realities and Consequences of U.S. Diplomacy* (Cambridge, Mass., 2002), p. 244.
31. Bacevich, *American Empire,* p. 6.
32. Bacevich, *American Empire,* p. 23; for a further critique by Bacevich, see his *The Limits of Power: The End of American Exceptionalism* (New York, 2008).
33. J. Record, *Making War, Thinking History: Munich, Vietnam, and Presidential Uses of Force from Korea to Kosovo,* (Annapolis, Md., 2002), p. 162. See also R. E. Neustadt and E. R. May, *Thinking in Time: The Uses of History for Decision-Makers* (New York, 1986).
34. Record, *Making War,* p. 77.
35. Z. Brzezinski, *The Choice: Global Domination or Global Leadership* (New York, 2004).

36. Z. Brzezinski, 'Hegemonic Quicksand', *The National Interest,* 74 (winter 2003–4), pp. 5, 14.
37. Brzezinski, 'Hegemonic Quicksand', p. 14.
38. R. D. Kaplan, 'Center Stage for the Twenty-First Century: Power Plays in the Indian Ocean', *Foreign Affairs,* 88, 2 (2009), pp. 16–32.
39. C. A. Kupchan, 'Misreading September 11th', *The National Interest,* 69 (2002), p. 28.
40. See conflicting articles by General Sir Hugh Beach and Julian Lewis MP in *RUSI Journal,* 154, 1 (2009), pp. 36–48. I would like to thank Julian for providing me with a pre-publication copy.

8 THE GEOPOLITICS OF THE FUTURE

1. H. Sicherman, 'The Revival of Geopolitics', *Intercollegiate Review* (spring 2002).
2. W. Hay, 'Geopolitics of Europe', *Orbis,* 47 (2003), p. 296.
3. J. Black, *What If? Counterfactualism and the Problem of History* (London, 2008).
4. P. Bobbitt, *The Shield of Achilles: War, Peace and the Course of History* (New York, 2002).
5. Bobbitt, *The Shield of Achilles,* p. 701.
6. Bobbitt, *The Shield of Achilles,* pp. 759–60.
7. Bobbitt, *The Shield of Achilles,* p. 815.
8. N. Ferguson, 'The End of "Chimerica"', *Standpoint,* 4 (September 2008), pp. 41–3.
9. Ferguson, 'The End of "Chimerica"', p. 42–3.
10. P. Tyler, *A World of Trouble: America in the Middle East* (London, 2009).
11. A. Garfinkle, 'Geopolitics: Middle Eastern Notes and Anticipations', *Orbis,* 47 (2003), p. 275.

9 CONCLUSIONS

1. R. Wakeman, *The Heroic City: Paris 1945–1958* (Chicago, Ill., 2009); J. Merwood-Salisbury, *Chicago 1890: The Skyscraper and the Modern City* (Chicago, Ill., 2009).
2. E. Genovese and L. Hochberg (eds), *Geographic Perspectives in History* (New York, 1989).
3. J. J. Grygiel, *Great Powers and Geopolitical Change* (Baltimore, Md., 2006).
4. For a critique, see D. Thompson, *Counterknowledge* (London, 2008).

5. C. D. Walton, *Geopolitics and the Great Powers in the Twenty-First Century* (London, 2007), p. 105.
6. M. Bassin and K. E. Aksenov, 'Mackinder and the Heartland Theory in Post-Soviet Geopolitical Discourse', *Geopolitics,* 11 (2006), p. 116.
7. L. Hekimoglu, 'Whither "Heartland"? Central Asia, Geography and Globalization', *Central Asia and the Caucasus,* 4 (2005), pp. 71–2.
8. G. Ó Tuathail, *Critical Geopolitics* (London, 1996), pp. 255–6.

SELECTED FURTHER READING

Akerman, J. R. (ed.), *The Imperial Map: Cartography and the Mastery of Empire* (Chicago, Ill., 2009).

Agnew, J., *Geopolitics: Re-Visioning World Politics* (London, 2003).

Barfield, T. J., *The Perilous Frontier: Nomadic Empires and China* (Oxford, 1989).

Black, J., *Maps and Politics* (Chicago, Ill., 1997).

Black, J., *A System of Ambition? British Foreign Policy, 1660–1793* (2nd edn, Stroud, 2000).

Black, J., *Great Powers and the Quest for Hegemony* (London, 2008).

Blouet, B., *Halford Mackinder: A Biography* (College Station, Tex., 1987).

Blouet, B. (ed.), *Global Geostrategy: Mackinder and the Defence of the West* (London, 2005).

Dodds, K., *Global Geopolitics: A Critical Introduction* (Harlow, 2005).

Flint, C., *Introduction to Geopolitics* (London, 2006).

Fukuyama, F., *The End of History and the Last Man* (London, 1992).

Fukuyama, F., *After the Neocons: America at the Crossroads* (London, 2006).

Gaddis, J. L., *Strategies of Containment: A Critical Appraisal of Postwar American National Security Policy* (rev. edn, Oxford, 2005).

Gray, C. S., *The Geopolitics of Super Power* (Lexington, Ky., 1988).

Grygiel, J. J., *Great Powers and Geopolitical Change* (Baltimore, Md., 2006).

Haushofer, K., *Geopolitik der Panideen* (Berlin, 1931).
Hugill, P. J., *World Trade since 1431: Geography, Technology, and Capitalism* (Baltimore, Md., 1993).
Hugill, P. J., *Global Communications since 1844: Geopolitics and Technology* (Baltimore, Md., 1999).
Huntington, S. P., *The Clash of Civilizations and the Remaking of World Order* (London, 1996).
Murphy, D., *The Heroic Earth: Geopolitical Thought in Weimar Germany, 1918–1933* (Kent, Ohio, 1997).
Ó Tuathail, G., *Critical Geopolitics* (London, 1996).
Ó Tuathail, G., S. Dalby and P. Routledge (eds), *The Geopolitics Reader* (2nd edn, London, 2006).
Parker, G. *Geopolitics: Past, Present and Future* (London, 1998).
Parker, W., *Mackinder: Geography as an Aid to Statecraft* (Oxford, 1982).
Sloan, G., *Geopolitics in United States Strategic Policy, 1890–1987* (Brighton, 1988).
Smith, N., *American Empire: Roosevelt's Geographer and the Prelude to Globalization* (Berkeley, Calif., 2003).
Stephanson, A., 'George Kennan and the Art of Foreign Policy', *The Economist* (June 1989).